W9-AQO-612

The Soldier's Pen

The Soldier's Pen

FIRSTHAND IMPRESSIONS OF THE CIVIL WAR

Robert E. Bonner

Hill and Wang

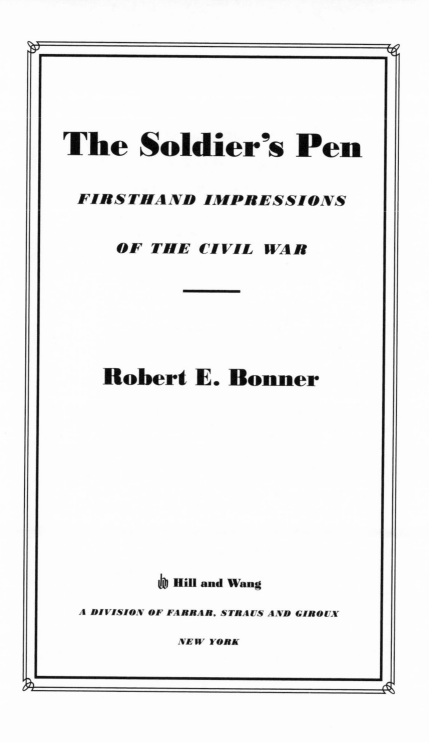

A DIVISION OF FARRAR, STRAUS AND GIROUX

NEW YORK

Hill and Wang
A division of Farrar, Straus and Giroux
19 Union Square West, New York 10003

Distributed in Canada by Douglas & McIntyre Ltd.
Printed in the United States of America
Published in 2006 by Hill and Wang
First paperback edition, 2007

The Library of Congress has cataloged the hardcover edition as follows:
Bonner, Robert E., 1967–
The soldier's pen : Firsthand impressions of the Civil War / Robert E. Bonner.— 1st ed.
p. cm.
Includes bibliographical references and index.
ISBN-13: 978-0-8090-8744-0 (hardcover : alk. paper)
ISBN-10: 0-8090-8744-8 (hardcover : alk. paper)
1. United States—History—Civil War, 1861–1865—Biography. 2. Soldiers—United States—Biography. 3. Soldiers—Confederate States of America—Biography. 4. United States. Army—Biography. 5. Confederate States of America. Army—Biography. 6. United States—History—Civil War, 1861–1865—Personal narratives. 7. Soldiers' writings, American. 8. United States. Army—Military life—History—19th century. 9. Confederate States of America. Army—Military life. I. Title.

E467.B66 2006
973.7′40922—dc22 2006004509

Paperback ISBN-13: 978-0-8090-8743-3
Paperback ISBN-10: 0-8090-8743-X

Designed by Jonathan D. Lippincott

www.fsgbooks.com

1 3 5 7 9 10 8 6 4 2

To Will, Matt, and Cameron Bonner

Soldiers, soldiers, soldiers, you meet everywhere about the city, often superb-looking men, though invalids dress'd in worn uniforms, and carrying canes or crutches. I often have talks with them, occasionally quite long and interesting. One, for instance, will have been all through the peninsula under McClellan—narrates to me the fights, the marches, the strange, quick changes of that eventful campaign, and gives glimpses of many things untold in any official reports or books or journals. These, indeed, are the things that are genuine and precious.

—Walt Whitman, "Soldiers and Talks,"
composed on August 12, 1863

Contents

Foreword

This highly original book by the historian Robert E. Bonner had its genesis in an archive with an extraordinary story of its own. The Gilder Lehrman Collection of historical documents, now on deposit at the New-York Historical Society in New York City, was born in 1990 when two collectors joined forces to pursue a vision. Richard Gilder and Lewis Lehrman, both businessmen, philanthropists, and lovers of American history, decided to combine their individual holdings, ramp up their financial commitment to unprecedented levels, and launch one of the most energetic and successful campaigns ever mounted to collect and preserve American historical documents. They and their agents sought out and purchased a range of items throughout the United States and Europe at such a rate that the collection became a magnet for material from every imaginable source, some of which no one had even known existed. Sometimes an acquisition was a solitary item, such as an 1859 abolitionist flag found within the wall of an Ohio tavern, a Ben Franklin document discovered in an old trunk, or a tickertape about the Kennedy assassination seen on *Antiques Roadshow*; and sometimes large caches, containing hundreds and even thousands of documents, came in at one time. The result is one of the nation's most valuable but least known archives. The collection now contains more than sixty thousand individual items and is still growing.

Numbers only begin to tell the story. Of his first encounter with the Gilder Lehrman Collection a few years ago, Pulitzer Prize–winning historian David Brion Davis wrote: "In the forty-odd years I had devoted to historical research . . . I had never encountered such a breathtaking single collection." Though containing scattered items from 1493 to the end of the twentieth century, the collection's strengths are in the eighteenth and nineteenth centuries, where indeed breathtaking treasures are to be found: four hundred George Washington documents, including his 1786 private letter calling for the abolition of slavery; fifty-three by Frederick Douglass, several unpublished and one of them a heart-wrenching letter of 1857 to his former master; almost five hundred Abraham Lincoln documents, including unique manuscripts of speech notes for his debates with Stephen Douglas that one imagines, from being carried in his hat or vest pocket, might still carry traces of Lincoln's DNA. There are rare copies of famous texts: an Emancipation Proclamation signed by Lincoln, a previously unknown 1776 South Carolina printing of the Declaration of Independence, Benjamin Franklin's signed copy of the Constitution, and scores of others, along with five thousand photographs from the nineteenth century (mostly taken during the Civil War), a comprehensive collection of presidential pardons, and the ten thousand founding-era manuscripts, still largely uncataloged and unexplored, in the Henry Knox Papers.

What makes the collection truly exceptional, however, are the thousands and thousands of documents that extend its scope so far beyond the iconic figures of American history. There are handwritten orderly books from the Revolutionary War, some of them anonymous, in which field officers record the day-to-day activities of their troops. There are manuscripts by and about women, such as the eighteenth-century correspondence between Mercy Otis Warren and Catherine Macaulay about America's founding and materials relating to the women's movement of the nineteenth and early twentieth centuries. There are more than one thousand documents connected with Native American history from the 1600s to the early 1900s, including individual pieces actually written in Algonkian, Cherokee, and Choctaw. There are thousands of documents connected with the history of slavery and abolition, and the lives of African-Americans, including the rarest item of all: what is believed to be the only surviving manuscript diary by an African-American soldier in the Civil War, that of William Woodlin, who served in the Eighth Regiment of the United States Colored Troops from August 1863 to the end of the war.

Here the story of the collection merges with that of how Robert Bonner came to write *The Soldier's Pen.* When Professor Bonner first approached the Gilder Lehrman Collection, he sought Civil War soldiers' letters that might illustrate or support parts of a book he was planning. But as he took the measure of some ten thousand Civil War soldiers' letters and diaries that lie in its vaults, most of them never before published, he saw that the collection was far more than a quarry for bits and pieces of evidence. In fact, the thousands of letters—from Confederate and Union soldiers, as well as African-Americans; from all parts of both North and South; from all ranks, during all phases of the war—were more than any single book could hold. Professor Bonner brilliantly reconceived his project as a distillation of the soldiers' collective experience of the Civil War—mental and emotional, as well as physical—as embodied in the lives of sixteen men he identified whose sketchbooks, diaries, and letters told particularly powerful stories.

Every reader will find something new in this book, because almost none of the material has ever been seen by the public. Perhaps as eye-opening as Woodlin's diary are two sets of unique visual materials: a satiric sketchbook kept by "George," a still-unidentified soldier in the Forty-fourth Massachusetts Infantry, and a set of nineteen watercolor sketches by the German-American Henry Berckhoff, infantryman in the Eighth New York German Rifles, who later reenlisted in the Fifth New York. These amateur artistic works give us new angles of vision, literally, on what ordinary soldiers experienced. But of course the same is true about each of the soldiers whose diaries and letters are now published here, from those of the English immigrant William Brunt, who captained the Sixteenth Regiment of United States Colored Troops and commanded a "contraband" (freed slave) camp in Tennessee, to Jeremiah Tate of Pickens County, Alabama, who survived four long years in the Fifth Alabama Infantry and went on to raise a large family after the war. Everyone will be touched by the pain and emotional intensity these documents convey. Among many such, perhaps the most poignant for me is the January 12, 1863, letter of Edward Ward, a young Confederate, who, after days of miserable suffering in battle, writes to his beloved sister that he has begun reading the Bible every night to console himself and asks her, even at a distance, to connect with him in spirit by reading the same chapters on the same days as he.

It is the emotional force of these documents, constantly pulling us in and connecting us with the inner lives of real people fighting the most harrowing war in American history, that makes *The Soldier's Pen* so powerful. It is the same intellectual and imaginative power that makes archives like the Gilder Lehrman Collection so rich with potential, and that in 1994 moved the two men who built the collection to devote it permanently to the public good by founding the Gilder Lehrman Institute of American History. Charged with serving as steward to the collection while also maximizing its usefulness to the public, the institute has drawn heavily on this invaluable resource to develop a broad array of programs that now reach into all fifty states: teacher seminars, history schools, traveling exhibitions, essay prizes, teaching awards, fellowships, lecture series, Web sites, print and electronic publications, and more. The collection has also been the basis for joint exhibitions and educational projects with historic Mount Vernon, Thomas Jefferson's Monticello, the Huntington Library, the National Constitution Center, the Meserve-Kunhardt Collection, the Gettysburg National Battlefield Museum Foundation, the Legacy Project, and the New-York Historical Society, with more developing every year.

We are particularly proud that the Gilder Lehrman Collection inspired Robert Bonner to create this profoundly important and wonderfully readable volume. *The Soldier's Pen* will be rewarding for Civil War specialists and enthusiasts, and of lasting value to students, teachers, and the general public for generations to come.

James G. Basker
President, Gilder Lehrman Institute of American History
Richard Gilder Professor of Literary History, Barnard College, Columbia University

The Penmen

In Alphabetical Order

HENRY BERCKHOFF was born on November 21, 1840, in Leidingen, Brunswick, Germany, and was working as a clerk in New York City in 1861. He left his mother's home on April 23, 1861, to enlist in the Eighth New York German Rifles. Upon serving his two-year commitment, he reenlisted in the Fifth New York in 1863. During the war he was involved in the construction of Camp Blenker in 1861, in the Shenandoah Valley campaign of 1862, and the Overland campaign of Virginia, where he was wounded in action by a rifle ball in August 1864. He then served in the regular army until 1894, suffering minor scrapes when he was kicked by a mule and, in a separate incident, fell on ice while in the line of duty. At sixty-four, reports that he was "rheumaticing, eyes sight failing, weak lungs, general disability due to old age" gained him a federal pension, which he held until 1905, when he presumably died, having never married or had children.

WILLIAM BRUNT was born in England sometime in 1823 and then lived in Illinois and Indiana before taking up work as a plasterer in northern Kentucky. There he lived in 1860 with a nineteen-year-old wife, Olive, and three children, two of whom were from a previous marriage. His pro-Union sympathies drew a hostile response from most of his neighbors, but these same convictions led to enduring friendships with Martha Cook, her brother Robert Winn, and others in the tight-knit Unionist community of Hawesville, Kentucky. After briefly working as a postmaster in Knox County, Illinois, Brunt joined the Eighty-third Illinois Volunteer Infantry on August 15, 1862, and was charged that November with overseeing the contraband camp at Fort Donelson. Experience recruiting black soldiers resulted in his appointment as a captain in the Sixteenth Regiment of the United States Colored Troops in December 1863, and he served in this position until the following May. He was then appointed the commander of the contraband camp at Clarksville, Tennessee, which was one of the largest such settlements in the entire South. He was divorced from his wife in April 1865 and was honorably discharged on February 1, 1866. His application for discharge indicated his desire to be "useful in the capacity as a private citizen in reforming and educating the negro character." No record exists of his postwar career or the date of his death.

WILLIAM CLEGG moved as a young man from his native North Carolina to northern Louisiana in 1859. On April 25, 1861, he joined the Claiborne Guards and traveled with them from Monroe, Louisiana, to New Orleans. By the end of that May he was serving in the Second Louisiana Volunteers in Virginia, where he witnessed few battles after recording his impressions of Bethel Church in May 1861. During the last three years of the war he performed detached service as part of a court-martial, and during the fall of 1864 he was deployed to North Carolina. He was released as a prisoner of war in July 1865 and returned to Louisiana, where he lived until early in the twentieth century.

DOLPHUS DAMUTH was born on April 10, 1839, in rural New York and then moved with his family to Fort Atkinson, Wisconsin, about twenty miles west of Milwaukee. He enlisted in the Twenty-ninth Wisconsin Volunteers in August 1862 and served in the Mississippi Valley (where he witnessed the siege of Vicksburg), in the Red River campaign, in Texas, and in the garrisoning of Memphis. He was discharged on June 22, 1865. On a march during the night of May 1, 1863, Damuth fell into an eight-foot ditch and suffered a back injury that hampered his postwar work as a farmer. Despite this injury, he received a promotion to sergeant and then to first sergeant of Company D over the course of the war. Damuth married Ida Curtis in 1867 and had five daughters and two sons by 1884. He died in Jefferson County, Wisconsin, on December 20, 1913, more than fifty years after the fall of Vicksburg.

CHRISTIAN MARION EPPERLY was born the son of a Virginia wagonmaker on June 27, 1837. He and his eleven siblings were reared within a devoutly religious community of Floyd County Lutherans. At the age of twenty-two, Epperly married Mary Phlegar, another committed evangelical, and the two were living in the home of Epperly's widowed mother-in-law when the Civil War began. During the war Epperly served both in the eastern theater, as part of General Henry Stuart's Horse Artillery, and in the Army of Tennessee, where he served after his transfer to the Fifty-fourth Virginia. He and his wife had two children during the war, a daughter named Larrigil and a son named Christian. Their hostility to the Confederacy was fairly typical for Floyd County, which became known as a haven for army deserters. During the postwar years the couple raised seven more daughters, and Epperly apparently worked as a farmer until his death in 1904. Mary lived until the age of eighty-five, and she drew a Confederate widow's pension from 1902 until she died in 1927.

The character of "GEORGE," or "GORGE," was likely based on the life of a real private who served in the Forty-fourth Massachusetts Infantry. Chances are good that it was the anonymous sketcher's own experiences that provided the basis for the exploits depicted in the book. Men in this Forty-fourth Massachusetts enlisted for a nine-month term in September 1862 and were deployed in coastal North Carolina that same October. The troops remained in this area for their entire service and took part in a series of clashes with nearby Confederate troops. By the time the regiment was mustered out in June 1863, thirty of their soldiers had died from disease and eleven had been killed in battle.

CHARLES J. C. HUTSON was born on February 11, 1842, on his family's Beaufort, South Carolina, plantation. After leaving South Carolina College before earning a degree, Hutson was briefly employed as a teacher. His service in the First South Carolina Volunteers led to his appointment as an adjutant in 1864. Upon his surrender at Appomattox

Courthouse, he was placed in the Capitol prison and then confined in a prison on Lake Erie, from which he was released in July 1865. He was admitted to the South Carolina bar in 1866 and entered practice with his father-in-law, William F. Colcock. Hutson served in the South Carolina legislature from 1876 to 1890. He was also a delegate to the 1895 constitutional convention that virtually eliminated black voters by passing a literacy test based on a demonstrated "understanding" of the state constitution. He served as a clerk of the United States District Court from 1895 until his death in 1902.

JAMES MAGIE was born in 1827 and lived until his late twenties in New York and New Jersey. When his first wife died in 1852, Magie moved to Illinois, and by the end of that decade his active support for the Republican Party had led to his association with the *Macomb Journal.* He continued to direct the paper after enlisting in the Seventy-eighth Illinois Volunteers in the late summer of 1862 and occasionally wrote letters from the field for publication in his newspaper. While stationed near Nashville, Tennessee, Magie served as a brigade postmaster. By the fall of 1863 he had lost this assignment as his regiment moved toward Chattanooga. Magie was promoted from private to sergeant while serving in Sherman's northern Georgia campaign, though soon afterward he was diagnosed with scurvy. Upon transfer to Charleston that same fall, he contracted yellow fever. He received a discharge after marching in the Washington Grand Review, and he then resumed work as an editor, first in Macomb and then in Canton, Illinois, and Chicago. He spent considerable time in the postwar years in Springfield, Illinois, especially during meetings of the state legislature there. He ran at least once (unsuccessfully) for the state senate and then died on January 12, 1893, leaving his widow, Mary, whom he had married in 1854, and two sons.

CHARLES MOREY was born into a large Vermont farming family in 1841. He entered the Second Vermont Infantry in the late spring of 1861 and spent nearly the entire war in the Army of the Potomac. Testimonials of respect from fellow soldiers helped Morey become an officer in the late summer of 1864. He was named captain of Company E later that same year. His regiment was among the minority of New England units that lent their support to the Democratic presidential candidate, George McClellan, during the election of 1864. A round of grapeshot hit and killed Morey during the Union's final assault upon Petersburg on April 2, 1865. By the time of his funeral in Vermont, Union troops controlled Richmond and Robert E. Lee's Confederate army was in retreat down the Appomattox River valley.

HILLORY SHIFFLET and his future wife, Jemima Cox, both were born during the winter of 1822–23 in Madison County, Kentucky. These two grandchildren of Revolutionary War veterans were married in 1843 and had six children over the next eighteen years. Their only son, John Breckinridge Shifflet, was born a few weeks before the bombardment of Fort Sumter. Hillory Shifflet joined the First Ohio Infantry as a private and kept this rank until he was killed at the Battle of Missionary Ridge on November 25, 1863. He was buried in the military cemetery in Chattanooga. Jemima lived until 1881, when she died in Dayton, Ohio.

DAVID V. M. SMITH was born in 1825. In 1850 he was working as a blacksmith at Post Mills, New Jersey, and by 1860 owned his own shop in nearby Elmer. He enlisted as a private in the Twelfth New Jersey Volunteers in the fall of 1862 and left behind his wife, Elizabeth, and three young children. Recurring sicknesses did not prevent him from taking part in the Battle of Chancellorsville or at Gettysburg, where his regiment was responsible for the capture of the Bliss barn. But chronic trouble with his legs worsened during the early fall of 1863, and Smith died in an army hospital on October 10 of that year.

JEREMIAH TATE was born in up-country South Carolina in 1829. His family relocated to Pickens County, Alabama, when Tate was a young boy, and he lived there and was working as a grocer in 1860. Shortly after the bombardment of Fort Sumter, Tate enlisted in the Fifth Alabama Infantry, in which he served until war's end. Among his assignments was a lengthy detachment late in 1864 as an army nurse. In 1866 Tate married Martha Speed, the widow of another Confederate soldier. The couple raised seven children, including one from Martha's previous marriage and two sets of their own twins. Tate managed to build a comfortable life as a mill owner in the 1870s before he contracted an unexpectedly fatal case of pneumonia in 1877. He was forty-eight when he died in March of that year; his wife was thirty-seven.

GEORGE TILLOTSON was born in 1830. In the fall of 1861 he became a corporal in the Eighty-ninth New York Infantry, named the Dickinson Guards after the former senator Daniel S. Dickinson. This unit first experienced combat as part of an assault on coastal North Carolina made by General Ambrose Burnside of Rhode Island. Tillotson's regiment was transferred to the Army of the Potomac in time for the Battle of Antietam; it remained in the Chesapeake region for the balance of the war. Tillotson rose to the rank of sergeant and then returned to civilian life in the late fall of 1864, having completed the three years of his commitment. He continued to farm after his service and took a noted interest in the activities of Union veterans' organizations. He lived on his farm in Greenville, New York, until his death in 1918.

EDWARD K. WARD was born in 1837, the son of Dr. R. D. Ward of Memphis, a noted doctor, druggist, and slaveholder. In May 1861 Ward enlisted as a private in the Shelby Grays, a company within the Fourth Tennessee Infantry. Within a year he had risen to the rank of second lieutenant, and he remained an officer through western campaigns with the Army of Tennessee. He was killed outside Atlanta on July 22, 1864, and reportedly buried in a nearby Confederate cemetery. Ward's younger brother Marshall, who served in the same regiment, lived until 1903.

LYSANDER WHEELER was born in Fultonville, New York, on May 29, 1837. In August 1862 he left his job as a ship carpenter in De Kalb County, Illinois, to enlist in the 105th Illinois Infantry. He was promoted to first corporal in the late summer of 1864 and assumed the rank of sergeant that same December, just as his regiment completed the March to the Sea under the direction of General William T.

Sherman. Wheeler returned to De Kalb County after the war and married Martha Bannister late in 1866. Three years later the couple's only child, a girl, was born. The family lived together in the same county until Wheeler died of heart failure in 1903, the day after his sixty-sixth birthday.

WILLIAM WOODLIN enlisted in the Eighth Regiment of the United States Colored Troops on August 20, 1863, while living in Syracuse, New York. Official records indicate little more about his earlier life than that he was born in 1841. After serving alongside other black troops in South Carolina, Florida, and Virginia, Woodlin's regiment was sent to Texas, where he suffered a sunstroke that was to afflict him long after his discharge. He was married in Syracuse soon after the war, and he and his wife had three children by 1870. Woodlin lived with his family in Michigan until 1871, when they moved to Centralia, Kansas. Two years later he returned to Michigan, where he reported working as a farmer, laborer, teacher, and book agent. He died on July 22, 1901, having outlived his wife by twelve years.

The Soldier's Pen

Introduction: "Glimpses of Many Things Untold"

The most lasting image of the Civil War soldier emerged during the last third of the nineteenth century, when Americans in the North and the South assured that posterity would remember some three and a half million ordinary fighters. As the ranks of actual Civil War veterans thinned, these men's younger selves rose atop monuments and gained immortality in stone and bronze. Tributes subsequently showered down on the common soldier focused on the hundreds of solitary statues that held vigil over town squares and busy intersections. Praise for the military service of these men has furnished themes for countless civic ceremonies, in spite of the fact that they went to war against one another. Pride in what each risked and lost has been expressed with particular intensity on Memorial Day, an annual commemoration begun in the wake of the Civil War.

The lavish attention devoted to the infantry private of the 1860s may not seem all that surprising in retrospect. For communities to honor defenders of their commonly shared values seems an obvious response. Yet in the context of the late nineteenth century, the elevation of the lowliest citizen-soldier over the statesman, the general, or the military conqueror was a strikingly novel gesture. Standing in uniform at parade rest with rifle at hand, this idealized soldier represented a new archetype, which proved to be a resilient part of the American culture of remembrance. By paying homage to this iconic soldier, the world's leading democracy found a way to celebrate all who bore the greatest sacrifices of war by entering the lines of battle.

Americans created three distinctive types in their postbellum efforts to valorize the citizen-soldier, and these have remained prevalent down to the present day. "Billy Yank" and "Johnny Reb" are the best known, and at times these are separated by little more than the fact that the first wore blue and the second was dressed in gray. Tributes to the African-American soldier introduced a third idealized infantryman, who would rarely receive as much attention as his white counterparts. It was not a nickname, a uniform, or any of those handful of striking monuments to black troops that elevated the archetypal African-American private to public prominence. This work was done by the words of Abraham Lincoln, whose tribute to a black fighter with "silent tongue and clenched teeth, and steady eye and well-poised bayonet" matched an imagined face and a warlike figure to the 170,000 enlisted men of the United States Colored Troops (USCT).

Distilling the mass of individuals into a trio of familiar characters reflected an important truth about the commonalities of army life during the American Civil War. Military service did have a way of grinding down differences and making members of large, seemingly undifferentiated groups into the human equivalent of a machine's interchangeable parts. The common soldier marched and ate en masse; he slept and bathed in shared quarters; his conduct was governed by standardized rules in force across thousands of miles; he formed the bottom of a chain of command organized by the nineteenth century's most intricate hierarchies. Perhaps most important, death and lasting injury were doled out randomly for all who engaged in combat or exposed themselves to the filth of the army camp. One of the earliest and most important lessons that soldiers learned was that the fates of military life respected rank even less than did the ordinary workings of fortune.

One of the central aims of *The Soldier's Pen* is to restore soldiers' individuality, which is often lost in the familiar triumvirate of Union, Confederate, and African-American troops. Collective portraits resonate not just in public culture but also in the development of a superb body of scholarship devoted to the common soldier. Historians over the last half century have produced enormously rich social histories of military life by discerning patterns, identifying leading tendencies, and establishing the basic parameters of the soldiering experience of the

1860s. This constantly growing body of writing, which draws from the same kind of firsthand testimonials sampled throughout *The Soldier's Pen,* has produced valuable insights into what it was like to serve during America's most costly war. In the details of such work one can find ample appreciation for soldier distinctiveness, though individuality is rarely a sustained theme.

There have been unintended consequences in even the best overviews of soldier experiences, and these reinforce the tendencies of public memorialization. Most historians have framed their studies by asking how and why "the soldiers" joined the armies and how "they" then made the fight and returned home. Posing questions in collective cannot help blurring the distinct personalities of each fighter and obscuring the living, breathing humans who were inside standardized military uniforms. This book offers a different approach by emphasizing how most soldiers stubbornly maintained their individuality in the face of common hardships and regimentation. Its point of departure is the basic fact that American armies of the 1860s were largely composed of citizens with no earlier military aspirations, who took up soldiering for a specific period of time and then returned to civilian life. It should not be surprising that the experiences of these men (and the cluster of women who surreptitiously entered the armies) should be complex or that they would sustain their civilian perspectives by maintaining regular ties with home. Such variety resulted from the simple fact that fighting forces were a broad cross section of a multivaried American society, which during the 1860s was more thoroughly mobilized for war than at any other time in U.S. history.

The documents collected in this book serve to remind general readers and scholars alike of the enormous diversity that prevailed within Civil War America and the armies that it raised. The strategy I have chosen is better suited to suggesting this truth than to establishing it definitively. The book focuses on the vivid lives of sixteen figures, all of whose wartime writing is located within a single archive. The resulting fine-grained portraits of distinct individuals have been gathered and introduced from a relatively manageable larger group. Such a limiting strategy allows for the development of characters across a number of thematic topics. Across a series of chapters, readers will learn how the same men faced soldiering and fighting, how they confronted the political questions that their military service sought to resolve, and how they used their pens to grapple with it all. The breadth of expression achieved by each of these individuals is a means of recovering the human dimensions of what too often seems a dehumanizing, even impersonal war.

In putting together this collection and situating documents within chapters, I have sometimes allowed myself to imagine the impossible, if only to understand what might—and what might not—be gained by extended interaction with long-dead soldiers. What would it be like, I have occasionally wondered, to invite the hundreds of sculpted privates down from their pedestals and listen to individual voices that were magically brought back to life? This thought experiment has allowed me to understand what the poet Walt Whitman meant when he offered his own evocative description of what it meant to talk with Civil War troops and hear them out firsthand.

I have concluded that Whitman was not only eloquent in his account of "talks with soldiers," which he first described in the fall of 1863 and then revisited in articles and books published during the 1870s and 1880s, but in most respects also right. The lessons he drew have informed my own sense of which documents should be included in *The Soldier's Pen*. Whitman emphasized, as I have in selecting documents and choosing images, those parts of soldiers' testimony that provide "glimpses of many things untold in any official reports or journal." Individual writing featured below conveys intricate stories, deeply felt emotions, passionate political commitments, and images in words and in pictures that still stir the imagination and leave readers with a lasting impression of what happened nearly a century and a half ago. Such material is, by its very nature, unavailable in the utterances of politicians or the reports of commanders.

It seems to me that Whitman was also correct in explaining how opening oneself to soldiers' words could lead to a heightened appreciation of the country's collective experience. "I now doubt," the poet confided after several months among the troops, "whether one can get a fair idea of what this war practically is, or what genuine America is, and her character, without some such experience as this I am having." This was a keen insight, and it suggests a crucially important point that I have also tried to keep in mind within each of the following chapters. Emphasizing individual voices need not keep readers from appreciating the larger picture, especially when there is enough context provided to understand each soldier's distinctive circumstances. As Whitman sensed, making a concerted effort to appreciate the parts and to set them in meaningful contexts can result in an increased appreciation of the broader course of American history during the early 1860s.

The back and forth of an imagined conversation with long-dead troops would surely provide a memorable encounter to anyone now living. Yet a communion in person, however bracing, would still not satisfy what might be our deepest urge, which is to gain a vicarious experience of war by hearing soldiers bear witness to the travails they suffered and the satisfactions they gained. As the writer and veteran Samuel Hynes has explained in his own meditation on *The Soldiers' Tale*, civilians can listen endlessly to those "who were there" without coming any closer to "being there" themselves. Appreciating the personal dimensions of enlisted life requires nothing less (and nothing more) than becoming a soldier. It strikes me (as a male who has never served in the military) that describing war shares something with conveying the experience of childbirth to those who have not lived through either. In both these instances even the most evocative language cannot make irreducibly complex human experiences fully available to the uninitiated outsider.

That soldiering and combat are fundamentally incommunicable may appear to be an unusual admission at the outset of a book featuring soldiers' impressions of war. Identifying this central truth is not meant as a disclaimer or a forecast of reader frustration, however. This acknowledgment instead helps establish the inherent tensions that mark soldier writing and explains why such documents merit careful consideration. How soldiers attempted to bridge the unbridgeable gap between themselves and civilian audiences produced enormously interesting results. Because of the intrinsic difficulties of the enterprise, writing forced even those who were not particularly adept with their pens to move beyond formulas and to perform the verbal and visual improvisations that best related their messages. The results were often extraordinary, as the passages and pictures that appear below will make clear. The more than 180 documents range from the poignant, clinical, and gruesome to the evasive, angry, and absurd. A tone of quiet resignation runs throughout many, signaling both the difficulty and the importance of putting meaningful thought and feeling into language that might be shared with others.

Whitman called attention to this tendency of soldiers to register their experience with a language of spare expressiveness. He explained how "the superfluous flesh of talking" had been "long work'd off" by fighting for most of those he engaged in conversation. There was "little but the hard meat and sinew" that remained in soldiers' autobiographical reflections. The simple eloquence of soldiers' language impressed Whitman, who hinted that their words formed a species of poetry that rivaled his own verse. One can appreciate what the poet found so fascinating and compelling about what he heard from those in the ranks. "The vocal play and significance moves one more than books," he explained, in terms that apply as much to soldiers' private writing as to their private talking. "There hangs something majestic about a man who has borne his part in battles, especially if he is very quiet regarding it."

While the busy pens of Civil War soldiers allowed some of the same "vocal play and significance" as did conversations, they left permanent traces that allowed later generations (including our own) to achieve the closest communion possible with actual nineteenth-century soldiers. As the following selections attest, reading such documents provides its own satisfaction by allowing us to eavesdrop on the innermost thoughts and feelings that soldiers committed to paper. Though historians are loath to admit it, there is an illicit thrill that comes with reading other people's mail. There is a sense of discovery, which can blur into embarrassment about trespassing upon intimacy, in peering into diaries and sketches that were created during private moments soldiers set aside for themselves. The fact that we are not the primary audience of this writing has a way of making our experience of their words even more "real" than if they spoke to us directly.

A second goal of this book, which works in tandem with its emphasis on soldier individuality, is to reflect upon the ways soldiers committed their impressions to paper. In giving permanence to their wartime reflections, these sixteen men created a series of self-authored memorials to the service of all common infantrymen. Individual families who secured these treasures understood that reading words composed from those long dead formed its own sort of tribute. Something about reading with an ear for the soldier's writerly voice becomes an act of public homage even more evocative than gazing upon a statue.

Surprisingly little has been written about Civil War soldier writing as writing. We lack any systematic treatment of the circumstances, the implications, and the unifying qualities of the voluminous written record compiled by ordinary infantrymen of the 1860s. This is not to say that diaries, letters, sketchbooks, and other written artifacts have been unknown to historians. Scholars have used this testimony regularly, turning to it as a repository of "evidence" that can be stitched together to support larger claims and to sustain generalizations. Snippets and choice quotes appear more often in historical writing than the lengthy extracts this book conveys. My approach intends to make far more clear than is usual the nuanced positions and the gradual evolution of ideas and images of men who changed over the course of their service. Perhaps later scholars will devote greater attention to the writing of Civil War soldiers as a cultural practice worthy of historical investigation. If they do, we may begin to understand how this distinctive body of work contributes not simply to American history but to a fuller appreciation of American literary expression.

To appreciate soldier writing as writing requires some basic classifications. The most important of these involve the three distinct forms used to record wartime impressions with ink and paper. Soldiers most often wrote about their experiences in personal correspondence composed at the front and sent home to family and friends through the mail. Civil War armies were drawn from an unusually literate population, and a postal service operated in both the Union and the Confederacy to assure regular written communications between the military and home front. Many, many more letters were sent and received by Civil War soldiers than during any previous war. While precise numbers are simply not available, we know that letters carried to and from the armies numbered in the tens of millions over the course of four years.

The flow of soldier mail during the Civil War was intense by earlier measures, but it fell short of the levels seen during twentieth-century conflicts. These later wartime communications were subjected to far closer scrutiny and monitoring, a fact that prevented them from including the open discussion of intimate and controversial topics typical of much Civil War correspondence. The military mail of the 1860s was unique in benefiting from a mass communications system that had not yet established a regular system of surveillance. What troops wrote would surely have been hindered by the perceived sensitivity of their intended recipients. But there seemed to have been hardly any fear that overt dissent, or even the discussion of unauthorized desertion, would be monitored or result in a soldier's punishment.

Diaries constituted the second most popular form of Civil War soldier writing. These were kept freely, with none of the restrictions on the practice that were imposed during twentieth-century wars, when private diaries were often banned lest they betray details by falling into enemy hands. While fewer enlisted men of the Union and the Confederacy kept journals than wrote letters, those diaries that have survived are marked by several distinctive traits. They convey a unique sense of immediacy by having been composed on a day-to-day basis (rather than in the rhythm of weekly reports that most correspondence through the mail followed). A notable quality of completeness distinguished such accounts, since these became finished products after an extended period of time, usually the passage of an entire year. Lines in diaries were assembled at a slow pace, and this meant that the most introspective of them were able to dramatize how individuals changed over time. The millions of words from surviving soldiers' journals varied in the quality of their observations, of course, and a great many diarists (probably a majority) were more intent on cataloging the weather or keeping account of a soldier's purchases and his debts than exploring the larger meanings of the war. The three journal keepers who appear in this book explore more compelling matters. Each of their writing voices attains a distinctive register all its own.

Soldiers did not limit their penmanship to words. Some of the most interesting letters and diaries contained drawings made from the front lines. These range from relatively crude stick figures to carefully rendered compositions, maps, and diagrams. Sketchbooks offer the most sustained examples of visual testimony, and two such documents are extensively featured throughout *The Soldier's Pen*. One of these is a watercolored account that a young German-speaking recruit compiled with considerable artistry. The second contains a series of caricatures that allowed an anonymous private to probe the darkly comic elements of a soldier's life. The work of these two soldier-artists provides a helpful counterpart to the illustrations made by the dozens of wartime professionals, whose images have long formed the basis of the war's visual catalog. Illustrations that appear in the following pages are different sorts of sources, not least because, with few exceptions, they do not seem to have been composed for publication. As was the case with the authors of the letters and journals in the book, a smaller intended audience hardly made such works any less important to their creators. For subsequent generations, their limited circulation only increases their worth as intimate firsthand impressions.

The expressive quality of these three different forms of soldier writing is every bit as evident as its testimonial value. Such inherently appealing traits have encouraged America's leading libraries to collect these and similar treasures for the public benefit. Dozens of collections have gathered army testimony that is now part of a collective national heritage. The volume of material that moves from private hands into public archives increases every year. It has become more and more common to have the correspondence or journal of a particular soldier find its way into print, especially in works published by academic presses.

Few institutions have placed as much value on documents produced by soldiers as the Gilder Lehrman Collection in New York City. Their curators have brought together some ten thousand pieces of writing by enlisted men. Through an ambitious acquisitions program, an uncommonly broad range has resulted, with hardly any major aspect of Civil War military history left unaddressed. All the artifacts featured in the following pages come from this rich trove; these come nowhere close to exhausting what is held within the Gilder Lehrman Collection. When placed within the context of other archival holdings, the following excerpts and reproductions represent a still more selective sampling.

Millions of common soldiers committed pen to paper between 1861 and 1865. The following chapters draw from writing done by sixteen such individuals, who are introduced in brief biographical sketches above. These men were chosen because of both the distinctiveness of their written responses and their broadly representative quality. In terms of the latter, it might be useful to speak of the group as a whole before sampling their individual writing.

The sixteen individual "penmen" were in several respects typical of the army rank and file. All were men, and all were born between the early 1820s and the early 1840s. None had previously served in the military, and only one chose to pursue a military career after 1865. This lack of experience was part of the reason why these men joined the infantry, which was the least specialized and largest branch of the military services that also included sailors, cavalrymen, and artillerymen. All sixteen enlisted without officers' commissions and were accordingly expected to march, camp, and fight as others commanded. A few weathered this experience and rose within the regimental hierarchy to become commanders themselves by war's end. Very little of their writing was done for publication; only two men shared sporadic reflections and reports that made their way into wartime periodicals. None of these figures experienced or wrote about captivity in military prisons, even though this was an increasingly common fate for those who served through the late stages of Civil War campaigns.

Within these general contours, the soldiers featured in the book convey a range of backgrounds that roughly match the variety within Civil War infantries as a whole. Of the six of these men who lived in the slave states in 1860, three were slaveholders, two came from relatively modest means, and one, a Kentucky Unionist, joined the Federal Army and became an enthusiastic recruiter of black soldiers. Among the ten soldiers from the free states were a free African-American from Syracuse, New York, a German-speaking artist from Manhattan, a Republican editor from rural Illinois, an anonymous satirist from Massachusetts, and an assortment of farmers and workers of differing ages, incomes, and levels of education. Within the entire group, nearly equal numbers were married and single. Of the four soldiers who died while in the service, three were killed in major battles while one died of sickness in an army hospital.

These men's experiences involved a range of military assignments, and each of them mixed combat with the less dangerous (though generally more onerous) chores of camp, garrison, and picket duty. Nearly half the men served in the eastern campaigns of Virginia, Maryland, and Pennsylvania. Their reports alternated between the daily drudgery of army life in the Union's Army of the Potomac or the Confederate Army of Northern Virginia and the searing experiences of facing their enemies at Antietam, Fredericksburg, Gettysburg, Spotsylvania, Chancellorsville, and Petersburg and in the Shenandoah Valley and Overland campaigns. The rest of this group saw combat across the wide expanse of territory between the Mississippi Valley and the seacoast of the Carolinas. The letters of a young lieutenant from Memphis, Tennessee, recorded the faltering Confederate effort in the West at Shiloh, Murfreesboro, and Missionary Ridge. The writings of two privates from Wisconsin and Illinois detail the Union perspective on the campaigns against Vicksburg, up the Red River valley, and across Georgia and the Carolinas during the last winter of the war.

As the book follows sixteen men through a variety of endeavors, their complicated personalities come into focus. Communications with home showed attitudes that ranged from the needy to the loving to the irritable. Responses to the hardship of camp and the horror of combat similarly show sixteen distinct ways of reacting to the least pleasant aspects of soldiering. While the documents produced by these men convey a wide range of learning, the depth of their reflections does not depend on the extent of their education. The same is true of their distinct political leanings, which show how each of these men, from the most worldly to the most innocent, cared about the larger issues that drew them to military service. All were committed to the notion that becoming a soldier did not make one less of a citizen. They realized that this was especially true during the greatest national crisis they or future Americans would ever face.

A final comment. As the selected documents reveal, there was a wide range of writing abilities across this group. Some readers may find it difficult to discern the meaning of the irregular spelling and grammar of some letters and diaries. I am aware of this challenge, but I have decided to alter even the most difficult documents as little as possible from their original appearance. The main editorial additions have involved the insertion of commas and periods. I have done so in ways that are consistent with the form that the written record suggests. To take the most common example, I have taken gaps between words or the beginnings of new lines as a signal that a new sentence or clause should begin. The difficulties of this process can be best appreciated by matching images of those actual documents that are reproduced with the printed transcriptions that appear in the Index of Source Material.

ONE

The Tender Lines of War

Before joining the army late in 1862, James K. Magie helped edit a small midwestern newspaper, where he made his living by circulating printed words to a largely anonymous readership. Not long after he became a soldier in the Seventy-eighth Illinois Infantry, Magie assumed another role in the wartime transit of information. The following letter explained how the thirty-six-year-old private had gained this enviable position, which he would use to assure the safe and speedy exchange of intimately inscribed sentiments between Union volunteers and loved ones back at home.

Franklin, Tenn
Feb. 17, 1863

Dear Wife—

I have a few minutes in which to write and I improve the opportunity. We have had no mail since we left Louisville. There has been so much dissatisfaction about Mr. Painter as Postmaster that he was removed this morning, and I was appointed in his place. In less than an hour I was promoted to the office of Brigade Postmaster. This gives me the privilege of going out or coming in just as I please. I am also furnished a horse, and I have the privilege of selling papers, envelopes, letter, paper, etc. by which I can make from 30 to 50 dollars per month. I shall go to Nashville tomorrow and bring out our mail. We are clear behind hand in news. . . .

As soon as I receive our mail and hear from you I shall write you again. I hope you received the $40 all right. . . .

Good bye my love.

Your affectionate
James

Over the next several weeks Magie made the most of his new assignment. Besides picking up and delivering his brigade's mail from Nashville, he delivered special parcels, completed minor errands, purchased newspapers, and brought back pens, pencils, stamps, and envelopes, which he sold to soldiers. Serving these needs gratified Magie, who bragged to his wife about his growing popularity with the troops. Yet helping men stay in better touch with loved ones had a more practical side, as the following letter confided.

Franklin, Tenn
March 1, 1863

Dear Wife,

. . . I am fearful all the time that some untoward event will happen to break in upon my present arrangements. If I can hold my position, and have the monopoly of the express and newspaper business for 100 days I can send you home $1000, which will buy us a snug little home. You need not tell the soldiers families how much I am making, for I don't let them (the soldiers) know that I am making so much, for it might create jealousness or the like. The feeling so far is high in my favor. They get their mail regularly rain or shine. They have found out that when the train fails I don't fail bringing the mail. The man who was trying to run me opposition, I think I will get rid of. The orders are very stringent against passing the lines. I have passes to go through the lines at any time. I think this will rule out all others. . . .

I have so little time that I cannot write you a long letter today. I start for Nashville in a few moments. . . . I will write oftener to make up for short letters.

Your devoted
James

Hillory Shifflet was the sort of soldier likely to resent Magie's calculation of personal profit. These two middle-aged midwesterners fought in the same armies, survived several of the same campaigns, and regularly corresponded with wives and children hundreds of miles away. Yet in other ways Magie, the Republican newspaperman, and Shifflet, a struggling farmer from southern Ohio, seemed to come from entirely different worlds. The following note suggests that the thirty-eight-year-old Shifflet had not been a regular letter writer prior to his enlistment. The emotions it expressed and the news it provided explained why he took up his pen every few weeks and, like thousands of others, drew sustenance from the written messages Magie and others helped to reach their destination.

January, 1862
Camp Wood, Heart County, Ky

Dear Wife,

I take my pen in hand today to let you no that I am well at presant and hope these few lines will find you and the children all well. I recev your letter last night which gave me greate satisfaction to her from you and that you was all well, but when the mail came I was vary much out of heart for I thot tha was no letter for me but when george open his letter I found yourn and I soon red it and the was a few tears fell from my eys. I cod not help it for I was so glad to her that you was doing as well as you was and I hope that you will still do well tell I come home and I hope that wonte be long. our union men have gain another greate victory on cumberland river. Tha kild a greate meny of the sesesh* than that is the place that Cit is and Ian Hardin, all the baker boys. The regiment tha was in had to dismount from thare horses and fight on foot but I dont no whether enny of them was kild or not. I look for a letter from them tomorrow. . . .

We had inspection this morning. Our company look better than enny of the rest. We had on our dress coats. I hav got a vary nise dress coat and look as well as you ever seede me. I shave ever

*This colloquial term for "secessionist" identified all Confederate enemies of the Union.

week and put on a clean shirt. I wash a shirt ever weeke. I have jest bin to the doctors and got vaxinated in my left arm George and Amos and Tom Westerman and Thompson Ennis and Tom Smith you sed you wanted me to send you my likeness. I will send it to you when I git pade of and tha captain told me that we wood git pade nex Tuesday or Wednesday and when I git hit I will send you twenty dollars. I will git twenty six dollars but will have to keepe some for I will neade sum. I neede a good deal but you neade it worse than I do so if I git it you may look for it nex Saterday. So you must do the best you can if I live to git home I will have rite smart of money unuf to give us a start to do well.

I want yo to right me as soon as you git this letter. . . . If you hante got no money to git postedge stamps I will sende you one that will do you till you git some. hit is a harde matter to git stamps her but I will send you one that will do you to send me a letter as soon as yo git this one. I want to her from you ever weeke hit dos me a heepe a good to her from you. . . .

I rote daddy a letter last weeke. I look for a letter in a day or two and I rote one to Irvin and expect to git one poty soon and then I will her all about the battle that Cit was in and I will right to you all about it. . . . When you Right, Direct your letter to the first Regiment of Ohio Volunteers, Company C, Captain Thurston, Camp Wood, Heart County, Ky.

Hillory Shifflet to Mima Shifflet

Over the course of his enlistment, Shifflet sent and received a steady stream of such letters. Like most soldiers, he continually asked for even more frequent communication. His last note, written three days before he was killed at the battle of Missionary Ridge, expressed love to his wife, "Mima," listed items that would make army life more comfortable, and suggested how these might make a safe journey through the mail.

Chattanooga, Tennessee
November 22nd [1863]

Dear wife,

I with Pleasure take my Pencil in hand to let you no that I am well at this time and I dwo hope when you git these few lines tha

> will find you all well and harty. I hante had no answer from my last letter I Sent you with ten dollars in it but I thout I wood right you a few lines and send you ten moore in it and I want you to right me a answer as soon as you git this if you git it a tall, for I will be uneasy about it tell I her and Mima, I want you to send me a par of yourn gloves for I cant git enny her and the best way to send it is to do it up in a nusepaper and put it in a invelope and direct it jest like you do your letters. And send some thread for I cant git a bit to sow my Buttons on my pants when tha Brak of. If you send them, send them soon as you can for I nead them mity Bad Mima. I cant right much this time. I am two or three letters ahead of you ennyhow. I hante no nuse only we ar looking for another fight ever minit. If you git this money I want you to git little Jonny a par of Boots and all of the rest what tha neade and donte forgit yourself. So Mima, let me no soon about it so I will close these few lines So farwell my Dear wife untell Death.
>
> Hillory Shifflet

Both Magie and Shifflet entrusted their most personal expressions and prized possessions to the large, standardized structures of the U.S. mail. They did so without much thought, since they had little reason to question the Federal postal service, which by 1860 had become the country's largest bureaucracy and one of the most effective communications systems in the world. Without such a reliable, rapid, and relatively cheap network for transmission, far fewer soldiers would have regularly committed their thoughts and experiences to paper. The Civil War would have drawn the same sort of written commentary from enlisted men as had appeared during the American Revolution and the Mexican War, when poor army mail service made diaries more reliable than letter writing. The fact remains, however, that the Civil War became a written war primarily because a regular exchange of letters allowed millions of personal stories to be recorded and preserved for posterity.

In fact, most soldier correspondence contained details that testified to the ease of sending and receiving mail. Given the high expectations about rapid and safe delivery, correspondents went out of their way to record those minor disruptions and inconveniences that resulted from the lack of stamps, the difficult conditions of camp, or the delay in sending money or other valuable items. Charles Morey, a twenty-year-old soldier from rural Vermont, was typical in complaining about the hardship of using a barrel for a desk, even though such an inconsequential constraint scarcely kept him from writing. Like many of those young men who had volunteered in the first weeks of war, Morey began his service with a stock of patriotic stationery that sustained his regular reports of a new life of soldiering. He also had time to keep five diaries that documented each new year's service with the Army of the Potomac, which was the largest of all the Civil War armies.

The South's mail service initially promised to be every bit as effective as the North's. After all, the U.S. government had implemented the same postal infrastructure on both sides of the Mason-Dixon line between 1790 and 1860. There was the same culture of correspondence in the slave South as in the free North, and Confederates' early enthusiasm for patriotic stationery matched that of their enemies. Private Edward K. Ward, the son of a noted Memphis doctor, druggist, and slaveowner, used his earliest letters home to broadcast his support for the Confederate president, Jefferson Davis.

At the beginning of 1862 Ward sent his sister the following letter, which blamed his lapsed correspondence not on Southern postal difficulties but on his own lack of spare change. He added an equally improbable excuse that letters had worn out in his pockets before they could be mailed. His sister probably was unconvinced by these explanations and may even have suspected that Ed's greatest concern was letting himself off the hook with those who had expected more regular army news.

Columbus [Ky.]
Jan 17 / 62

Dear Sister,

Most certainly your school is a model one where strict etiquette is preserved in all things. So that you could not consistently write until you were written too, or you have thought it was not worth the pains or you would have written before now. I have written you one or two letters, and carried them in my pocket until they wore out, waiting to borrow five cents to pay postage

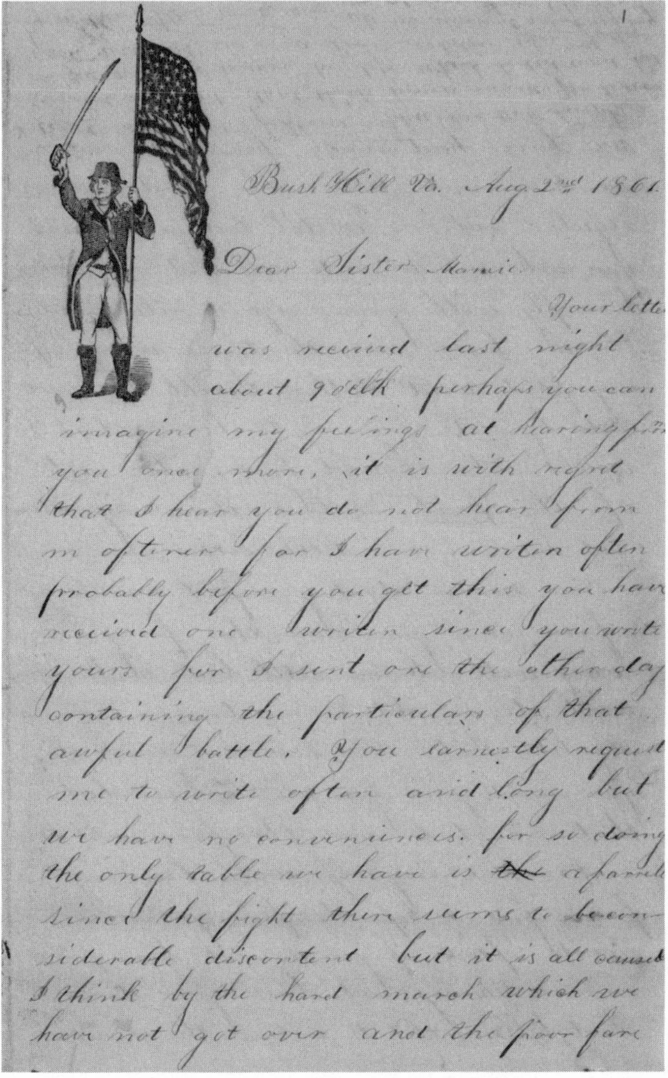
1

Bush Hill Va. Aug 2nd 1861

Dear Sister Mamie

Your lett

was recived last night
about 9 o'clk perhaps you can
imagine my feelings at hearing fr
you once more, it is with regret
that I hear you do not hear from
m oftener for I have writen often
probably before you get this you hav
recived one writen since you wrote
yours for I sent one the other day
containing the particulars of that
awful battle. You earnestly request
me to write often and long but
we have no conveniences for so doing
the only table we have is ~~the~~ a famil
since the fight there seems to be considerable discontent but it is all caused
I think by the hard march which we
have not got over and the poor fare

Figure 1. Charles Morey to his sister Mamie, August 2, 1861.

on it—Haller is up here and brought the only silver I have seen in two months. . . .

I don't know where you are. Every time I hear from home it seems that you are there just ready to start, and I never know where to direct my letter. Now if you have not got excuses enough I will give you more next time for that is one thing my female friends say I am never without. I shall not attempt to give you the news for fear of telling you something you have already heard. I am very well with the exception of one ear which has been deaf and roaring for some time. . . .

I must stop for the police guard have ordered my light out twice and I don't want them to again. My love to all the girls. Write soon and tell me all the news they tell me Somerville is a good place to hear Memphis news.

Your aff. brother,
Ed

Confederate troops would in time face unique challenges in keeping up correspondence with home. Federal occupation of communications routes and the surrender of key cities like Nashville and New Orleans hindered the flow of mail to and from the Rebel armies. Such failures of the official mail service often forced soldiers to find other means to transmit their news. From the very beginning, Ed Ward of Memphis had sporadically entrusted his notes to individuals traveling back and forth to the army. (The stampless envelope with the Jefferson Davis im-

Figure 2. Patriotic envelope sent without stamp by Edward Ward to his sister, June 20, 1861.

age no doubt fell into this category.) His habit became a necessity when Federal troops occupied his hometown in the spring of 1862 and blocked the official lines of communication between his family and Rebel troops.

Worsening the situation was the provision in the 1861 Confederate Constitution that required mail service to become self-sustaining within three years. This measure effectively ended the previously large subsidy for postal service, which had been an indispensable factor in the success of the U.S. mail. Slower and more irregular service resulted almost immediately, as did the cost of using the mail. Many poorer Confederate soldiers responded by deliberately rationing their correspondence. Marion Epperly, a middle-aged Confederate private from southwestern Virginia, met these challenges by squeezing as much ink as he could on every note he composed. In one letter sent home in 1863, Epperly used a single sheet of paper (and a single ten-cent postage stamp) to convey five different notes to various members of his extended family. Regardless of the difficulties, Epperly insisted that the mail service continue, even if it meant that government officials had to resort to extraordinary means to preserve a soldier's right to the mail. However the following letter traveled, it apparently did arrive at his home in the Blue Ridge Mountains, and it was among the dozens that he was able to read and to cherish when he returned home to his family after the surrender of the Confederate armies.

Camp Near Marietta, Ga
June the 29th, 1864

My Most Dear Companion,

. . . I haven't gotten aney letter from you sins the one dated the 2nd of this month. I have written you som 4 or 5 letter in the month, but I am afeard you haven't gotten them as the Yankees has possession of the Railrode and have burned a Grate many Bridges on the Rode. but I hope our letters will go from high Point to Floyd C.H. by Hors back I hope the Postmaster will see that our letters will go throo soon and you will get them in due time. . . .

I still remain your tru Husband til Death,
C. M. Epperly

Confederate soldiers' frustration with the mail was worsened by the pinch of the widespread paper shortages across the South. At a time when some Southern editors were forced to issue their newspapers on wallpaper, letter writers and diarists invented new ways to record and circulate their wartime impressions. Surviving letters suggest that the initial stock of patriotic stationery ran low early in 1862 and that even basic paper and envelopes became rare. Resourceful soldiers still had a range of other materials, however. The thirty-three-year-old bachelor Jeremiah Tate, who had been a grocer in Pickensville, Alabama, prior to his enlistment, began to reuse the envelopes sent from home. He was equally inventive in converting an appointment book into stationery and even commandeering personalized letters and envelopes captured from the enemy, bearing the return address of the Twentieth Maine Volunteers.

Whatever the challenges of the mail, few soldiers were inattentive to the importance of staying in touch. Americans often insisted that the flow of information was as vital to the nation's existence as the circulation of blood was to the fate of a living organism. Civil War letter writers similarly believed that long-distance relationships would wither if not sustained by a regular exchange of sentiment. What a letter said was important, of course, but so too was the way that its arrival expressed a basic commitment to an ongoing conversation. In this way, wartime mail was part of an evolving relationship, which writers developed over time. Such relationships influenced what sorts of observations soldiers made in their letters and how they decided what to include and what to filter out.

The perspective and voice of each Civil War letter depended on the participant at the other end of this imagined conversation. The thirty-one-year-old private George Tillotson of New York struck a variety of different poses in letters he wrote while serving in coastal North Carolina and northeastern Virginia over the course of his three-year enlistment. During an extended period in the middle of the war he became an outspoken critic of Republican policies, and with his alienation came some nasty racial views that he expressed in angry letters to antislavery in-laws. Yet when Tillotson sat down to write his immediate family, a more tender side emerged, if only for the time that it took to put words onto paper and the paper into the envelope. Despite his reputation for fearlessness in battle, Tillotson was capable of great warmth in these family exchanges, as can be seen in his note to his daughter Georgianna, sent February 16, 1862, and in his determination to share, as in the following letter, an important occasion with a much-missed wife.

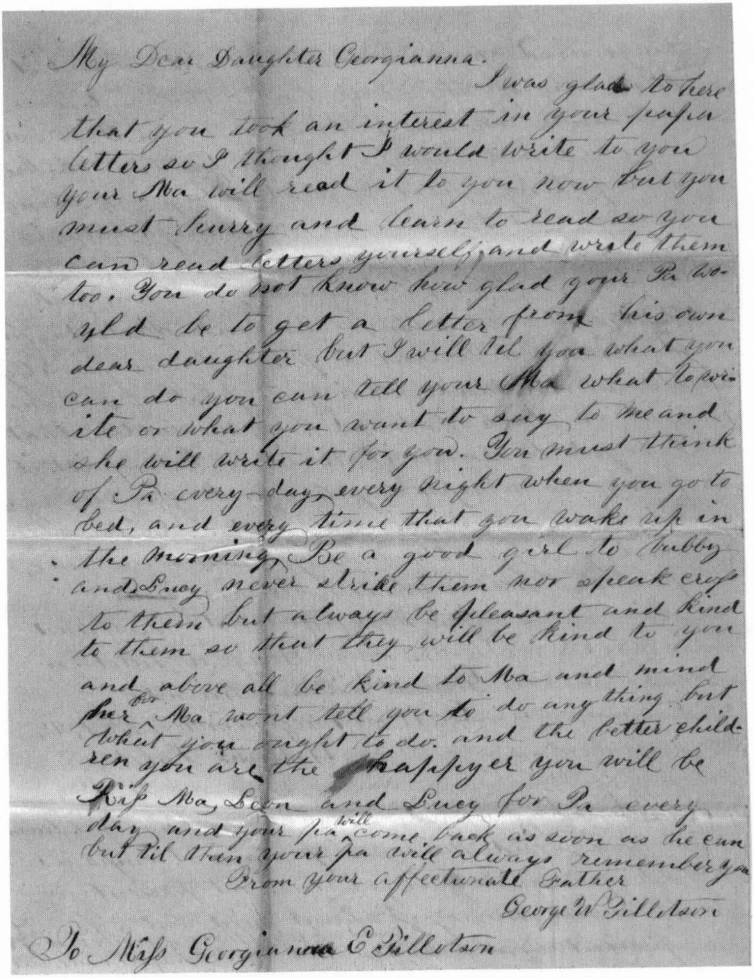

My Dear Daughter Georgianna.

I was glad to here that you took an interest in your papa letter so I thought I would write to you your Ma will read it to you now but you must hurry and learn to read so you can read letters yourself and write them too. You do not know how glad your Pa would be to get a letter from his own dear daughter but I will tel you what you can do you can tell your Ma what to write or what you want to say to me and she will write it for you. You must think of Pa every day every night when you go to bed, and every time that you wake up in the morning Be a good girl to Bubby and Lucy never strike them nor speak cross to them but always be pleasant and kind to them so that they will be kind to you and above all be kind to Ma and mind her for Ma wont tell you to do any thing but what you ought to do. and the better children you are the happyer you will be Kiss Ma, Leon and Lucy for Pa every day and your pa will come back as soon as he can but til then your pa will always remember you

From your affectionate Father

George W Tillotson

To Miss Georgianna E Tillotson

Figure 3. George Tillotson to his daughter Georgianna, February 16, 1862.

Folly Island
Sunday
October 11, 1863

My Dear Wife,

. . . It is the tenth anniversary of our wedding. I could not resist the impulse to pen a communication since it is not possible to hold a closer communion in person. Nor can I help contrasting the experiences of today and ten years ago, although in one respect they are similar. The old love is experienced the same or in a stronger degree, and is more holy from the addition of other loves growing out of it. But when I consider the distance in space and time that I am and am to be separated from the object of that love, I can't help, dear wife, from feeling a melancholy which causes a choking sensation and a moistening of the eye. Could I but annihilate time, and space, I would soon be with you. I am now the only man in Co. H that has a family (that they take any interest in at least) although four others has (or had) families. . . .

Kiss the children for me and imagine a few enclosed for yourself from

Your loving and True Husband,
Geo. W. Tillotson

The mail exchanged by some other couples lacked such warmth or intimacy, especially in marriages already marked by a high level of distrust. Absence sometimes might have softened feelings, though in other cases, frictions persisted and were more than evident in written correspondence. In the following letter, the New Jersey private David V. M. Smith urged his wife to move past earlier difficulties, arguing that his sufferings as a soldier should earn him a fresh start. He began the letter with instructions about running his blacksmith shop in Elmer, New Jersey. This attempt to conduct business from afar was pursued by many such older, more financially established enlisted husbands and fathers.

October 28 / 62
Camp Johnson

. . . You say that you have Rented the Shop. Be sure that you got the right account of things. I had expected to come home this week, but there is talk of a general move by the army on the Potomac so General Wood has forbid any more furloughs being granted for the present. But if we don't move from here, I think I should be at home before a great while for I long to see you and the Children. try to keep them all alive until I can get there and for God's sake and for my sake and for every body else's sake that has anything to do so or say about our troubles and misfortunes, don't write any more about it nor about the liquor that I have bought and what I have drank for it pains me to have it brought up in my mind and I can't Read about it without shedding tears and I must say something in reply. I think if I could see you we could alter the face of things very much for I am sure you would see a sober man and one that does not want to quarrel with you. You don't speak in your letter as if you wanted me to come home but I don't think you mean so. Let us try to Bring about a good feelings and say nothing more about the past. . . .

Direct as before and if we move it will follow the Regiment. Tell me about the shop and see that Adams keeps the Barn the fence and sheds in good Repair. And I Remain your Husband and to your children a Loving Father,

D. V. M. Smith

We know of his wife Elizabeth's objections to his drinking only because David Smith urged her to cease making this a topic of concern. His wife's part in these exchanges was lost with the letters she sent to the front. This in itself said little, if anything, about Smith's feelings toward his wife. Families at home had drawers and chests to stow away letters from the army; soldiers were expected to dispense with all but the most essential gear. We shall never know for sure, then, if Elizabeth Smith objected to her husband's parenting advice expressed in the following letter. At the time that Smith offered his suggestions, Charley was thirteen years old and Annie was eight, while Rufus was a mere four.

Camp near Falmouth, VA
Feb 13 / 63

Charley my son,

. . . I want you or your Mother or both of you to write to me & when you write send me word what 16 ounces of Solid gold is worth as I do not know myself & I cannot find any one that does and it is quite a question here in the army. I think you had better not go to school to much so as to injer your health as for Annie your mother must use her own judgment on her. & as for Rufus tell him to mind his Mother and begin to chew tobacco until I get home if he does then I don't know that I have any more good advice to send you but try to be as useful at home as you can & mind your Mother. . . .

I must now close my letter hoping it may find you all well & getting along first rate. . . .

D. V. M. Smith

Written instructions, whether they concerned parenting or business transactions, depended on the prevailing assumptions with particular families. These might be supplemented by a trip home, which troops made with some regularity, especially early in the war. Commanders rarely developed a standard and consistent policy on furloughs for their troops, though they realized how much soldiers valued the chance to reacquaint themselves with civilian life. Letters were filled with information about requested leaves and the campaigns taken by enlisted men to secure them, through additional services, special pleadings, or pledges to reenlist. Correspondence also indicates the prevalence of so-called French leaves taken by soldiers in both Union and Confederate armies. Such unauthorized absences, which rarely extended for more than a week or two, usually resulted in a minor punishment, as long as a soldier returned to his unit on his own initiative. Unauthorized leaves could often blur, if there were indications that they were intended to be permanent, into the far more serious crime of desertion, which could draw a death sentence.

Husbands and wives also shared news about other members of their local communities in an attempt to preserve the sense of common purpose that had drawn many of them into the army in the first place. Most companies consisted of neighbors who were intent on gossiping through the mail about what was going on both at home and in camp. Communications were not "private" in any meaningful sense, and most letter writers knew that what they recorded was likely to be read aloud. This regular circuit of information meant that behavior could be easily monitored from a considerable distance. Minor instructions and friendly reminders that came through in correspondence had to be taken seriously, since there were multiple sources to verify how soldiers acted in the camp and to convey what civilians were up to back home.

Wartime letters brought their expected quotient of genuinely sad news as well, and these resulted in some of the most poignant messages that would be saved for posterity. Receiving the mail was normally a fairly predictable experience, whether it brought joyful expressions of love or nagging from an unhappy partner. The most consequential news was often unexpected, even if nearly everyone knew that dark tragedy could lurk within each unopened envelope. Despite the perceived immediacy that written conversation made possible, the delay between posting and receiving a letter produced bittersweet irony when there was a mishap involving either the writer or the recipient. The twenty-four-year-old Dolphus Damuth returned an unopened letter that his sister had written to her sweetheart, who was a fellow private in Damuth's Wisconsin regiment. The following explained how Jesse Smith had died of measles before Maria Damuth's letter had arrived. Dolphus could do little more than to assure her in his next letter that he had "fixed up the grave of Jesse as best I could."

March 3, 1863

Dear Sister,

When we got back there was four letters for Jesse. I looked at them and saw one was from you. I thought you wouldn't like to have anyone open it so I will send it to you. Dave asked him before he died what he should do with your picture. He said give it to Maria. These words were about the last he ever spok. I have it and will Send it to you by mail. I think I shall send his death to the Chief. I will answer all my letters before long. Elva must be a good girl and I will bring her something when I get back from the war. All is well.

From Dolph Damuth

The early interchanges between Charles J. C. Hutson and the extended network of his family and friends brought bad news in the opposite direction, informing the members of the First South Carolina Infantry of an unexpected civilian death. Not long after he enlisted as a nineteen-year-old volunteer, Hutson became engaged to Emmeline Colcock, a distant cousin and a proud member of the same low-country planter class to which Hutson belonged. With the blessing of both sets of parents, the two teenagers pursued their relationship primarily through the mail. Hutson wrote his fiancée on September 1, 1861, how much he appreciated such correspondence.

A few days after he wrote this note, reports of Emmeline's sudden illness reached Hutson's regiment in Virginia. He sent a last letter that did not arrive until after she had already died of typhoid fever. Bonds forged through a prolonged period of grieving led to a series of letters between Hutson and Emmeline's father, which culminated in Hutson's postwar marriage to his dead fiancée's youngest sister. The following letter, which explained how dangers at home made Hutson's own lot worse, brought his future father-in-law to tears when he opened it just hours after his eldest daughter's death.

Richmond, Va.
Saturday Sept. 7, 1861

I had just sent a letter to the P.O. dear sweet Em., when the intelligence of your sickness through your Father's and Cornelius' letter reached me. . . .

O we know not of the trials and hardships of a soldiers life, until we hear of the sickness of those whom we love most in this world. Far away from sweet Home, among the unsympathizing, it is very difficult to bear patiently the trials we are called to endure. I know not what to do, I know not what to think, for you dear Em. may be ill, and I must be ignorant, painfully unconscious of your suffering in a land now distant from me. O! that

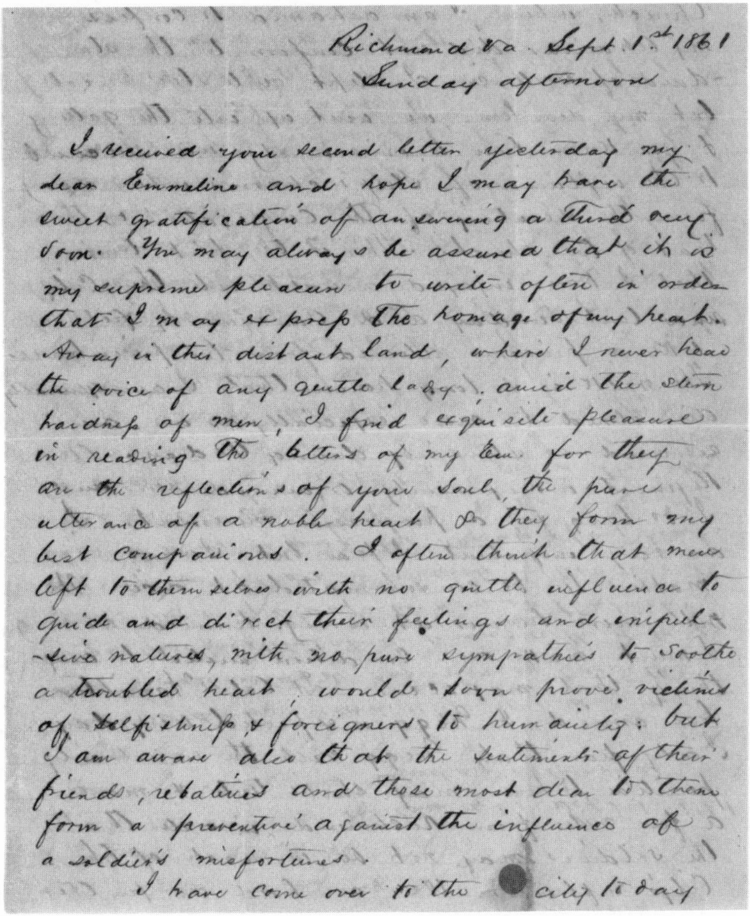

Richmond Va. Sept. 1st 1861
Sunday afternoon

I received your second letter yesterday my dear Emmeline and hope I may have the sweet gratification of answering a third very soon. You may always be assured that it is my supreme pleasure to write often in order that I may express the homage of my heart. Away in this distant land, where I never hear the voice of any gentle lady, amid the stern hardness of men, I find exquisite pleasure in reading the letters of my Em. for they are the reflections of your soul, the pure utterance of a noble heart & they form my best companions. I often think that men left to themselves with no gentle influence to guide and direct their feelings and impulsive natures, with no pure sympathies to soothe a troubled heart, would soon prove victims of selfishness & foreigners to humanity: but I am aware also that the sentiments of their friends, relatives and those most dear to them form a preventive against the influence of a soldier's misfortunes.

I have come over to the city today

Figure 4. Charles Hutson to his fiancée, Emmeline Colcock, September 1, 1861.

I could be transferred upon the wings of the wind to Carolina's City that I may know how my dear Emmeline is. . . .

Your letter, which I received on Thursday had just elevated my spirits, just invigorated me with mental and emotional food & prepared me for life's stern duties when I was soon called to distress and mental suffering. . . .

I must close—I anxiously await news of you—O! that I

could hear of you being well—or that I could bear your sickness in your stead—My love to your father & the boys & girls at home & believe me ever,

Your fond and Loving—C.-

The bulk of soldier mail was directed either to immediate family members or to actual or prospective lovers; such letters were also far more likely to be saved than less intimate correspondence. Other written interactions did survive, however, and these could contain striking depictions of crucial aspects of the war. The British-born plasterer William Brunt used the mail primarily to sustain his ties with Martha Winn Cook and Robert Winn, who were the recipients of all the extant letters composed while Brunt served as a white officer of black troops. Brunt and his correspondents forged ties based on ideology rather than blood lineage or romantic interest, and most of their letters recalled what they had suffered as committed Kentucky Unionists during the secession crisis. Brunt's following note expressed his mixed emotions about his adopted hometown of Hawesville, just south of the Ohio River. After the election of Abraham Lincoln, Confederate sympathizers had driven Brunt, then in his late thirties, to Illinois, where he briefly served as a postmaster before volunteering for service in the Union army.

Fort Donelson, Tenn.
July 26th / 63

Dear Friend Martha,

I received your kinde letter in which you speak of Robert returning to his Regiment. I was glad to get it & to learn that you were all well at home. . . . Give my love to him & Mattie when you write to the rest of the faithful from Hawesville. I think the day is breaking. A few more blows like the fall of Vicksburg & Port Hudson and the rebellion will be on a parr with our loss in the Bull Run fight. I would like to visit Hawesville and hear J. C. Martin & Co. sputter now. Perhaps I may yet have the pleasure of a visit to my old stomping ground. I think I shall have no cause to blush for any thing I have done there. Would to God those that used to taunt me had as little to regret or rather that they had done as little evil as I did while there. But verily they have their reward their day has past & Perjury, perfidity, Treachery & Treason begin to show their fruits. This fruit seemed sweet to them while eating it but it will be wormwood to digest. Let those who sow the Whirlwind reap the storm. . . .

Tell your Father I don't feel hard towards him for not writing some in each of your good letters but still I would like to have a line from him occasionally, but as long as you write I will excuse him & consider the letters you write as family letters on condition that my letters to you are looked upon in the same light. I don't doubt his friendship because he don't write. I think his firm manly course in the dark days, will ever keep his name fresh in my memory, & secure to him & his my best wish through life & beyond it as far as mortal wishes can effect anything. Give my love to him & your Good Mother also to Bessie & George & to Robert's Family. Remember me to Robert Kays Family & to as many of the Union Club members as remained faithful to there first love. I should dearly love to have you all for neighbors once more but it is useless to speculate in the future for no man knoweth what a day or an hour may bring forth. . . .

My sheet is nearly full & poorly written for I am on Pickett & am writing on my Port Folio sitting like a Tailor in our tent in the N East corner of the Old Rebel Fort About 80 Rods west of our new Ft. I have a fine view of the old battle field & when I look at the strength of the Rebel works & think of General Grants victory I think that the Bull Run disaster was thoroughly wiped out by his glorious achievement here.* It was a very strong place & strongly Garrisoned. I must close. Please give my compliments to Mrs. A. D. Hawley & her sister. They wer good Union Women. I heard that A. D. Hawley is Dead is it so & does Mr. H still live there. Please write soon.

Yours truly,
William Brunt

*On February 16, 1862, General U. S. Grant captured Fort Donelson, thus opening the Cumberland River to Union gunboats. Federal forces replaced the Confederate defenses with their own fort a short time later.

While conveying news about their own well-being and emotions, soldiers also used their correspondence to address the course of the war and the nature of their army experiences. Letters written by single men to their parents and siblings offered stories meant to interest, entertain, and impress their recipients. Such notes had a good deal in common with the travelogues that young men had earlier produced when they left home during times of peace.

The Confederate private Jeremiah Tate lacked the sophistication and spelling skills of many Civil War correspondents, but his keen eye for detail was evident in the string of jaunty notes he sent to his sister back in Alabama. As he left home just days after the Confederate bombardment of Fort Sumter, the thirty-two-year-old began what would be a regular set of descriptions and stories. One of the first letters explained his first weeks as a soldier and told of ever-present scenes of parting. He closed his composition with a view of the Alabama capitol, which had recently housed the Confederate Congress.

Montgomery, Ala.
May 12, 1861

Dear sister,

I seat my self to inform you whir I am and what I am doing. We left Pickensville on last sunday evening we landed in mobile on tuesday evning & lay over until Wednesday mornin we then got abord of the St. Nicholas & started for Montgomery. . . . We had cum to the conclusion that we would not be cald to our supprise the call came and we had but a few hours to prepare for starting. I could not git out of the company on honorable terms so I cum to the conclusion to see them out for it shall never be said that Jerry was a coward & wood not fight for this cuntry. it is a hard life to live but we have to put up with it.

I have witnessed friends and relatives parting frequently. I never witnessed parting until the day we left Pickensville there was the largest crowd I ever saw in that place. We have one hundred and two men in our company and as good harted boys as ever lived any whir the boys was very serious for severall days whilste home was fresh on their memorys for the last few days they seem to chir up and pass off the time as pleasantly as possiblly. You must excuse my short letter ill composed for my mind is so frusterated. when I get to Pensacola I will write to you and give you a full history of my travails give my love and respects to all in quiring friends. Direct your letters to fulton Florida in care of captain SV Ferguson.

Yours affectionately JM Tate.

from whir I am sitin I can view the Capitol of Ala rite soon.

Union soldiers used their early letters to draw attention to the exotic nature of a region most entered for the first time. Lysander Wheeler, a Sycamore, Illinois, recruit in his mid-twenties, drew upon his preconceptions about the slave South during his first days in the bluegrass region of Kentucky. Along with a description, he used the following letter to his family to evaluate African-American loyalties. His remarks came just weeks after President Abraham Lincoln had adopted a new policy that helped move the war for the Union into a full-fledged assault upon slavery.

Sunday
Oct 5 / 62
Shelbyville [Ky.]

Dear Parents and Sister,

. . . This is a nice country we are marching through now down east style. good dwellings and there is lots of slaves here withal, at most every house the niggers are out to the road with the white women and some white men we ask the niggers all sorts of questions a good many say Massa is in the Secession Army. Two or 3 volunteered to go with us, went a little ways and backed out, they are all about like the one Dustin has as regards their manner of talking. They are well brought up for niggers every thing looks as we've saw Southern life represented. The nigger women with a big white hankerchief on their heads and it is fun to see 10 or a dozen nigger children dancing around in the door yard with as little clothes on as possible. They seem to be happy as clams they all say they are for the union. . . .

Lysander

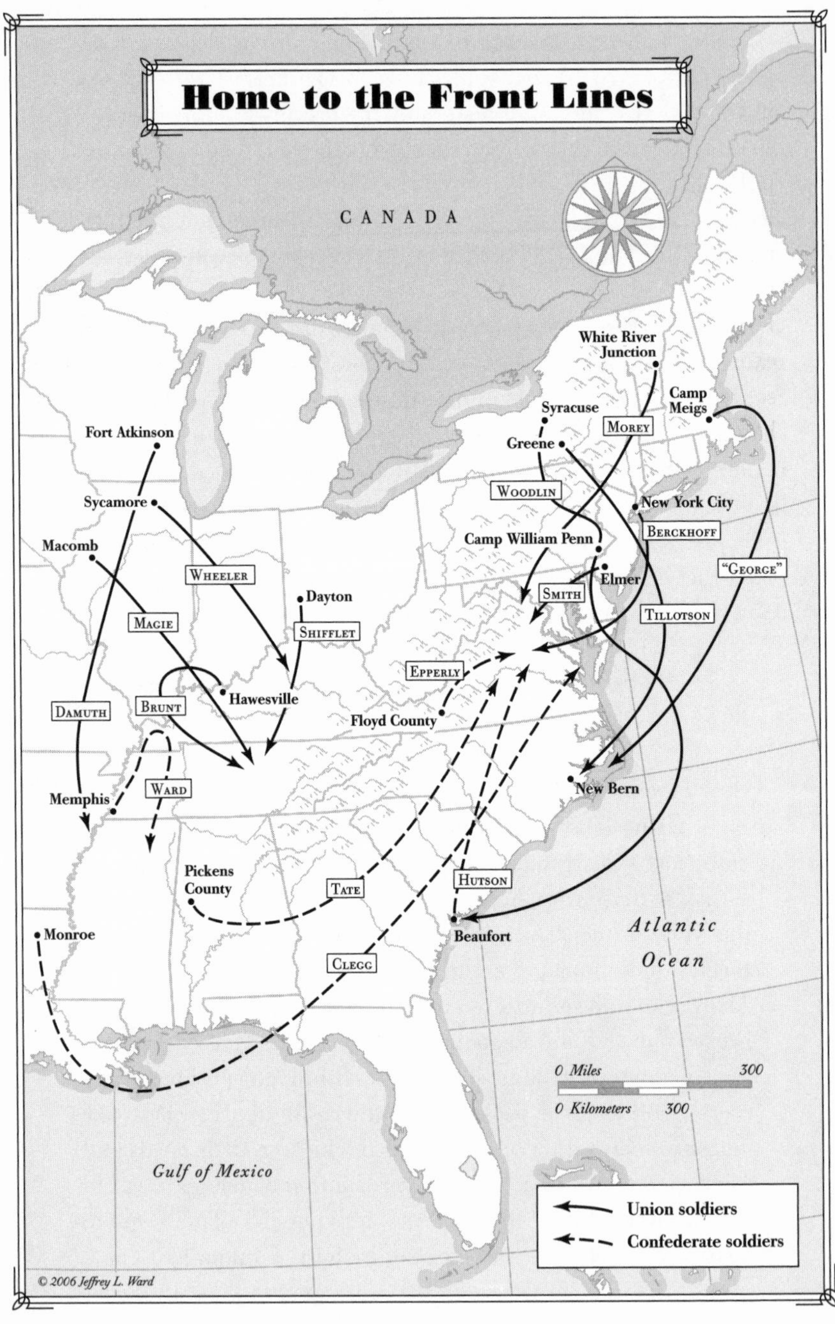

Home to the Front Lines
CANADA
White River Junction
Camp Meigs
Syracuse
Morey
Greene
Fort Atkinson
Woodlin
New York City
Sycamore
Berckhoff
Camp William Penn
Macomb
Elmer
"George"
Wheeler
Dayton
Smith
Magie
Shifflet
Tillotson
Epperly
Hawesville
Damuth
Brunt
Floyd County
New Bern
Memphis
Ward
Pickens County
Hutson
Tate
Beaufort
Monroe
Atlantic Ocean
Clegg
0 Miles 300
0 Kilometers 300
Gulf of Mexico
Union soldiers
Confederate soldiers
© 2006 Jeffrey L. Ward

Letters sent from the more exotic Deep South conveyed an even greater sense of wonder. Three months after Dolphus Damuth enlisted in the Twenty-ninth Wisconsin Infantry, he found himself on the Mississippi River, where he proudly noted increasing signs of Federal supremacy. After describing his new circumstances, he closed the following letter with a crudely racist aside. Like most white soldiers, Damuth regarded blacks as inferiors, though his views, like those of soldiers more generally, proved to be remarkably fluid as the war progressed. Damuth's sense of his own racial superiority did not prevent him from expressing strong support for emancipation and the arming of black soldiers, or even from considering how he might lead former slaves into battle.

Camp Bryant
November 7, 1862

Dear Friends,

I sepose you are all anxious to here whear we are and how we are getting along. . . .

I went after landing and found a good place to camp in a thicket of Cotton wood saplings. The boys went to work and built a comfortable brush house and here we are on the banks of the Mississippi. I in command of 27 men doing guard duty in an enemyes country and the best feeling lot of boys you ever saw. We have just been down to the river and had a good wash. The water looks very dirty but it tastes good. Thear is no large boddies of Rebbles here but the country is full of Gurilliaes who skulks around and take off our pickets. . . .

There will be a large army start for Vicksburgh some time but not until all the new Regts gets here from Wis. Then I sepose we will have a fight if we whip them out thear then the river will be open to its mouth and I think we can clean them out thear it is about 300 miles to Vicksburgh we will have to march thear I belive but we are good for it if we feel as well as we do now. . . .

. . . when I was coming down this river I wished you all could see what I saw. The old Forts whear our men had fought and gained and the gun boats and evry thing in that line that we had read so much about and wished that we could see was before us. But the country is a hard looking place and the people looked as if they were half starved but the Blacks are fat, they cheer us evry whear we go. They all know what is going to happen the 1st of Jan what don't we will tell as we go I hope you will all write when you rec'd thus and send me a paper with the Election returns in. You don't find any Bryan Democrats* down here. They are all damn abolitionists down here.

Sate you must write me a letter right off or I will spank you when I get back. I will send you a little niger in my next letter if you want.

My love to all good By,
Dolph Damuth

Damuth's enthusiasm reached an even higher register the following spring, as he followed the Union army toward Vicksburg. He wanted to share some of his wonder at this lush semitropical otherworld with his large farm family on the Wisconsin frontier, even though he knew that they were more concerned with his military duties than his collecting of flora and fauna.

April 15, 1863
Milliken's Bend La.

Dear Friends,

I sepose I have a chance now to write a few lines that will reach you. . . .

This is the most beautiful place I ever saw. Such fruit trees of all kinds peaches are a quarter grown Apples are as large as Robbins eggs the Gardans are full of flowers of all kinds. I will send you a rose and an other kind. They will likly be wilted but you can see a rose that grew away down South in Dixie.

But I sepose you are thinking of Something beside the beauties of the South. It is about the fight that is about to take place. I sepose you think we soldiers are trembling in our Shoes for fear of being in the fight but I can tell you and truly to that

*Damuth likely had in mind the Wisconsin lawyer Edward G. Ryan, a prominent Democrat, whose incendiary antiabolition speech had made headlines just a few weeks earlier.

such is not the case. I don't believe thear is ten boys in our Co that really don't want to be thear or have any dread of it. I am just as contended here as I would be at home and knowing and thinking as I do now a great deal more. So when you hear that Vixburgh is taken and the 29th was in the fight and fought like men I should think you ought to be proud of us and things look like it now. . . .

No more at present,

From Dolph

By sending a rose itself, rather than a mere written description, Damuth acknowledged that new sights and experiences could not be conveyed with words. William Clegg of Louisiana seemed to have agreed when he sketched a flower in his 1865 diary. Like other soldiers with drawing skills, he recorded the rich environment around him with vivid images.

Other soldiers used sketchbooks to compose a series of visual depictions. These now furnish one of the most powerful means of seeing the Civil War through the eyes of those who fought its battles. A small

Figure 5. Sketch from William Clegg's 1865 diary.

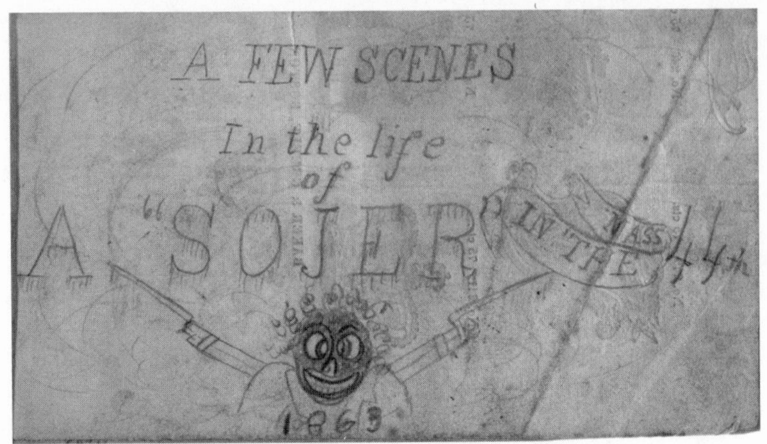

Figure 6. Title page of "George"'s Scenes, 1863.

Figure 7. "George" cutting his foot.

notebook containing nearly forty pages allowed one anonymous soldier in the Forty-fourth Massachusetts Infantry to record what would otherwise have been forgotten details of this unit's nine months of service. Most of the slim handmade sketchbook involved the cartoonish misadventures of a Massachusetts private named George, who was very likely an autobiographical figure. Whatever the case, "George"'s exploits revealed the comic absurdities of camp life and the travails experienced by a common soldier.

The sketched encounter between the Forty-fourth Massachusetts and a local alligator recorded the unit's surroundings on the North Carolina coast with tall-tale exaggeration. An even more prominent theme

Figures 8 and 9. "George" is eaten by a Carolina alligator, then escapes.

of these pictures was the presence of African-Americans. The Federal presence at New Bern attracted former slaves who experienced their first taste of real freedom by mingling within a free black community that had numbered several hundred at the beginning of the war. The sketchbook's cover emphasized this central black presence by featuring the caricatured face of a local African-American.

The nineteen watercolors created by Private Henry Berckhoff were vastly more accomplished than the sketches of the Massachusetts soldier. The best of these are among the most moving renderings of Civil War soldiering that now exist. Berckhoff left no written account of how he composed these scenes, nor did he indicate whether he planned to sell the work or simply share it with a smaller private audience. He was serious enough about the work, however, to finish what began as pen-and-ink drawings with a subsequent application of watercolor paint.

Berckhoff's scenes go beyond detailing the personal experience of a single soldier as they follow the collective life of his regiment. His sketchbook opened with the departure of the New York German Rifles, which General Louis Blenker raised among Manhattan's German-speaking community in the spring of 1861.

The series concluded when this same unit was dissolved in 1863, even though Berckhoff himself reenlisted and fought with another reg-

Figure 10. Detail of Henry Berckhoff, "Marching to the seat of war 27 May 1861."

iment for the last two years of the war. Deciding to include scenes only from the first stage of his service, Berckhoff sustained the coherence of a group portrait. This tendency to subordinate the individual to the regiment was evident within each of Berckhoff's individual compositions. Even the apparently solitary figures who stand picket do so close to other troops, with the sentry in "Bivouac on the Potomac" guarding a row of sleeping bags and that of his relatively late "RailRoad guard near Brooks Station" marching a short distance from a snowy campfire.

More is known about Berckhoff himself than about his watercolors. Military records document both his Civil War experiences and his subsequent four decades of service in the regular army. These records indi-

Figure 11. Detail of Henry Berckhoff, "RailRoad guard near Brooks Station February 1863."

cate that he was a twenty-year-old clerk upon his enlistment in April 1861. His halting English in official communications suggested that he continued to speak the German he had learned in his native Leidingen; this may be a clue to why he conveyed his experience with finely wrought images rather than in words. While he never married, he did maintain contact with his mother, who lived in New York during the war and who died some time before Berckhoff retired from the army in the 1890s. Unlike other Civil War artists, Berckhoff did not use his drawing skills as a means of advancing his career. He seemed never to have requested assignments as a mapmaker or an architectural draftsman, which would have allowed him to escape the routines of common soldiering.

Berckhoff's ability to balance description, narrative, and reflection in his watercolors was realized in many of the diaries soldiers used to document their military service. Among the most interesting of these artifacts was a journal written by Private William Woodlin of the Eighth United States Colored Troops (USCT). This New York private ventured south in the fall of 1863, several months after the Federal government had begun to enlist African-Americans. Woodlin's experiences began just outside Philadelphia at Camp William Penn, where he entered the service as an infantryman and an army musician. From entries he made in his diary we know that Woodlin, who enlisted at the age of twenty-two, was highly literate and a talented horn player. These also indicate he likely worked as an agricultural laborer before joining the ranks.

The following selections were recorded at a relatively early stage of Woodlin's enlistment, when his regiment journeyed to South Carolina by ship, trained in the Carolinas, and took up their assigned duty at Fernandina, Florida, a port that was safely under Union control. Like white Northerners journeying into unknown territory, Woodlin was captivated by the new sights, smells, and tastes of the Deep South. His distinctive exactitude was everywhere evident, from his careful numbering of a captured alligator's teeth to his precise description of how quinine, a common remedy for low-country diseases, might affect a soldier's health.

[January] 23rd [1864] Passed Charleston at about 9 A.M., an occasional gun fired; and saw smoke rising from various points.

24th Landed at Hilton at 9 A.M. formed in line and march outside of the Entrenchments and encamped.

25th We went into the woods and practiced Home, Sweet Home, and another Quick Step, but had no tents to sleep in as yet. . . .

[February] 6th We had a very pleasant sail all day and made Fernandina about 6 P.M. and coaled, and our cooks went ashore and made some coffe for us. We weighed anchor about 5 A.M. on the 7th. . . . The 54th Mass. Landed first and exchanged shots with the rebel pickets no one hurt seriously. Some half dozen rebels taken prisoners. We marched about ¼ of a mile from town and encamped for the night. I sat up all night to cook my meat.

8th Our men went out on a scout and got corn, molasses, and other things. there were also quite a No of Rebels captured during the night. Some of the men went into town and got oranges from some of the citizens, also some Banannas. . . .

[March] 4th Did some heavy practicing and about 10 A.M. we were ordered to join the rest of Our Reg on the South side of the town; on reaching here, we rec'd the old familiar huts of the servts of the Old Reb who formerly lived here which we cleaned out, making a fine place to practice. . . .

15th Rained last evening & changed into very cold weather for this season of the year saw a blue bird last evening cook a catfish head this morning very good. . . .

[May] 29th We had good success at singing at church. Mrs. Bude sang Alto for us. The boys belonging to the picket boats brought down an Aligator head which they had killed. It was 14 ft. & 9 inches long. His mouth contained some 79 teeth, they were taken out and his jaw made into rings and other ornaments by the boys. The bones look much like ivory. . . .

[July] 2nd Very warm all day. Still sick. . . . The effects of quinine on the system. If taken in large doses it is apt to effect the head unpleasantly and produces virtigo deafness and stiffness of the joints. . . .

4th There is no work done here of any consequence today as 9 of the boys went to Jacksonville no boats passed this day. The boys killed two Alligators and did various other funny things.

The Louisiana private William Clegg, the last of the penmen chronicled here, also began a diary with a record of his travels. Making his way east on train, boat, and foot, the young North Carolina native traveled from Monroe, Louisiana, to the Chesapeake Bay, taking him farther than any soldier featured in this book. Perhaps because of the distance covered, Clegg sought out the familiar when he arrived at Yorktown, Virginia, in the spring of 1861. The following entries demonstrated both Clegg's eye for detail and his staunch Confederate patriotism.

> May 24 [1861] about day break took the steamer for Yorktown (a part of the regiment proceeded us) at which place we arrived about 11 o'clock a.m. Pitched our tents the same evening within the old intrenchments of Cornwallis. Very few fortifications as yet thrown up. Negroes busy at work on the river batteries both on the York and Gloucester sides. Saw a good many things about Yorktown. Interesting on account of their connection with the scenes of 1781—marks and reminiscences of the last battle of the Revolution are still visible there, in fact there are many incidents connected with the place to render it interesting. . . .
>
> July 4th Camp in a fever of excitement on account of rumors from below, a battle expected in a day or so. This is the first 4th dawning on our glorious Confederacy, but what a change has come upon the country. "The home of the free the land of the brave." We see a disrupted Union and feel sensibly that after all, no written constitutions and laws framed by the wisest of our ancestors no common country made sacred by the blood of our forefathers no brotherly share in past victories is proof against a separation that wreaks its passion in slaughter and furnishes with the victims of the battlefield so many proofs of the fact that our once the best of all human governments is a failure & was but an experiment. . . .
>
> July 6th I have spent many a pleasant hour while at Yorktown sitting on the breastworks in front of the river, watching looking down into the bay and around on the beautiful scenery. My mind in the meanwhile wandering to those dear loved ones far away, and musing upon scenes present & past in my life. . . .

> 13th October 12 o'Clock I am now sitting on the banks of James River looking at Newport News which is about 5 miles distant. Four large vessels are in sight lying out opposite the point. . . . I can see the enemy's flag on the point. That once proud emblem of liberty now disgraced and carried at the head of armies in the futile attempt to subjugate a free enlightened & brave people. While I am looking upon this I see dense clouds of smoke burst up from the woods & darken the horizon. This is the enemy burning the homes of our citizens, and visiting the horrors of war upon our defenceless women & innocent children.

Clegg's journal entries were marked by an unusually developed historical imagination and a contemplative stance toward the pageant of war just then commencing. His writing established the largest contexts available, as he drew on the contrasts between past and present and the looming battles between good and evil. His emotions were directed less toward home or family (details he mentioned only in passing) than toward national celebrations and symbols. By noting these items he measured the distance between a recent past within the United States and a future outside it.

Such lines had a tenderness all their own. Their poignancy did not depend on whom Clegg addressed or even what he described. His diary explored with unusual self-consciousness what it was like to stand at the crossroads of history. The other penmen also found solace in realizing that later generations would value their communications, descriptions, and reflections. As they penned even the most intimate lines, they had posterity always in mind.

TWO

Army Life and the Comforts of Home

As he neared the end of his second year in the Confederate army, Jeremiah Tate wrote his sister back in Alabama, "Whi shood I use the word truble?" That was a word "that a solger never thinks of for thar is one truble after another heapt upon his mind til he has becum so accustomed to it he never thinks but what evry thing is all right."

Like most soldiers, Tate realized that becoming an army private had guaranteed what seemed to be an infinite supply of difficulty. Veterans later reminisced fondly about the world of camps, tents, and rations they had survived as young men. At the time, however, the discomforts of soldiering mattered most, and these brought forth bitter complaint or sulking resignation, or some combination of these two. The best that most could manage was to leaven their misery with a dose of humor. Tate appreciated the comic side of the soldier's predicament and wrote in the following note how well-told stories of hardship might bring a good chuckle in the future.

Orange C.H. Va
Aug the 7th 1863

Dear Cousin Darcus,

To pass a way a few of the lonely and desolate minutes of a camp life I have cum to the conclusion to write you as thare is nothing that I can think of that wood afford mee more pleasure than to convers with you by letter as I kno that it is impossible to speake verbaly, if I was only permitted to spend a few days at home I cood tell you of many little instances that has occurd in the army since I saw you that wood amuse you and make you laugh. . . .

J. M. Tate

The Civil War's massive volunteer military helped make army life a topic of dark humor. The written records of soldiers at the time were in fact the beginning of a comic sensibility that has remained part of the response of the "grunt" to modern war for the next century and a half. Union and Confederate armies each had men who could confront the unpleasant novelty of lousy food, shelter, and sanitation by making jokes. Laughter could overcome for a bit the soreness, tears, and heartache that were bound in the end to return. The same wry perspective could bring a light touch to the routines of subservience that wore upon men who were not used to such regimentation. With the important exception of former slaves, few Civil War soldiers had ever been subjected to the absolute authority and perpetually demeaning circumstances of enlisted life.

The absurdity of soldiering was the main theme of the exploits of "George" captured by the anonymous private of the Forty-fourth Massachusetts. This regiment's adventures with Carolina alligators probably had a basis in reality, but translating them into a fantastic tall tale was what made them entertaining. Most of this sketchbook's comic scenes were conveyed without farfetched embellishment. Picketing in the rain, losing food over the campfire, and injuring oneself while chopping a tree were likely to have actually happened. Soldiers facing these mishaps would have responded in exactly the way the cartoons depicted them, only their expressions being exaggerated for comic effect.

Comedy worked best among those who had actually experienced the challenges of enlisted life. The story of "George"'s service is littered with inside jokes, which suggest that the intended audience of these scenes were fellow soldiers of the Forty-fourth. Conveying the frustrations of army life to those at home usually required a different approach, and here previous expectations and earlier conversations shaped what was put in writing. Before George Tillotson wrote the following two letters, he had bragged that training with the Eighty-ninth

Figure 12. "George" on picket.

Figure 13. "George" and his comrades in the Forty-fourth Massachusetts "lose every bean."

New York had not been nearly so bad as he had feared. What changed his mind was his shipboard transfer to coastal North Carolina, the same area where the Massachusetts private "George" served. A difficult trip aboard a dreary steamer caused Tillotson to express his first real longings for comforts only his family could provide.

At sea
Jan 9th, 1862

Since I have missed the chance of sending this ashore at Annapolis I will write a few lines more. . . .

We are getting along very slow. The steamer Eastern Queen is towing the two ships that carry our regiment but last night they had to lay to and cast anchor on account of its being dark and rainy. This morning we started but had to stop again because it is so foggy they cannot keep the right channel. We have to take to our living on ship board about as we can ketch it for there is but two stoves to cook for 7 companies so about all they can do is to make coffee twice a day and cook meat once. the rest is sea buiskets which is a kind of very hard cracker. They taste pretty much like any other cracker but I have about put my jaws out of joint chewing them but today they delt out pilot bread which is very much like soda crackers. I am very glad that the children remember and want to kiss me don't let them forget. Last night I dreamed of being at home as I often do and sweet were the kisses what I took all around. . . .

Write as soon as you get this. . . .

George W. Tillotson

Off Hatteras inlet
Jan 22nd, 1862

Dear Wife,

It is with feelings of uncertainty that I undertake to write to you for the prospect of sending a letter home looks rather dubious at least for the present. We left Fortress Monroe a week ago last Tuesday morning and arrived here the next day before dark. The day that we started from Ft. Monroe was quite pleasant with a fair wind but the next was rather rough and I got somewhat wet by a big wave that came on deck while I stood by the bullworks holding on to the ropes, giving me my first taste of salt water. We are lying now where we first stoped ten days ago about three miles outside of Hatteras inlet. The rest of the fleet is all inside they towed all but us in yesterday. Since we came here the soldiers have had some work throwing out ballast (sand) which took some three days and nights with about 70 men at work at a time. I worked 12 hours at they say ten cents an hour but we have not yet the pay. . . . Myself with lots of others were taken with seasickness the day we started from Fortress Monroe and I don't believe I have got over it yet for this eternal rocking heaving rolling bobing keeps head rong side up all the while. Maybe you won't believe it but if I ever was homesick in my life it is now and I think it is a general complaint among the soldiers if I can judge from their countenances. . . .

I don't think that if these soldiers were discharged that one in a hundred could be got to enlist again if there was any prospect of being put on board ship one month. No one on the ship knows how long we are to stay on it but I am afraid we shall all be more anxious to get off of it than we are now before we do. No one has been off the ship except the Colonel and some sailors the next morning after we got here. . . .

You cant imagine how much I would give to here from home and how much more I would give to see home . . . but then I suppose the satisfaction will be all the sweeter for waiting. But then I would not insinuate that I am sorry that I enlisted though perhaps, maybe. like enough I would not enlist again to be candid I don't think I would. . . .

Your affection husband
Geo. W. Tillotson

The burdens of travel caused many soldiers to regret they had ever joined the army in the first place. Moving increased the actual distance between a soldier and his family while it drew attention to the chasm between military life and the comforts of home. Whether men traveled by boat, foot, or train, the likely result was sore bodies, empty stomachs, and queasy heads. The monotony also encouraged recollections of the world a soldier had left behind and the loaded question "Do they miss me at home?"

In the following letter Lysander Wheeler described how he and a friend managed two days of hard marching that first took them into Kentucky. It was appropriate that Wheeler wrote of this experience

Figure 14. "George" wonders: "Do they miss me at home?"

with as much pride as complaint. During the last year of the war his feet were to carry him and the rest of William Sherman's army from Atlanta through Savannah and the Carolinas to Washington, proving he could handle marches most could not even imagine.

Sunday
Oct 5 / 62
Shelbyville [Ky.]

Dear Parents and Sister,

. . . Fryday we took up our line of march our Regiment with 4 or 5 others and Cavalry and Artillery and marched 16 or 17 miles marching nearly all night—got up yesterday morning started about 11 o'clock A.M. and went 16 or 17 miles farther marching about 33 miles in all carrying knapsacks. Yesterday lots of boys pulled off their drawers and threw them away and the road all along was strewn with shirts, vests, handkerchiefs, etc. All I saw picked up was a pocket inkstand I picked up myself and I gave that away. Lots would have thrown knapsacks away if allowed to tho they belong to Uncle Sam—they won't allowed to. We do not know whether we march to day or not, the first night 50 of our company fell behind but got in most of them the next day. but Darius and I kept up without any trouble. Darius does not carry his knapsack so I put my blanket in his that saves me from carrying and sometimes he helps me carry my gun. Each man has his own gun to carry 40 rounds of secesh pills* 3 day provisions and canteen of water but the provisions grow lighter and so does the water. . . .

Lysander

The most painful journeys came when a soldier was hurt or sick and needed to reach medical care provided at a distant hospital. Charles Hutson discussed such a move in the following letter to his father, written during his second year in the Confederate army. Part of a shell had hit Hutson in the lower part of his stomach during the fighting around Richmond that became known as the Seven Days' Battles. After a short stay at a local hospital, he was sent on a harrowing journey by rail to a sanctuary that was less crowded with dead and dying patients.

Vaughn's Hospital
Farmville, Va.
July 8, 1862

My dear father,

. . . I came out to this place about 75 miles from Richmond on Sunday & have been here ever since. We were treated horribly by the Richmond authorities; having been crowded in

*_Secesh pills_ was a colloquial term for the bullets that would give "Secesh" Confederates their needed medicine.

box cars with no seats and provided with nothing to eat. We starved from dinner hour on Saturday until Sunday evening, having been accidentally detained at the Junction nearly a whole day, in an almost starving condition—I bought a few apples which stayed my appetite and enabled me to get along—This is quite a nice place for a hospital. . . . The ladies are very kind also—and their attentions remind me of dear old West Perryville and the short time I spent there with you all in April. . . .

The young Hutson was not accustomed to such rough treatment. Raised on a Beaufort plantation by a family with an illustrious revolutionary past, he had in the late 1850s attended South Carolina College. There he had cultivated the art of letter writing as part of a larger repertoire of social graces and even corresponded in Latin with college chums. During his first year of service Hutson concluded that such unusual refinement would not hinder his effectiveness as an infantryman, despite the far more meager circumstances of his new life. In the following letter to two female relatives, Hutson explained how the upper echelons of Southern society would in fact make the best of all troops. They knew more about mastery, even of themselves, than those who slavishly used their bodies as mere machines.

Camp Huger
Friday November 1, 1861

Dear Sister—Dear Emily

I received your two letters with one enclosed from Miss Frances on Wednesday and have determined to merge my two answers in one. . . . We received on that evening such a bountiful supply of the good things of life, relating both to intellectual and physical comfort, that I am quite apprehensive of an injury to our moral status, when it has all vanished. We will create disaffection in our midst. But really in a style of life like this, one needs a stimulus now and then. . . .

My philosophic ideas with regard to health have been developed very satisfactorily to me & I have observed very closely. The men who lead an inactive life at Home and are ill-prepared for hardships there, make the best soldiers, particularly if they are educated. The adaptation of their minds to meet the various scenes, trials, and hardships of a soldier's life is an important fact. Now we who have been accustomed to no hardships have done most of the duties incumbent upon the company and have very seldom been sick while the robust at home have suffered & pined away. It is really melancholy to see Alston's "Horry Rebels"*—Their minds are accustomed to one beaten channel at Home & like a negro, by merely mechanical powers, they lived very well—but the slightest variation from that path completely puts them out.

I think unconsciously we are receiving an excellent education: the education of the will and desires for we must exercise a great self-control not to grumble inwardly over the position given our Regiment & its consequent inactivity. We are becoming Stoics like Capt. Haskell, who won't learn to smoke because he wishes to carry out the Stoic dictum to feel independent of the want of anything and to enjoy that independence. Charley Pinckney & myself had a long argument with him, we arguing that the pleasure derived from the positive enjoyment of anything is preferable to the pleasure derived from the sovereignty of wishing nothing—merely a comparative question. . . .

I am ever Yours affectionately,
Charles J. C. Hutson

Near the end of his first winter in camp, Hutson was still amused by the primitive conditions of camp life. The following letter to one of his dead fiancée's sisters whimsically began by insisting that his transformation into a soldier need not be permanent. He then described some of the routine duties of camp life and the disruptive influence of regimental politics that came after a broad reorganization within the First South Carolina. His complaints about the lack of combat were typical for this period, when troops in Virginia were experiencing a lull in the fighting that had lasted since the Battle of Bull Run the previous July.

*Hutson uses the nickname of the First South Carolina's Company F, whose captain at the time was Thomas Pinckney Alston.

Camp Huger
Suffolk Va.
February 6, 1862

Dear Minnie,

. . .We are becoming quite accustomed, however, to the "barbarian" life which we have so long led. It would be worth any one's while who has been accustomed to the ease of life, to take a survey of our log houses, their ingeniously made furniture and the habits of their occupants. I am afraid sometimes that having become so entirely strangers to ceremony among ourselves, we will be poor specimens of refinement when we return home. But as one who learns to swim never forgets, I hope when we go back to Rome, we will easily do as Rome does.

We have become a finely drilled and disciplined Regiment and can vie with any in Virginia or So. Ca. Indeed from Mr. Langdon Haskell's account, the troops in our state are in a universally drilled condition: he gives a very laughable account of the dress parade of a Tenn. Regiment in Gregg's Brigade. But the Government won't give us anything to do; while many of our men grumble at times considerably. . . .

I am still a distinguished Corporal, having been promoted backwards from a Lieut.—But it has taught me some good lessons. Office-seeking even in the Army has become the order of the day and patriotism has been quietly put away for afterthought. There are few who do not sincerely wish for the close of this war: the war is at such a stand-still and men have so little fighting to do, that the first bursts of enthusiasm have quietly died away and stern duty alone keeps up the willing spirit.

Your affectionate Cousin,
Charles J. C. Hutson

Measuring the distance between camp life and home was never a mere question of miles. Even after soldiers became accustomed to new routines, they continued to compare unfamiliar experiences with their former lives. Those who had grown up within slave societies appreciated how army life reversed typical patterns by introducing members of a self-conscious master class to deprivations and to a state of powerlessness usually associated with their own black "servants." Such comparisons became a running theme in Edward Ward's letters to his sister, which also made clear that Ward had at his disposal a black slave provided to him by his father. All three of the following letters were written while Ward and the rest of the Second Tennessee Infantry were camped in northern Mississippi. Though some of his remarks hinted at his disaffection, his letters at this stage were still more playful or resigned than truly embittered.

Tupelo
June 14th / 62

Dear Sister,

. . . Well Sis, I say confound this war. I despise the whole business and if ever I get into another I want somebody to have me put in a lunatic asylum. I often wish I was a negro with a good master. We keep nearly starved, and get nothing but buscuit and occasionally some fresh beef, well there is some hopes for us yet as the blackberry season is coming on. The only difficulty is there is So many of us here there may not be enough to go around. Aint a pity I can't get any more good vegetables, or fruit, or anything of that kind. Well I reckon we will come out all right after awhile. . . .

. . . We have at last succeeded in getting a boy but Pa was badly cheated in him. He has fits every now and then and is half sick the rest of the time and don't know anything about cooking, though that is no material objection at the present there is nothing to cook. . . .

Your aff. Brother,
Ed

Camp near Tupelo
June 18th / 62

Dear Sister

. . . You ought to see me now if you want a hard looking case (your beau idea probably of a highwayman or brigand on the plains of Arabia). I am almost as black as a negro, whiskers have all grown out all over my face without regard to shape and form, and my hair has become crisped and wirey. I will say I am ashamed to see a looking glass, you know I used to be such a nice young man for a small tea party. I did not know you had a picture of mine. I wish the ladies could decide which they prefer whiskers or no whiskers. At any rate I shall first make my appearance as the "Brigand Chief." George looks pretty near as hard as I do. . . .

Write soon to your aff. brother,
Ed

Tupelo
July 11th / 62

Dearest Sister,

. . . This is Saturday and like the negroes we have this day for washing ourselves, and clothes, cleaning of our camps, arms, etc. . . .We still have our own cooking to do—which goes powerful hard with me. It is true Pa sent us up a boy, but he is no account and sick most of the time.

I am sure I never drink anything and occasionally I do take a little game of draw poker just to pass the time when I am not drilling or studying Hardee's Tactics.* . . . I have had all my whiskers shaved off, and got George to cut my hair and he made such an awful cut of it that it will take it 12 months. I am afraid for it to grow out again right. Write soon and direct your letters as heretofore,

Your affectionate Brother,
Ed

Marion Epperly represented an altogether different South from that of Hutson, Ward, and other young slaveholders. Like many poorer Confederates, Epperly drew sustenance from an evangelical culture that had become increasingly popular among American "plain folk" during the early nineteenth century. As a result of these religious con-

*Confederate and Union infantrymen alike depended on this 1855 manual of rifle tactics, which was written by the future Confederate general William J. Hardee just before he became the commandant of the U.S. Military Academy at West Point.

victions, his string of letters registered a disgust with the moral filth he saw in the off-duty activities of a wicked regiment. This indirect testimony furnishes a glimpse of the manly world of gambling, drinking, and swearing that most soldiers left out of their letters lest they upset disapproving parents and wives. Though Epperly had only been in the army for a few months, he closed the letter with thoughts of joining the stream of Floyd County deserters.

Hanover C.H. Va
July 27, 1862

Dear Mary if I could Just be at home this beautiful Sabbath day you dont no what a happy beeing I would be wee cant hear and see any thing here but cursing and swairing and card playing Sonday and every day. I seames to me sometimes like it cant be possible that I can stay with such a crowd of men; but I stil put my trus in god hoping he will soon deliver me from this plase it seams to me lik it wouldant be any harme for a man to try to get rid of this plase and get to a better one if he could.

Dear Mary I sent By Mr. Roblerson for you to send me a little Butter and a culple Lbs of Soap as he was coming to Floyd in Search of Some of our Floyd Boys that runaway from this company a weak or so ago; but I supose the present conditions of thing wont give you a chanse to send them to me; I would a bin very happy to com with them men if I could of got the chanse; they found out that Pelham was going to Send some one after them and get him to detail them to go with the officer that was sent with them. I believe I will press a furlow and come aney how they cant but take my life from me if I doo. . . .

I Remain your Tru Husband until Death,
C. M. Epperly

Army food served as a constant reminder of what soldiers gave up when they volunteered. Even those with the strongest aversion to the camp staples of hardtack, beans, coffee, and pork came to realize that some nourishment was better than going without food altogether. Rations were all too often in short supply, particularly among Confederates, as the war dragged on. Both sides felt the pinch of limited food when troops were on the march or when supply lines were disrupted. Dolphus Damuth explained in this letter from 1863 how hunger triggered powerful thoughts of home. He wrote while participating in the siege of Vicksburg, whose even hungrier Confederate defenders were to surrender by early July of that year.

May 9th, 1863
In camp on the road to the Jackson & New Orleans Railroad
20 miles South of Vixburgh

Dear Sister

I rec'd your of the 20th the 5th I wrote one to you the day before but I dont know but it will ever get to you. Some of the mail that was sent came back it is very uncertain about letters going now days but it will do no harm to write them. . . .

We started from whear I wrote you last on the 6th at 6 o'clock . . . we drew 4 days rations at the river the one day before the fight. a great many of the boys lost thears in the fight and we have not drawn any thing until yesterday except fresh meat and a little corn meal. I can tell you it has been rather tough for the last few days. I lived mostly on sweet corn popped. Barney went out to kill a Sheep and give me som as usual. I dont think any one has Suffered by hunger yet but when a felow gets up in the morning with nothing to eat but popcorn it will make him think of his mothers cubbord. I have found what Aunt Myra told me was true that I would think of mothers cubbord before I got home and I have a great many times. . . .

Our Col. Read to us yesterday Gen Grant's Order Complimenting the Soldiers for the Great victory achieved at the Battle near Port Gibson and the hard Ships they had passed through without a murmur. . . . Yesterday Curtis got back with the rations we was very glad to See him and the boys that went with him they had a hard time they had to march all the time night and day to get out of the reach of the Rebels.

Soldiers hoping to improve their diet regularly requested that home-cooked food be sent through the mail. Some of these instructions were quite specific. Marion Epperly closed a note to his brothers by ordering them to "send me a good fat opasum or too." Hillory Shifflet was not so direct, but he still enjoyed the parcel sent from his wife in the spring of 1862. Eating turned his mind toward his family in the same way that hunger had done for other soldiers. The condition of these delicacies did not lessen his appreciation for them. Food that would have brought grumbling if served at home was still greatly valued by those accustomed to camp fare.

March the 11th 1862
Camp Andy Johnson
Davidson County Tennessee

Dear wife,

I take my pen in Hand this Beautiful evening to let you no that I am well at presant and hope when you git these few lines tha will find you all well. I can tell you that I got my box you sent me this evening and was glad to git it for I hante had nothing fit to eat for three weeks. I found everthing all right nothing spoilt but the chicken it was spoilt and the pies was a little moldy on top but tha ar mity good. I hante tasted the cakes yit but I no tha ar good by the way tha look. I will try them to night the boys all sworm around me like bees. I give them a pese a pie a pese. The box was on the rode one month but I will eat the cakes if tha was on the rode two months. It puts me in mind of home. I hante heard from you in a month and I want to her from you mity bad but I want to see you a heepe worst and I think I will see you in a short time if everything goes on as we expects it will but the prospect is now that we will have a fight. last night the rebbles attacted our pickets and our men kild six of them. . . .

I want to see you and the children mity bad if the war donte end vary soon I will come home on a furlow so I will see you all as soon as I can but I am in good helth at this time and I hope you and the children all is. . . .

I am mity glad that I got your box. Tom Smith got his the same day. I want you to do the best you can and right as soon as you git this letter. Derect your letters to the First Regiment of

Ohio Volinteers Company C in care of Captain Throuston via Louisville and Nashville.

Hillory Shifflet to Jemima Shifflet

Food from loved ones was one way for soldiers to reestablish familiar comforts within the army and to narrow the gap between a soldier's military and civilian lives. Another was to make living quarters as much like home as possible. Charles Morey sent a sketch of his winter tent in Virginia to reassure his sister back in Vermont about his own health and safety. The sturdy walls, chimney, and clothesline conveyed that he would be both cozy and clean as bad weather approached.

The diary of Confederate private William Clegg documented the effort required to transform soldiers' rough camps into more bearable accommodations. The following entries were made during the fall of 1861, when his Louisiana troops (and most of the rest of the eastern armies) were in the midst of several months of relative inactivity. A spurt of December activity came while there were reports of enemy threats. Despite the disruptions, winter quarters were still ready by the time Christmas was celebrated far from these men's homes.

Figure 15. Sketch of Charles Morey's winter quarters, 1862–63.

11th October Still cloudy and threatening rain. Our camp reminds one of a hog pen. Reading Shakespeare, Campbell & Nap & his Marhsl. . . .*

14th October Resting in morning. Battalion drill at 3 ½ PM. An order was read on dress parade . . . that the troops are forbid building winter quarters at Fortress Monroe, and Newport News and their commanders say they will go into winter quarters in Yorktown. . . .

9th Nov. We marched for two hours in a hard drenching rain. we spent the night on wet ground in the open air. I left camp sick and spent a horrible night. . . .

14th to 20th Nov. Still sick in camp very disagreeably situated & suffering a great deal.

Dec. 3rd to 6th Still at Dr. Martins. . . . The Reg is building winter quarters near Camp Pelican.

7th Dec. Went to town with Dr. Martin. I am under many obligations to him and his lady for their kindness to me while at their house. They are true Virginians & the kindest people I have met in the state. Stayed all night with Ben O'Rear at the College Hospital. Ben is a noble fellow

8th Left for camp in the Ambulance & arrived about dark. Roads very bad. All the surplus baggage & best tents were ordered to Williamsburg. Some of the boys have their huts built.

9th In camp the Regt engaged in felling trees between our camp & Young's Mills.

Tuesday 10th Dec. The Reg. still cutting trees. All the extra baggage and best tents were sent to Lebanon Church about 12 miles above this place.

11th Dec. More baggage and tents sent to the rear. Some of the Messes moving into their huts. Half of the comp'y's cutting trees.

12th Reg felling trees between this place and Young's Mills. Very cold.

13th Reg felling trees. Started to have logs for our house & the wagon broke down.

*J. T. Headley's *Napoleon and His Marshals*, which had been published in the 1840s, enjoyed new popularity during the Civil War.

14th Hauled logs for our hut in the morning. On fatigue duty in the evening.

15th Regt's inspection & review. John Leseuer left for Home—Boys busy on their huts.

16th On Guard at the Col's tent. Put up our house. Pretty handwork too. Camp Pelican.

17th Dec Busy with our hut about 3 PM we were ordered to pack up, put our guns in good order & be ready for an attack to night which the officers seem to expect. Every thing is now ready for a hasty move. I am afraid we will leave our new huts but hope we will give the enemy an opportunity of forcing us from them.

18th to 21st Busy working on our hut nothing very interest transpiring in camp. reg't now in their winter quarters. . . .

25th Christmas and a very dull one to me. Some of the boys in the Reg very happy. At night I was detailed on guard, had a very comfortable post by the fire. Camps were very quiet considering the amount of whisky drank and the number drunk.

Most soldiers had their own comfort in mind when they devoted attention to their quarters. But creating a proper home also had a collec-

Figure 16. Detail of Henry Berckhoff, "Building Fort Blenker September 1861."

tive aspect, and this sense of common endeavor was a primary theme of Henry Berckhoff's depiction of the quarters of the New York German Rifles. "Camp at Roache's Mill" (see color insert) showed how his regiment's first military home was a tidy row of shelters nestled within a peaceful landscape of mountains and trees. The tents of enlisted men and the larger headquarters of the foreground were surrounded by evidence of peacetime activity, with the mill on a stream indicating the camp's location and the railroad tracks and roads showing routes of approach. Unlike any other view in Berckhoff's sketchbook, it did not include any actual soldiers in the composition, a decision that intensified the picture's overall tranquillity.

Berckhoff's subsequent visions of camp life were brimming with human activity. By the fall of 1861, the Eighth New York had already joined several other units in the hard work of surrounding Washington, D.C., with fortified defenses. Berckhoff's sketch of Fort Blenker's construction showed men in a variety of tasks, as they chopped and hauled trees, dug dirt, removed stumps, formed terraced earthworks, and placed cannons and tents at the fort's highest positions. Soldiers apparently did not have the help of horses or mules in completing this backbreaking work during what seemed to be a warm, sunny day. They provided the brawn, while officers in red caps on the lower right directed their efforts and monitored the fort's progress.

"Morning scene at Camp Hunters Chappel" took a similarly busy set of activities to establish an idyllic view of soldiers' own time. Its closer range, which allowed for a detailed etching of individual soldiers, made this one of Berckhoff's most accomplished pictures. The activities featured in this scene each took place within an orderly environment that the public associated with German recruits. These troops' reputation for cleanliness and discipline made their camps a favored destination of military and civilian observers wanting to inspect these well-ordered all-male villages. Each of the scenes that Berckhoff included established the importance of clean water to a successful camp. The stream crowded into the bottom left of his picture was used for bathing, for washing clothes, for drinking, and for cooking. As a result, it became the focus of morning activity, just as tents and fires drew soldiers at night and parade grounds and drilling fields hosted their daytime assemblies.

Figure 17. Detail of Henry Berckhoff, "Morning scene at Camp Hunters Chappel October 1861."

Figure 18. Another detail of Henry Berckhoff, "Morning scene at Camp Hunters Chappel October 1861."

Figure 19. Detail of Henry Berckhoff, "Bridge building at New Market 5 June 1862"

The commanding position of officers was a recurring theme of Berckhoff's pictures, which showed regimental leaders in a generally positive light. Army life was saturated with a sense of hierarchy, which determined how a common soldier would relate to his superiors and how he would perform his range of assignments. Berckhoff set off the officers in his pictures by featuring their distinctive red hats and by depicting their pointing gestures of command. An outstretched arm signaled instructions that were meant to be obeyed, whether in the context of the camp or the battlefield or in the passage of a wagon toward a river crossing.

Ordinary soldiers expressed a range of attitudes toward the officers who directed their every activity. Leadership among volunteer troops grew from perceptions of a man's standing within his local community. During the early stages of the war enlisted men chose their lieutenants and captains in elections held at the company level. Such rituals of democracy helped fighting men extend their sense of themselves as civilians, a perspective often at odds with military notions of absolute authority. Even so, there were well-defined barriers between men of higher rank and those from whom unquestioning obedience was required.

The Kentucky Unionist William Brunt was less concerned about the potential for friction across ranks than were many soldiers, in part because he sensed a bond of mutual respect that united all men under arms. The following letter discussed the officers of his first unit, an Illinois regiment in which Brunt served as a private. He seemed to be as comfortable at this stage in following orders as he would be in giving them when he became a captain of black troops.

Ft. Donelson Tenn
June 11th, 1863

Dear Friend Martha,

Your kinde & welcome letter of May 31st came to me yesterday while I was on Pickett. I feel very thankful to you for writing twice to receiving a letter once from me. I am really sorry that you did not get my letter descriptive of our fight on the 3rd of Feb. for I think it would have been interesting to you. I have thought of writing several times since But have been very busey. . . .

I don't believe that abuse from the Officers over me can ever make me forget my sacred Oath & duty to our glorious cause. I believe I would suffer death from sheer abuse rather than desert our dear old Flagg. But dear Friend Martha Thank Heaven I have nothing to complain of in this respect For our Officers are as generous as they are brave. I have never had a harsh word from one of them yet nor do I know of more than one or two cases of unjust conduct on the part of Regimental or Company Officers towards those under them. I feel proud of our regiment for this & I cannot help but attribute our efficiency to the kind considerateness & noble bearing of our Officers toward the truly patriotic men under them. It is a fact that purely Patriotic motives brought both men and officers into the field. There is a strong warm attachment between Officers & men & a mutual pride in each class for the other. This makes it pleasant for all concerned. . . .

Please write soon, give me all the news as usual.

Yours Respectfully,
William Brunt

Initiation into the army life of routine and obedience began with an intense period of regimentation in training camps. In the following entries the African-American private William Woodlin began what became a yearlong diary with an overview of life at Camp William Penn, just outside Philadelphia. His written notes described the problem of regulating misbehavior and suggested how the military authority held by white officers commanding black troops built upon and extended America's persistent racial hierarchies. Woodlin understandably emphasized the special role he played in the pomp of military routine, since his enlistment as a corps musician required him to learn the songs that would help both to organize drills and reviews and to lead his troops through the streets of Philadelphia and Manhattan.

1863 Journal

Nov. 18 General review of troops here by Gen. Casey.

26 Thanksgiving day. A present of $100 made to the Reg which was laid out in apples, pies & coffee. Speeches by Gov. Cannon of Del. A gentle[man] from Eng. and some others.

27 went over to the Barracks to carry a flag pole, the whole Reg.

28 A very heavy rain and a cold one followed by a cold snap of 3 days, which is just beginning to ease up this the 2nd day of Dece towrd evening.

Dec. 5 We have had Battalion drill for the past two days under our two Field officers. on the third there was a great row in Camp from there being a little liquor brought in. On the fourth one of our Corps had his stripes ripped off for leaving the ranks without leave.

6th Sunday cold but we had an inspection which was hard to endure. in the afternoon we had a meeting where I sung again as usual with others.

7th We did not drill much to day, but in the evening there was a great row, from a drunken man being struck by an officer with his sword. One of our men knocked the Capt. down; two were sent to the guard house from this Co. . . .

[January] 8th [1864] Today the band went out on dress

parade for the first time, and played yankee doodle and old Joh Brown. It went off well, though very cold.

9th We had a new chord given us to practice in today and I had my gun stock varnished. On the 8th we got our new knapsacks & traps, fine but small.

9th The news came that we were to move to South Carolina soon.

10th We were all on inspection nearly all day; the Col said that we were to give up our guns, who belonged to the band.

11th We did not play at all as the members were nearly all gone. Shank among the rest. Whiskey held high sway here all day. At night some 100 new recruits came in, with a semblance of a Band with them, and a poor one at that.

12th We were called up and dressed up in our Zouave Suit* today, and played for Dress Parade. We also got our leggins; and gave up our guns, who belong to the band. We did not have very good success. . . .

14th We went out in the road to practice twice today; a ball whizzed over our heads, which made quite a sensation amongst us.

15th We played for guard mounting this morning and stopped.

16th We rec'd orders to pack up this morning at roll call to be ready to move at a moments warning. fell in at 10 A.M. and the start was put off until 1/2 past 1 P.M. When the whole Reg was formed in line, and march out in review before the 22nd. Band Playing Yankee Doodle. Paraded through Front & across Walnut Strs and took the carrs for New York where we arrived at about 9 A.M.

17th Paraded through Cort & Broadway down Canall Strs to the wharf where we shipped at night.

Once the first stage of training was complete, troops moved nearer the battlefield, where the regimentation of soldier life continued. In

*Zouave suits were designed to resemble the brightly colored baggy uniforms worn by French colonial troops in northern Africa. These enjoyed some popularity among white troops early in the war and experienced a brief resurgence when the first USCT regiments were raised.

these settings, highly staged military reviews showed soldiers their place within the larger structure of authority and allowed them to receive face-to-face orders from the very top of the military hierarchy. Such direction was impossible during battle, when the demands of modern bureaucratic command separated the highest officials from their troops. Soldiers' commentary about these reviews and other regular drills and orders often led them to reflect on military routines more generally. In the three excerpts that follow, the Illinois editor James Magie expressed impatience with what he considered to be nonsensical military protocol, Charles Morey of Vermont conveyed his sense of awe in a direct encounter with the commander in chief, and the anonymous Massachusetts sketcher turned military pomp into a subject of ridicule.

Franklin, Tenn
Feb. 17, 1863

Dear Wife—

. . . We have a new order, similar to the one we had in Louisville when we were there in September last. The regiment is required to get up at half past 5 in the morning, and stand to arms until half past 6, with knapsacks strapped upon their backs. The teamsters are also required to have their teams hitched up and they also have to stand an hour. The sense of the order no one can perceive. . . .

Your affectionate
James

Figure 20. "The Kernil" of the Forty-fourth Massachusetts, as seen by "George."

Tuesday [July] 8th [1862]

Weather very hot but [the Second Vermont] remained in camp nearly all day but just before night we were called out for review and the booming of canons announced the coming of the commander-in-chief of the army "Honest Old Abe" and he arrived at our camp just after dark but the moon shone bright and his honest countenance gives the men confidence but as he past us we were as mum as though we knew him not, yet he smiled on us and passed quietly by with uncovered head and after he returned we returned to our tents and rested quietly.

If army enlistment changed ordinary life in countless ways, so too did it alter how men faced death. Soldiers were far more likely to suffer a violent fate than were civilians, of course, and the most severe wounds brought quick deaths on the field of combat. Other fatalities took more time, however, and thus drew death into the world of the camp and the hospital. The rudimentary state of Civil War medicine assured that operations made on minor combat wounds were likely to do as much harm as good, especially since there was no appreciation for how germs were bred by unsanitary conditions. The filth of army hospitals was well known among the troops, as can be seen in the following grisly aside made by the New York farmer George Tillotson to his wife.

Pleasant Valley
October 14th, 1862

Dear Wife,

. . . Amos and Wiley Holdredge were both wounded at the battle on South Mountain. Wiley I understood was dangerously wounded in the bowels. Worden has been with his company all the while and is yet. Dont know but I could afford to loose a leg for the sake of going home but it would be rather a dangerous experiment to try here at least, for almost every one of our regiment who have had a leg amputated have since died. But then what could we reasonably expect of wounds that is left without dressing until maggots crawl out of them. . . .

Your Own, George

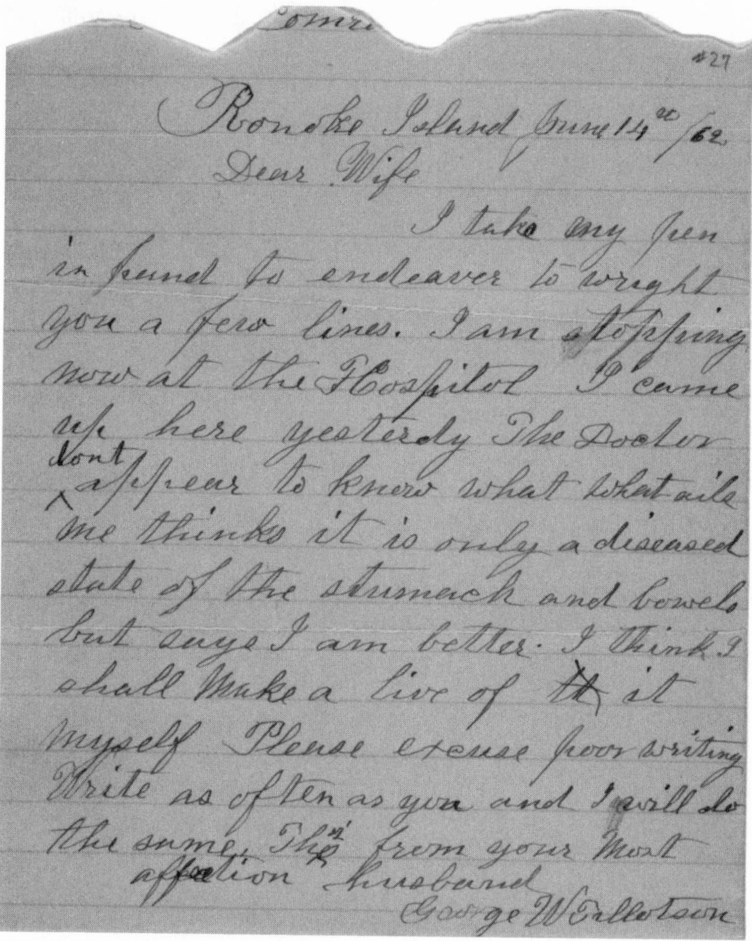

#27

Ronoke Island June 14th /62

Dear Wife

I take my pen in hand to endeavor to wright you a few lines. I am stopping now at the Hospitol I came up here yesterdy The Doctor dont appear to know what what ails me thinks it is only a diseased state of the stumach and bowels but says I am better. I think I shall make a live of ~~th~~ it myself Please excuse poor writing Write as often as you and I will do the same. Thy from your most affection husband

George W Tillotson

Figure 21. George Tillotson to his wife, Lib, June 14, 1862.

Tillotson spoke from experience since he had suffered through a prolonged hospital stay a few months earlier in what he considered the worst aspect of his soldiering career. These weeks surely produced his most recognizably pained writing, as shown in his letter of June 14, 1862. Symptoms from what turned out to be typhoid fever lingered until Tillotson died nearly fifty years later. As his experience showed, the exposure to a new disease environment was among the gravest threats to a soldier's health.

The most common cause of sickness was diet and the improper sanitation of army camps. Approximately two-thirds of all Civil War fatalities came from maladies contracted in these conditions. In the following letter to his wife and children the New Jersey blacksmith David Smith discussed his own recurring symptoms while explaining the devastating toll that a sickly encampment had upon the rest of his regiment.

Camp Near Falmouth, Va.
March 25th, 1863

Dear Lib,

. . . I was taken with a Distress in my head & breast & then I could not write. & I have been under the doctors hands ever since & am yet. But I am getting better & hope soon to be well again. Although a good many gets sick that never gets well again. we have a funeral in the Regiment nearly every day on an Average. Last night we had 3 & one of them was Corporal of our company by the name of John Gardens from near Black River Township NJ. It rained quite hard at the time & it was between sun set & dark but we have to bury them the same day they die. We are looking for a battle or to move every day & God grant that we may have something for I believe we shall soon all die if we lay here. . . .

I must now close for my head pains me much & the paper is full. I am looking for a letter from you to day. I yet & ever remain your affectionate Husband & Father,

D. V. M. Smith

Smith and his fellow soldiers soon moved away from this diseased locale, though it hardly mattered in his case. He suffered poor health from the beginning of his enlistment, and his letters home regularly reported aliments that may have resulted from his earlier abuse of alcohol. By 1863 his sharpest complaints concerned his legs, which caused him ever-greater pain after that summer's long march to Pennsylvania and back. What finally caused him to enter an army hospital, however, was a case of dysentery, the term used to describe various intestinal diseases.

Even though large army hospitals were widely associated with sickness, injury, and death, the care they provided offered more opportunities for tender affection than common soldiers found anywhere else beside home. Most of the hundreds of thousands who were admitted to hospital care recovered during their time there. A good portion suffered through the last stages of a fatal wound or illness. David Smith relied on letters to let his family know about his declining health and his last days in a Union hospital in Virginia. His fate was documented in the following two notes, the first of which was written in his own hand from the camp. The second, which Smith presumably dictated, came from a hospital and had been written by a nurse.

Au. 14, 1863
Camp Near Bristol Station near the Orange and Alexandria Rail Road Va.

Dear Elizabeth and Family,

. . . This morning I feel very bad my legs are swelled very much & pains me badly my bowels are in an awful condition & my stomach is as sour as if I had been drunk for a week. So you can guess a little about how I feel, we expect to move today or sometime very soon but I am in hopes we are not going very far for I am not able to go on a long march. . . .

I cannot eat bread & salt pork when I feel as I do at present. Write as soon & as often as you can & I will do the same. So I bid you all good bye for the present.

From your affectionate Husband,
David V. M. Smith

September 26, 1863
Stanton General Hospital Washington

My Dear Wife,

I am now in this Hospital at Washington. I write now to let you know where I am and that my health is very bad. I am pretty sick at present but with good care. I hope to be well again before long. This is a very good Hospital, it is one of the best in the city we have better care here than we would in the Field. . . .

From your most affectionate husband, D. V. M. Smith

Soldiering life had taken its toil, and Smith died on October 10, 1863, at the age of thirty-eight. Details worked out after Smith's death required a final exchange of letters between the army and his mourning family. Elizabeth Smith and government officials used the mail to arrange for his corpse to be sent from the hospital to his home, so he might be buried in a New Jersey cemetery. In his last instructions to Smith's widow the responsible official warned her not to open the casket. The delay in its transfer meant that when Smith's body finally arrived home, it would be in a state of advanced decomposition.

When Smith's family first received news of his death, they would likely have thought less of his dead body than of his soul and the possibility of its ascent to heaven. Victorians understood the afterlife as an ideal domestic home, associating the eternal resting place of believing Christians with the warmth, safety, and nurturing that were so conspicuously absent from the life of a soldier. Those still in the ranks no doubt tempered fears of miserable death like that suffered by Smith by reflecting upon its compensations. Soldiers who made the ultimate sacrifice brought honor to themselves and their families, and their example of suffering lent strength to their cause. They were also rewarded by relief from the aches, pains, and indignities that survivors continued to experience. Such trials were the stuff of army life. They were what made soldiering a burden and what made interactions with home a source of constant longing.

THREE

Combat, Bloodshed, and the Traces of Battle

Two months before dying in an army hospital, Private David Smith wrote to his wife about the fighting at Gettysburg, where he and more than 150,000 other soldiers had just concluded the most celebrated battle in American history. In the following report Smith emphasized how hard it was to convey this searing experience with a letter.

Camp Near Bristol Station
near the Orange and Alexandria Rail Road Va.
August 8th, 1863

Dear Elizabeth,

. . . I hope that we shall never get into another fight like that at Gettysburg Pa for it was awful beyond Discription. I cannot discribe it with my pencil but if I don't get to come home myself this fall I will try to give you or Charley a Slight sketch of it but I think you would not care to Read the details of the fight as it was. I will just say I sit on my knees by the side of Stone fence & loaded & fired my gun until I had blisters on my fingers as big as 10 cent peaces from Ramming down the loads & my gun was so hot I could not touch the Barrel with my hands & so was most the other I never wanted to load & shoot so fast in all my life before. . . .

The previous December Smith had experienced another scene that challenged his powers of description. Loading the Fredericksburg

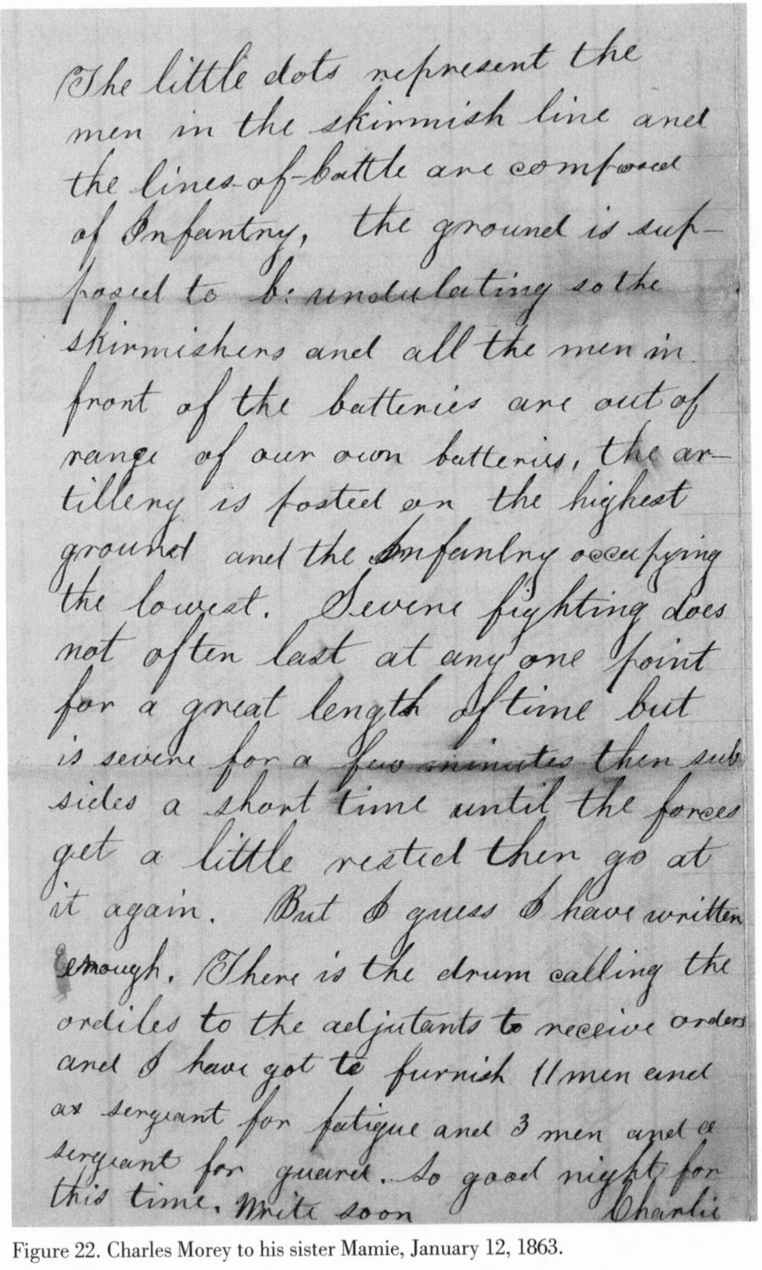

The little dots represent the
men in the skirmish line and
the lines-of-battle are composed
of Infantry, the ground is supposed to be undulating so the
skirmishers and all the men in
front of the batteries are out of
range of our own batteries, the artillery is posted on the highest
ground and the Infantry occupying
the lowest. Severe fighting does
not often last at any one point
for a great length of time but
is severe for a few minutes then sub
sides a short time until the forces
get a little rested then go at
it again. But I guess I have written
enough. There is the drum calling the
ordiles to the adjutants to receive orders
and I have got to furnish 11 men and
a sergeant for fatigue and 3 men and a
sergeant for guard. So good night for
this time. Write soon Charlie

Figure 22. Charles Morey to his sister Mamie, January 12, 1863.

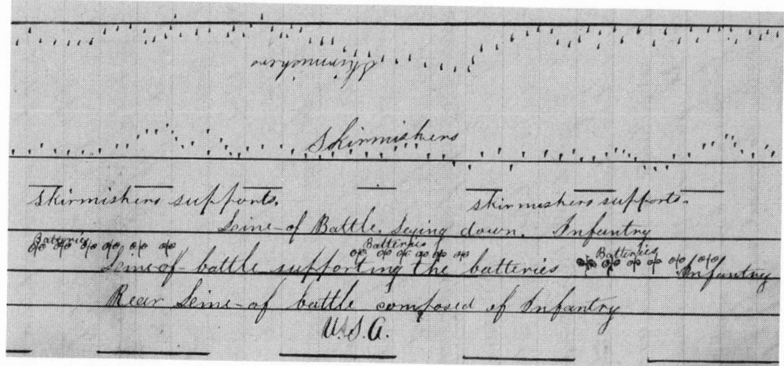

Figure 23. Charles Morey, sketch of skirmishing, in his letter to sister, January 12, 1863.

wounded into boats through the night was "the most heart sickening job I ever undertook," Smith recorded on that occasion. "I will not try to Discribe it at present." This overpowering episode, like that of Gettysburg, made Smith realize that some aspects of the war were better explained in person. Or perhaps not explained at all.

Doubtless a good many soldiers left out the nearly indescribable horrors of battle from their wartime writing. But the fact that most recorded their impressions of combat testifies to the powerful urge to document such singularly dramatic experiences. When writing letters, combat veterans kept their intended audience in mind and often focused, as Smith did, on the immediate details of where one stood and what marks were left on blistered hands or other parts of one's own body. Some detailed the general progress of events or tallied the names of those killed. When the Vermont private Charles Morey wrote to his sister on January 12, 1863, he used a strikingly abstract sketch to show how soldiers faced one another with deadly fire. Unlike the actual chaos experienced by himself and other ordinary soldiers, this schematic overview used small jots of skirmishers to clarify how armies coordinated lethal force against one another.

The blobs of ink that Morey used to depict skirmishing were a great deal more dangerous than they appeared on paper. In real life these marks were actual men, who discharged deadly efficient weapons toward the enemy while they exposed themselves to a withering hail of bullets and artillery fire that came in return. Recent advances in military technology changed battlefield conditions by making combat faster and more treacherous. The infantryman's primary weapon was his rifled side arm, which spun the newly developed minié balls toward a target with five times more accuracy than the best smoothbore muskets could boast prior to the 1840s. The most advanced of these new rifles allowed for far more rapid firing. Some offered a repeating feature (which permitted several bullets to be shot before reloading) while others allowed ammunition to be loaded at the gun's breech rather than through its muzzle (a notoriously slow process). There were similarly important improvements in some of the Civil War artillery pieces, the batteries of which Morey also included in his diagram. If shells delivered from these cannon reached their targets, their destruction came in wide swaths rather than with the directed precision of rifles. At close range, the preferred ammunition for such cannon was either grapeshot—a cluster of medium-size balls—or canister packed with small bullets, which had an effect similar to that of a shotgun.

David Smith's letter about Gettysburg showed the ultimate result of the war's massive firepower. After noting the overpowering awe he had felt during the height of the battle, Smith shared at some length a macabre adventure story. With this, he shifted attention from the battle itself to what the field was like after the Union forces had taken effective control. The excerpt that follows was part of the same letter of August 8, 1863, quoted above.

> . . . after the battle was over some of our fellows went in among the dead to get their Haversacks. They came back with short or longcakes whichever you may call them & some good biscuits. I tried to beg some but that was no use so the captain told me I was about as stout hearted as any of them I had better go and get some as there was plenty on the field. So I took my gun in one hand & my knife in the other & I started on the hardest mission I had ever been on. the ground being nearly covered with the dead and wounded, the wounded crying for help & water & to be killed & so on that I could not stand it so I cut 2 Haversacks off 2 dead men picked up as many guns on the field as I could carry & went back to the stone fence again. I got cakes & good fresh mutton well cooked enough for 6 or 8 of us.

> The Rebel sharpshooters was popping away at us all the time but they did not hit me & when we buried the dead there was loads of cakes laying about the battle field.

Writing about mangled corpses, wasted life, and the plundering of the dead required more fortitude and greater creativity than relating any other aspect of soldiering. If army life usually lent itself to contrasts and comparisons with the familiar world of home, being surrounded by death was a world apart, especially for those taking part in the killing. While it took particular skill to share this irreducible experience of soldiering with the uninitiated or the squeamish, there were challenges even for those who kept diaries or made sketches of combat presumably for their own benefit. The difficulties of tracing battle on paper was not simply a matter of communication. There were inherent challenges in using words and images to explain the elemental violence of war.

William Clegg struggled to make sense of military sacrifice while documenting one of the Civil War's earliest battles. Shortly after the Confederate victory at Bethel Church, Virginia, in June 1861, Clegg took up his pocket-size diary and drew a bird's-eye view of the topography, which he included next to a written description of that day's events. The diagram helped him track the grid of movements just as Charles Morey's sketch had made sense of the clash of opposing armies. Clegg's fervent Confederate loyalties led him to supplement his map with a justification of the dead soldiers, whose sacrifice he believed had transcendent value.

> June 10 I visited the battle field [of Bethel Church] while the dead were still upon the field and saw bones mangled in almost every imaginable way. The enemy carried most of their dead and wounded from the field. Great pools of clotted blood could be found all over the field, proving the unerring aim of our gallant rebels.
>
> . . . A circumstance connected with the fight is worth remembering which is as follows. A house behind which the enemy were taking shelter was ordered to be burnt. A young man from one of the N.C. companies volunteered to do it in the face & under fire of the enemy—while he was on his way to perform

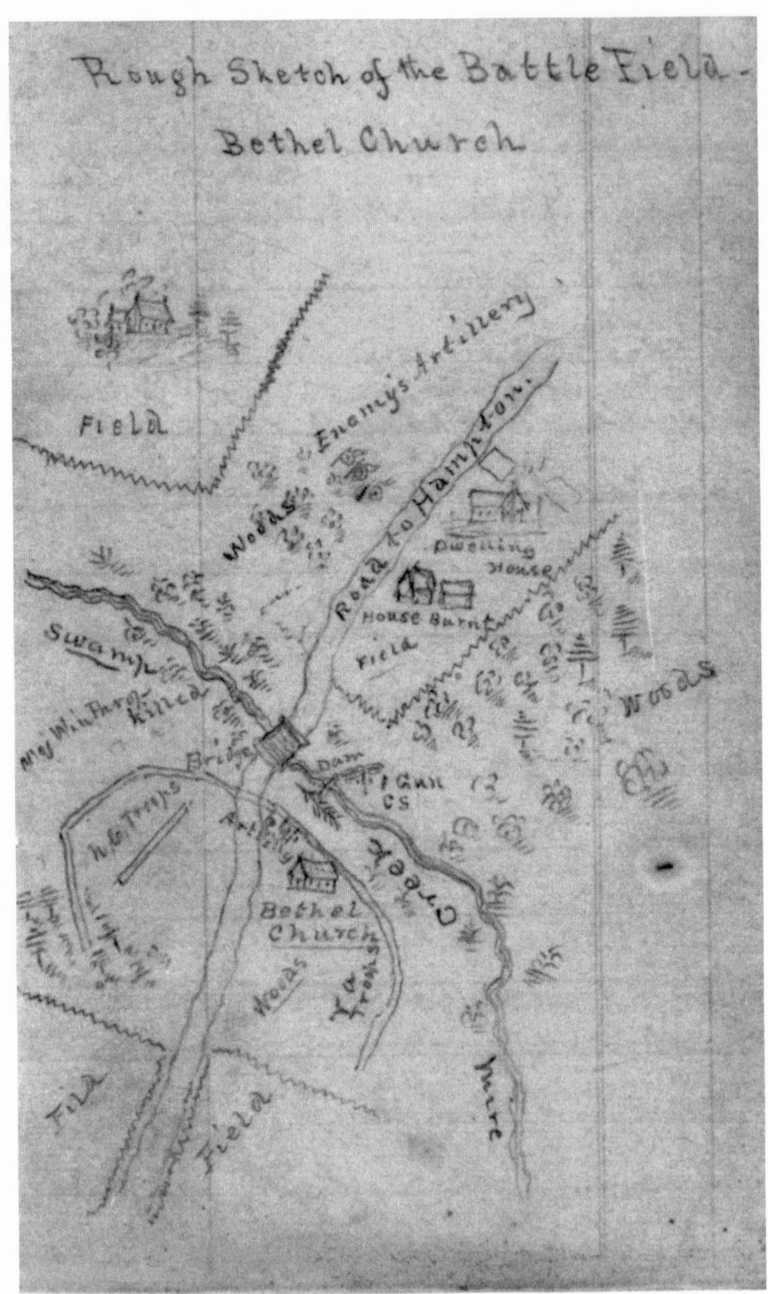

Figure 24. Sketch of Bethel in the 1861 diary of William Clegg.

the noble task he rec'd his death wound & was the one on our side that was killed, thus sacrificing his life cheerfully in the noble cause. The young man's name was Wyatt. . . .

About 6 P.M. the whole of the troops were ordered to return to Yorktown at which place we arrived about 11 o'clock at night, making a distance of 32 miles marched by our regiment that day. The night march and the scenes connected therewith are long to be remembered by me. 'twas truly an interesting sight & one that we ought to be thankful for, to see our noble soldiers marching with steady step, & determined air followed by the beautiful artillery corps with their beloved pieces, preserved but a few hours before from annihilation by the merciful interpositions of Providence.

While soldiers could gain perspective on battle from an aerial view or from patriotic conviction, what most clarified combat experience was the simple passage of time. The immediate noise and smoke of battle disoriented soldiers who were in the midst of the fight, as did the rush of adrenaline that came with the awareness of immediate danger. Most common soldiers found it nearly impossible to place their own actions with the larger sweep of events until after the fighting had stopped. Gaining additional information in the aftermath of a battle helped them overcome the immediate confusion. The harrowing ordeal could be further distilled by committing summary reflections to paper. Writing done for whatever audience was a means of imposing order on chaos.

Two sets of records made by Private Charles Morey of the Second Vermont showed how one soldier gradually absorbed the significance of the Battle of Gettysburg. His first written account of this battle came in the following daily entries of early July 1863, which contained a series of provisional and unorganized details. Conspicuously absent was any sense of how this story would end.

July 1 [1863] we were mustered for Pay by our Col. we remained on picket all day obtained plenty of bread and milk from the inhabitants near the town march at 8 o'clock p.m.

July 2 We marched nearly all night last night and all day we arrived near the battle ground near Gettysburg Penn. at night and took up position on our left flank at dark. Hard fighting toward night.

July 3 We took up a new position in A.M. and laid in a road on the left all day. Exceeding hard fighting on the right in p.m. Genl Hancock took 6000 prisoners Genl Longstreet reported killed.

July 4 We held the same position to day as yesterday, no fighting of any consequence. Our cavalry went around on the extreme left and in rear of the enemy.

July 5 Enemy left us last night and we started in pursuit and came up with the enemy near Fairfield a little skirmish and some shelling no fighting of any consequence, camped for night.

Monday 6 We marched from Fairfield to Emmitsburg after dark tonight in a terribly muddy road men suffer immensely camped about midnight.

July 7 We marched from Emmitsburg MD to the top of South Mountain terrible rainy and dark in evening awful suffering mud terrible, rain all night.

Morey was apparently dissatisfied with these notes, which contained too many obscure details, as well as some inaccuracies (the most glaring being the report of Longstreet's death). At some point in the weeks that followed, Morey composed a lengthy addendum in the back of his diary, where there was a section for "Memoranda." This more writerly account relied on drama, suspense, and figures of speech that were lacking in earlier notes. Knowing the larger context helped him convey a sense of one of the Union's most important victories.

William Woodlin's first experience under fire drew him to record his own notably breathless account. Like Morey's first record of Gettysburg, Woodlin's description of the Battle of Olustee, Florida, was more attuned to specific details than to the larger context or significance. In the following journal entries this musician of the Eighth USCT narrated the Union defeat in what was one of the few consequential military events during the winter of 1864. In presenting the bare details of this setback, Woodlin avoided a larger reckoning with what this clash meant to the history of his regiment or to the reputation of black soldiers.

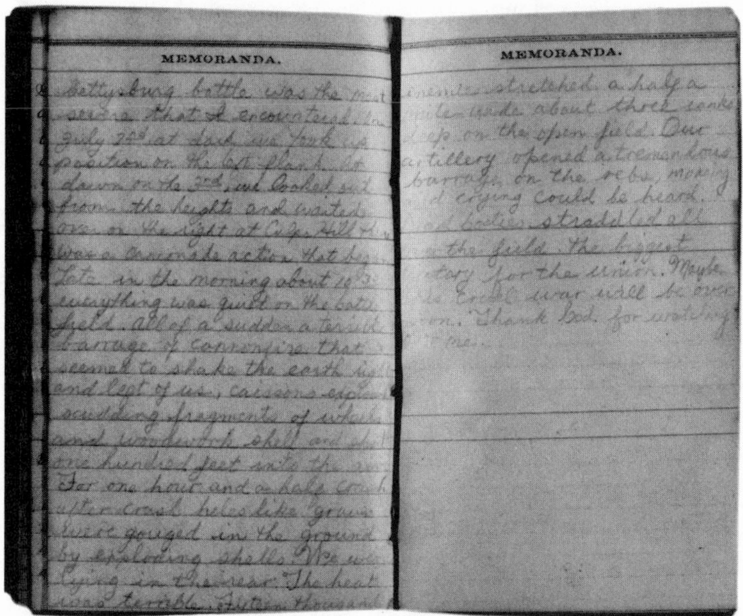

MEMORANDA.

Gettysburg battle was the most
severe that I encountered. On
July 2nd at dark we took up
position on the left flank. At
dawn on the 3rd, we looked out
from the heights and waited.
over on the right at Culp's Hill there
was a cannonade action that began
late in the morning about 10:3[illegible]
everything was quiet on the battle
field. All of a sudden a terrible
barrage of cannonfire that
seemed to shake the earth right
and left of us, caissons exploding
sending fragments of wheels
and woodwork shell and shot
one hundred feet into the air.
For one hour and a half crash
after crash holes like graves
were gouged in the ground
by exploding shells. We were
lying in the rear. The heat
was terrible. Fifteen thousand

MEMORANDA.

enemies stretched a half a
mile wide about three ranks
deep on the open field. Our
artillery opened a tremendous
barrage on the rebs, moaning
and crying could be heard.
[illegible] bodies straddled all
the field. The biggest
victory for the Union. Maybe
the Civil war will be over
soon. Thank God for watching
me.

Figure 25. Selection from Charles Morey's 1863 diary.

[February] 20th [1864] We rec'd our rations last evening and got underway about 1/2 past 6 A.M. at a quick step on the left of the division, passed Sanders Station about 11 A.M. about 12 m. (as near as could be learned) from B's Plantation; we had a very rapid as well as fatiguing march; passed through a'deal turpentine forest. after this halt we were ordered forward, & soon could hear the roar of Canon & the rattle of Musketry ahead of us, we were hurried up to the line of battle at the double quick and our Reg was place in the center and rec'd the hottest fire that was given; The Col. fell the Major wounded a Capt, & several lieutenants. the band and Drum Core went up to the front ahead of the Cavalry and were exposed to a very hot fire: for a while when we fell back to the R.R. until we were in danger of being taken by a flank movement of the Rebs: we got away however and had another station for a while: when we were again move a mile farther from the Battle field, which was in the front of Lake City. we built some fires there & was halted by the Division Dr. for a while after which we move on untill we reached the station. we left in the morning 8 am blow the scene of action nearly worn out with fatigue and cold. we reached there about 1 A.M. that night and stayed untill daylight.

21st we again moved on this morning to Baldwinsville, and made short halt and formed in line of Battle, ate little & again moved on through swamp & water . . . on to Camp Finnegan, where we stoped a short time and then turned to the left to the R.R. where we had rations issued to us & moved down the R.R. a mile. turned off again halted to get hard tack & got none. we then turned to the left through Swamps & some very fine land; saw more cattle that had seen anywheres else, we reached our Camp about Sundown, and had a good nights rest, though we were in danger of being attacked at any moment. . . .

25th All quiet till about 12 A.M. when an order came in for us to move as quick as possible to Jacksonville as the Rebs were on us, we of the band & Drum Core went directly into town, where Troops were coming from Gunboats and from the front all the time: and rifle pitts were thrown up. . . . we are under the com'd of Brig Gen Fields now formerly of the 54th Mass Reg' and are going to be in reserve across the river. there are six Colored Regs here at present, four of whom are from the North.

It was a full eighteen weeks later when Woodlin next referred to this battle. He recorded the following facts without even mentioning the name Olustee. By including this information in quotation marks, Woodlin indicated that the tally came from an official report rather than his firsthand experience.

[July] 5th "This Reg lost 320 men killed, wounded & missing. 29, killed, 76 taken prisoners and the rest wounded."

Woodlin's subdued reaction likely had as much to do with collective embarrassment as with personal pride at being forced to retreat by Confederates. Olustee became a touchy subject for black troops who were aware that the Confederate victory there might be used to cast doubt on their record of proud achievements. Over the summer of 1863 African-American soldiers had shown heroic valor at Milliken's Bend, Port Hudson, and Battery Wagner and had in the process done much to silence their white critics. The effectiveness of the USCT was not yet a definitive fact for the most skeptical whites, and the setback in Florida would be a step toward greater racism evident during the summer and fall of 1864.

Henry Berckhoff showed how the passage of time could improve a soldier's perspective on battle. His watercolor depictions of combat began with an initial faltering attempt to draw "Gen. Blenker at the close of the Battle of Bull Run." This composition was flawed in several respects, but its greatest distraction was the separation of its title character from his troops by an ill-defined clump of green foliage, whose splash of bright color drew attention away from the picture's more important elements. Thematically, this scene was also the least successful in Berckhoff's wartime portfolio, since by showing the regiment providing protection during a disastrous retreat, it failed to provide any hint of the wider rout of Union forces that occurred that day. Even the individual figures were handled with uncharacteristic clumsiness. Mounted officers appear in a series of wooden poses, while three different lines of infantry are either obscured (behind Blenker and behind their fire) or placed too far in the distance to be easily recognizable. The picture crowded the best-drawn figures into the extreme right of the pic-

Figure 26. Detail of Henry Berckhoff, "Gen. Blenker at the close of the Battle of Bull Run 21 July 1861."

Figure 27. Detail of Henry Berckhoff, "Battle on Manassas Plains 2nd Bull Run 29 August 1862."

Figure 28. Detail of Henry Berckhoff, "Cavalry skirmish near Aldie 28 November 1862."

ture, but even here the Confederate cavalry were awkwardly submerged in a sea of gray and green undergrowth.

More than a year later Berckhoff captured the spectacle of combat with the same vivid detail that distinguished his views of camp life. "Battle on Manassas Plains 2nd Bull Run" effectively used a panoramic perspective to convey the grandeur of a smoky, noisy landscape. This picture offered both a depth of field and a range of individual activity. Within the frame of exploding shells, distant mountains, and broken trees were Union soldiers busy marching, firing, commanding, grieving, and suffering. The picture even includes two stretcher-bearers removing a crumpled body from the field of battle and toward the margins of the composition. "Cavalry skirmish near Aldie," which Berckhoff composed a short time earlier, showed that he had also improved his rendering of larger figures in battle. The stiff horsemen of his First Bull Run scene gave way to the more energetic mounted figures locked in close combat.

Many letter writers tried to convey combat with the same vividness achieved by the most compelling diaries and sketches. But when soldiers sat down after a battle to write a letter, the expectations of their recipient were uppermost in their mind, and this consciousness of audience profoundly influenced what letters included and left out. Those at home cared less about how a battle was mapped than how combat felt and what it meant for those who had survived the ordeal. Soldiers' letters responded to this interest by explaining the full range of sensory responses to battle. These remain among the most powerful testaments to the reality of America's first modern war.

In one of the early battles on the Atlantic coast, George Tillotson told his wife not only what it was like for him to be under fire but also how his own response mixed ferocity with an unexpected sense of satisfaction. His coolness in the face of danger subsequently marked his experience at the Battle of Antietam, the topic of the second excerpted letter. During what was the bloodiest day of the entire war Tillotson's own self-confidence grew along with his pride in his unit. His concluding reflections indicated his growing familiarity with different varieties of enemy firepower.

Roanoke Island
May 22 [1862]

Dear Wife,

. . . If you want to know just how I felt when I went into battle it would be hard telling exactly but in the first place I felt most d---d tired. Other ways I felt well enough, wasn't at all afraid. the idea that we could be whipped by any number of the rebels did not come into my head at all even after the Zouaves were driven back among us and I heard some of them say that they were all cut up and that the day was lost. <u>I couldn't see the</u>

point. When the bullets were whizzing around our head like a nest of hornets, I suppose I felt about as Lieutenant Colonel Robie expressed himself when he was forming the line of battle for the second and last charge. Some of the men were inclined to dodge when the bullets came to close their heads. Robie cryes out "Never mind those little fellows, boys; they wont hurt you, but stand steady in line if a ball should come and sweep down every man of ye." As we were going in on the last charge I stepped over a man of the 21st Mass whose side was all torn open by a rebel shell and who was just uttering his last prayer to God for Mercy. I must say that I felt some "savage," but the savage turned to a smile when after we had gone a rod or two beyond a bullet whistled by the back of my head so close that I felt it and I looked around and saw the eyes of the man behind me stick out. . . .

Accept the love of your Dear old man,
Geo. W. Tillotson

In camp seven miles from Harpers Ferry and 1 ½ mile
from the Potomac River in Maryland
September 24th, 1862

My Dear Wife,

. . . Colonel Hawkins who has been to New York and just returned says that this brigade has got as good a name as any in the service and General Burnside says that ours is the best brigade in his whole command. Maybe you think that I am bragging but still I think so far we have been as good as any of them while under fire. . . .

I tell you what Dearest when the real tug of war comes it is easy to pick out the cowards. The morning of the 17th when the rebels were shelling us out several of the boys run out of the ranks so far that they didn't find the regiment again for several days. Three of our company ran away and some of the other companies. George Sherwood has not got back to his company yet. For my part I kinder liked to hear the shells come whew bang and then hear the pieces scatter around us, for all I knew that if any of them hit a fellow they would hurt. Where a shell

> bursts directly over head there is not much danger of it but it if bursts twenty rods ahead of you then look out for the pieces. . . .
>
> Ever your loveing Husband,
> George W. Tillotson

Among the range of responses that combat produced, humor was in relatively short supply. Even so, the anonymous sketcher of the Forty-fourth Massachusetts tried to draw forth a laugh by showing how "Gorge" was "blown up by a shell" at the Battle of Goldsboro, North Carolina, in late 1862. Like modern cartoon characters, "Gorge" emerged from the explosion only slightly worse for the wear and was able to join the rest of his friends in the journey back to the Federal position at New Bern. There seemed to have been little that was funny about their collective gloom after this raid, which inspired what was the most sober picture in the entire sketchbook. While the coordinated operations against Confederate targets achieved their primary objectives, there was little sense of elation from the troops that helped assure a minor Union triumph.

The first time that Hillory Shifflet recorded being under fire, he emphasized the fatalities of acquaintances and friends. Shifflet had missed the colossal fight at Shiloh, where many western soldiers were initiated into battle, and thus was still without combat experience until the fall of 1862. At that point his Ohio regiment took part in

Figure 29. Battle of Goldsboro, as seen by "Gorge."

Figure 30. "Gorge"'s return from Goldsboro, December 1862.

driving back the Confederate invasion of Kentucky, an effort that culminated with the Battle of Perryville, which occurred just two days after he sent his wife the following letter. Shifflet subsequently saw battlefield action on a regular basis until he was killed at the age of forty by a Confederate cannonball in Tennessee. Fighting had already become less and less a theme of his letters before his death in the fall of 1863, however. He had turned his attention to issuing requests from home and expressing what was his growing opposition to the political course of the war.

October the 26, 1862
Taylor County, Ky.

Dear Wife,

I take the opportunity to right you a few lines this morning to let you no that I am well at this time and hope when you git this few lines tha will find you and the Children all well. . . .

I sepose you hird about George Ennis being killed—was shot through the heart and dide instantly. I was right clos to him and my cap box was shot off of my belt and fore bullets holes in my blouse and my gun barrel shot off at the brech and hit started me so that I had to leave the field for a lille while but I got another gun and went back but the Rebbles run we whip them bad by that morning the like to killd me. but tha didn't but tha will never come enny nerer with out kilen me. My leg was sore for two weeks but hit is nearly well now so I must close. hit is dredful morning could and the snow is fore inches deepe . . . and I am nearly bearfootted. My feete is on the ground so I am in a bad fixe you made a pend but I cant help it. So you do the best you can. I donte no when I will git home I am interely out of hearte So good by my dear wife untell death,

Hillory Shifflet

Marion Epperly waited even longer for his first taste of battle. The evangelical Virginian came under enemy fire during his third year of service, when he took part in the Army of Tennessee's unsuccessful attempt to block General William Sherman's advance toward Atlanta, Georgia. In telling his wife about the bloody Battle of Resaca, Epperly had less to say about this experience than might have been expected. He accurately tallied the losses incurred during his regiment's failed counterattack and pointed out it was a "serious time" in witnessing the death of comrades. But his letter included nothing at all about his own experience or even what part he took in the day's events. Though Epperly was in many ways disaffected from his fellow soldiers, their deaths still brought a sense of solidarity and of sympathy for their sacrifices.

Camp Near Ash Station, Ga
May the 22an 1864

My most dear and Effectionate Wife,

Throo the cind Providens of a murciful God I am blest with a opportunity of writing you a few breafe lines. . . .

Dear Mary, I must now tell you something about the time here wee have had som verry hard fighting to doo sins I last written to you—wee have been fighting an scirmishing nearly every day in this month. wee had som tolerable hard fighting to doo at Dalton about the 8 and 9 of this month and wee had to fall back to Resaca about 15 miles whair wee taken another stand and on the 15 wee had another verry heavy ingatement which a large number of our Regt was kild and wounded. ther was about 419 kild and wounded which was dun in about 10 minuts time in making a charge on the yankees whair they wer three Calloms deep. wee had to fall back. this number was lost out of a bout 5 Companies wee had 5 men kild out of our Companey an 8 or 10 wounded. . . .

Dear Mary, I can tell you it was a serious time to see so many of our dear Boys fall to the Ground and be cut to peases by Bomshells, and minney Balls; we ar now about 40 miles from Atlanta and I sepose will go thair befor they will make another stand or at least our men is compeld to fall back and I Beleave the yankees will flank them out of that plase, I don't think wee can Get men a nuff to stand them a fight soon again. Ther is missing out of this Regt. 250 men kild wounded and missing . . . some of them is taken prisoners and I cant tell what has becom of the rest. I must soon close as I havent' much room to writ and have no mor paper nor money to Buy with. . . .

I stil Remain your tru Husband as ever til Death,
C. M. Epperly

Most combat accounts described battling between opposing infantries under circumstances chosen by commanders. These climactic encounters subjected soldiers to the most concentrated attacks and were thus the touchstones of veterans' later reminiscences. Yet during the war itself most men realized that danger existed outside the context of the transfixing battles. Families of soldiers who were killed in an ambush, a raid, or a rifle pit during a siege appreciated that there was nothing minor about an incident that cost them a loved one. Nor was the fire of Confederate guerrillas any less deadly than that of Rebel infantrymen drawn up in regular order. In the following letter written near the middle of the war, William Brunt explained how occupied Tennessee had become a breeding ground for such guerrillas. These men were dangerously unbound by war conventions, even though they attempted to use certain provisions, such as the loyalty oath and the parole, to their own advantage.

Ft. Donelson Tenn
Sept 13th 63

Dear Friend Martha,

I received your kinde and welcome letter some time since. . . .

We have good times now scouting after the Gurrillas. But they are very shy. we brought in two Gurrillas & 8 good Loyal Cittizens on our last scout & the gurillas were pretty saucy at first but want to take the Oath & be released. But they will probably be held as hostages for two of the 13th Wisconsin Boys that were captured by the same band that these two belong to. Iff the Wisconsin Boys are not released soon we shall believe the report of the cittizens which is that the Gurillas killed them & then they will have to travel the same road. . . .

Well Martha, the Gurillas are getting scarse here. One band led by a desperado has been disbanded by the leader at the request of the Citizens who were getting tired of feeding & clothing them & once in a while a cittizen gets shot while in there company. The last scout we had a Gurilla & a Cittizen were riding along together they accidentally run on a squad of our men lying in wach for Gurillas near this mans house our men fired at them killing the cittizen & wounding the gurilla in the left arm, but he being mounted got away. The Cittizen's horse was also killed dead upon the spot. I think the Rebels must begin to think about peace. . . .

Please write soon. Yours truly, William Brunt

Earlier that same year the Illinois soldier James Magie had been called north from Middle Tennessee to help meet that surprise raid that John Hunt Morgan's calvary made into Kentucky. Since Morgan and his men held regular commands and were sanctioned by the Confederate government, they were not guerrillas in the strict sense of the term. But they did draw military attention away from the battlefield by targeting lines of supply and communication rather than massed concentration of Union troops. In the following letter, written shortly before his appointment as brigadier postmaster, Magie explained his capture of a leading Confederate, which he accomplished through his own masquerade. Though his account was marked by a sense of excitement, it also shows that he was aware that by blurring the lines between combatants and noncombatants, he might have been prosecuted as a spy.

Headquarters 78th Regt. Ill Vols
Camp at New Haven, KY, January 4, 1863

Dear Wife,

I have an opportunity to write a little while this evening and I improve the occasion by writing to you. During the recent excitement occasioned by Morgan's raid in this section of the state, we have been cut off from communication with the Northern states and hence have received no letters. . . .

In the estimation of all the citizens hereabouts we are all heroes, and there is much talk over the manner in which we made them skedaddle. I went this forenoon over the ground where the rebels were during the fight, and found the fences, trees and bushes were riddled with bullets. The rebels sent some of their balls and shells into the town, and did some damage. Of course all the women and children in the houses in range of the shooting had previously left. There is considerable talk about the arrest of Floyd Price. This is the noted rebel that I captured and brought into camp. I was seen by several in New Haven and on the Bardstown Pike, but I was all the while taken to be a rebel. I was fixed up in true butternut* style, and I walked different, and acted different, so that those who saw me then and have seen me since have not recognized me as the same. It has leaked out that the rebel who was seen on the Bardstown pike one morning about 9 o'clock was nobody but a Union soldier and he was the one who captured Price.

. . . I met with so many adventures in the two days when I was playing the rebel that it would fill a large book if I should write it all out. If I had been captured by the rebels and they had known that I was a Union soldier I would have been shot without ceremony. . . .

Your ever dear, James

Magie's escapade put him in a position of grave danger, since soldiers disguising themselves as civilians were likely to be executed if

**Butternut* was a term Republicans like Magie used to describe those conservative residents of the Ohio River Valley who were friendly to the South. The name came from local dyes (taken from butternuts) that were used to color homespun dress.

captured. A few months later Magie witnessed the full gravity of such an infraction when he sketched two Confederate spies who were hanged within his own camp. This event, which was transacted with great ceremony before the assembled Union troops, inspired him to sketch the Confederate corpses hanging from a tree. Making a visual record of this execution was an unusual gesture. Magie did not illustrate any of his letters, nor did he ever mention a particular interest in drawing. In this case, however, he sent the original sketch to *Harper's Weekly*, one of the most popular Northern magazines, which then published a woodcut based on his drawing. Magie never indicated his reasons for documenting or circulating this image. Perhaps he was moved by the awareness that under slightly different circumstances, it might have been his body that was dangling from the end of a rope.

War almost of necessity forced soldiers to confront their own mortality and to consider how their own deaths might appear to those around them. Amid such widespread carnage, many soldiers re-

Figure 31. Execution of spies as depicted in *Harper's Weekly*, prepared from a sketch by James Magie.

sponded by finding solace in traditional Christianity and in its promise of eternal life in heaven. While Protestantism was already a formative cultural influence in the antebellum United States, the Civil War helped evangelicalism achieve even greater resonance within American society. Among the fruits of the war were the first use of "In God We Trust" on U.S. money and the institutionalization of Thanksgiving as a national holiday. Within the armies the expansion of Christianity was evident in an effective chaplaincy corps, a series of evangelical revivals, and a vigorous publishing campaign mounted by church groups in both the Union and the Confederacy.

Edward Ward's spiritual striving may have been shaped by such larger trends, but the most direct cause was what he and the rest of the Confederate Army of Tennessee experienced at the Battle of Stones River during the opening days of 1863. As the following letter to his sister explained, the young Memphis soldier had helped blunt a major Union offensive on December 31, 1862, the bloodiest single day of the war in the West. In the days that followed this clash, the Union successfully regrouped and forced the Confederates to retreat from Murfreesboro. Ward spent half a week exposed to the elements and to massive shelling. The misery of these days led him to turn from the chaos of war to a better knowledge of the Bible.

Camp near Shelbyville January 12, '63

Dear Sister,

I have written a great many letters home lately and am in hopes you have received some of them. The last letter I received came direct by a friend and was dated Dec. 9th. I have written to you once since the battle of Murfreesboro giving an account of the battle. Thanks to a kind providence I am again safe and so is Marshall. . . .

It was pretty cold sleeping Sunday & Monday nights with only our blankets. On Tuesday it was raining pretty much all day and was very disagreeable. Our forces engaged the enemy on the right and drove them back with great slaughter capturing a great deal of their artillery. We still remained in line undisturbed except at times by their shells. But Wednesday the 31st day of Dec. it came our time and as usual we played our part well. This day the engagement became general along the whole line. About 9 o'clock our first line charged the enemy we followed up and were soon in a very hot place. We fought them until night driving them through a cedar woods into an open field. We would have followed up this retreat but he had his artillery in a strong position well supported and it would have cost too much to have driven him from it. We held the battle ground from which we had driven him Wednesday night and Thursday, Friday and Saturday the enemy could be plainly seen fortifying and did not fire a shot as we quietly withdrew our forces Sunday morning at 2 o'clock. For three days Thursday, Friday and Saturday we lay flat down on the cold wet ground under the most terrific shelling I ever saw. Besides it was raining and a groan or scream occasionally would show the mangled corpse of someone who had paid his last sacrifice to freedom. . . .

Sis I have got a great deal better since the fight. The first of Jan I commenced reading the bible through. I commenced in the 1st chapter of Genesis and read two chapters every night. So about dark if you would know what I'm thinking of turn to your bible and read with me. This is the 12th and tonight I read from the 23 and 24 chapters of Genesis. . . .

I would give anything in the world to see Pa and Ma and you all once more. Write as often as you can to your aff. Brother,

Ed

Christianity answered profoundly human needs by providing comfort for the grieving and by allowing both sides to see the ultimate outcome as part of the mysterious workings of Providence. Christianity also raised questions about the sinfulness of soldiering, and not just in terms of bawdy camp life. Could the message of Christian peace and justice be squared with service that required soldiers to kill? When did such violent destruction betray God's wishes? How would soldiers who crossed the line into sinful violence be called to account by a higher power?

Few soldiers faced up to these issues as honestly as the Confederate private Jeremiah Tate of Alabama. In the following two letters

Tate probed some of the darker aspects of the war from the perspective of a believing Christian. In the first, he imagined how soldiers might not be punished for wartime sins, a supposition he followed, without any sense of irony, with a gleeful consideration of how black Union soldiers might soon be murdered. The second letter moved from his consideration of whether he would be sent to hell in the afterlife to a description of a very real inferno—complete with burning bodies—in the woods around Chancellorsville in the spring of 1863. In passing, Tate also noted the accidental death of one of the Confederacy's greatest heroes.

Camp Graces Church Near Fredericksburg
March the 15th, 1863

Dear Sister,

. . . I am all moste purswaded to believe that solgers are not accountable for there deeds hereafter; for if they have to endure all the truble, triles and tribulations of this unjust war and then be punisht in the world to cum wo be unto them in the day of there reserection. . . .

I hear that old Hooker has several regements of darkes in his army. I do hope to god that they may sho themselves in the next battle if they do I am confident that there will be nun that will escape. Without they do it by fast running.

Jere Tate

Camp Graces Church near Fredericksburg Va
May the 10th 1863

Dear Sister Mary,

I once more have the exqisit pleasure of writing to you and informing you that I am in tolerable helth at presant, as good as cood be expected from the hardships and exposure that I have under gawn in the late battles on the Raperhanack River, sum twenty miles from this place.

. . . Stonewall being our foremon and Rades his second, gave the orders to move forward and attact the enemy, we had not gawn more than one quarter of a mile before we cum in contact with the enemys Picketts the firing comenst, volla after volla of musketry was pourd in to them, whitch soon put them to flight, and in this way we drove them several miles throug the roughfest woods I ever saw, capturing a number of prisnors, and many other valuable articals, night came on the thick woods prevented from pursuing them further that night, hear we campt on the battle field. . . .

Mary I can assure yo of the fact that I have no recollections of the time when I was so near run to deth, I hadent eat any thing for two days and night so Monday and Tuesday I was not able to turn a wheel I had to give it up but I helt out til the fight was over. On Sunday I witnest the awfullest sight that the eyes of man ever beheld. That was I saw many of our poor wounded that was burnd to det afte they wer wounded, and all so hundreds of the enemy, it was caused by the woods taking onfire from the explosions of shells, the ambulance core could not bare the wounded of faste enoughf so those that was left burnd for there was no time to put out the fire.

Our commanding General was wounded in Saturdays fight, that is Old Stone Wall Jackson he was shot by our own men axidently. . . .

The enemy was on thre sides of us and thare was but one little gap to run out at we made it safe. The balls came thicker around us than ever you saw June bug around a peech tree. Expected evry minit for one to strike me but I came out safe the tide of affairs soon changed and the yankes wer going the other way as fast as quarterhorses, there loss was mutch grater than ours. . . .

I will close my short letter by saying that I never want to git in to another as hard a fight for I can assure you that it was a warm place on Sunday, May the 3rd. Write soon and give the nuse. I wod write more but have lost so mutch slip and feel so bad that I want to take a nap. I have bin like a founderd horse ever since the fight. Notthing at Presant I will write again soon,

Yours truly, J. M. Tate

Such harrowing experiences turned some soldiers away from war altogether. Most merely tried to deal with the necessary consequences of causes they struggled to justify morally. Tate might have himself been comforted by the fact that the burning woods of Chancellorsville was an unintentional tragedy and had not resulted from any conscious design to inflict suffering. Whatever the case, his moral response to the suffering of others had severe limitations, as the following two letters indicate. The first, written in the spring of 1864, indicated his macabre hobby of making jewelry from the bones of enemy corpses, a practice he and other Confederates used to indicate their contempt for Yankees, who they believed bore full responsibility for their own suffering. The second letter, written after the bloodiest period of the war, expressed pity for the Union soldiers who had unsuccessfully called for help while lying wounded on the field. This gesture of sympathy for the enemy passed, however, as Tate ended by bragging about his own role as a Confederate sharpshooter.

Camp 5th Ala Regt Near Orange, C.H. Va
April 6 / 64

Dear sister Mary,

. . . I rote to darcus last week and inclosed a bone ring in the letter and I will enclose one in this for Ma made by my own hands with an old knife. those sets are pure silver. the bône was found on the Battle field of Seven Pines and all so Darcases was of the same. I have one for you that was found on Mine Town that I will forward in my next letter. Tell the old lady to except this ring in remembrance of her only son and when his sweet harts came to see hir, she can show what hir son did in the army of Northern Virginia. This closes my short epistol, except my best wishes.

Camp 5th Ala Regt Near Hanover Junction
May 23, 1864

Dear sister Mary,

. . . We moved down near the ford and attacted the enemy at eleven o'clock and the fight raged with <u>fury</u> for several hours at whitch time we succeeded in driving the enemy from his pursition we then went to work and soon had the hill fortifide about sunset the enemy made another assault but was repulst and driven back, hear we remained from thursday til sunday morning they attacted our lines each day during our stay at this place but was repulst with grate loss, our loss was cumparitively small, in my company thar was one kild and four wounded two taken prisoners, it was a sight that is seldom seen to gase upon the did bodies of the enmy and to hear the cries for assitence and water, as they lay between our lines for two days and nights and neither party could get them out, or give them any releaf, it was enough to brake the hart of the most harden to hear those cries. . . .

I have spent evry other night at the skirmish line since the fight comenst, I am most broke down for the want of sleep. The sharp shooters has had the hardest time of any, one consilation is we have had the chance of taking revenge out of the vandals, they never have courage to fight until they are made drunk, then our boys mow them like they wir grass. I will close. Write soon as I am ever anxious to hear, the last letter that I received was dated in April so nothing more at present yours truly,

Jer. M. Tate

It took a special kind of soldier to become a sharpshooter since this assignment required both skill and a willingness to draw a bead on unsuspecting victims. Not everyone had the stomach for this kind of killing, which removed any uncertainty whether it was one's own fire or that of another soldier that had struck a particular enemy. Effective sharpshooters tended to develop a calculated indifference to the casualties they inflicted, which could easily lead them to become numb to dangers they faced in return. In these two letters to his sister, Dolphus Damuth explains how killing others helped reduce his own fear. He wrote these while his regiment helped keep the Confederate Army of Mississippi under siege at Vicksburg. During periods of prolonged siege, troops were careful to protect themselves within fortified trenches they dubbed rifle pits.

Near Rear of Vicksburgh
June 9, 1863

Dear Sister,

The boys all sez today is Sunday and I sepose thear is such a day down here. . . . I never have Seen a day Since I have been South that realy seemed like our old fashion Sundays that we used to have up north but like that as well as a great many other things we have to go without down here in Dixie.

We are in the same place as when I wrote you last we are on duty 4 hours each day as Sharp Shooters. yesterday I saw a great many Rebels Sticking thear heads up over thear rifle pits then we would give it to them we have got as good rifle pits now as they have. . . .

. . . we have got used to hearing the big guns that we don't care any thing about it when we go up to Shoot at the rebels we go as we use to for Co drill all the boys feeling as light harted as if they were at home going into the field to work. . . .

Yours Truly, Dolph

Send a few stamps

June 20, 1863
Rear of Vicksburgh

Dear Sister,

I rec'd a letter from you & one from John night before last. the first I had heard from home in some time. I was very glad to hear from you once more. . . .

Last night our Co was on picket or out post duty we were in front of our rifle pits a great ways we could here the rebels sing Methodist hymns. I think they are like all devils very pious when they get in a dangerous place. we had a very peacable time. Capt sat up the first part of the night and I the last part but I think we both slept all the days allowed. we came down to our quarters at 4 this morning. The Col. Told us to get our breakfast as Soon as we could and go back into the rifle pits.

Capt didn't feel very well & Curtis was on picket in the rear So the Col said I would command the Co. he said they was going to bombard them in six hours all along the line and they did. Such a nois I never heard before, but hope I shall agane tomorrow. The object of our going into our rifle pits was we thought they might try and break out of thear pen and if they did it we would be ready to bag them. but we watched in vane they didn't Show thear heads I was in hopes they would try and get out but they know better than to try any such game. . . .

From Dolph

Soldiers seeking justifications for their wartime deeds looked to ideological vindications from which both sides drew sustenance. Patriotism held a soldier to his own cause and justified a soldier's willing death for a greater good. Disgust toward the enemy could prove an even more powerful motivation. As the war entered its final year, Union soldiers became increasingly convinced that they were serving as instruments of God's justice against deeply sinful slaveholders. Lysander Wheeler visited this theme of divine retribution in a letter written outside Atlanta. His reflection immediately preceded the raid made by Sherman's army toward Savannah, where Wheeler and his fellow troops were welcomed as liberators by slaves and condemned as destroyers by white Confederates.

Chattahoochie River
Wednesday Evening
November 2nd, 1864

Dear Parents, Bro and Sister,

I seat myself this evening to write you a few lines happy to inform you that good health is still spared by god's blessing. . . .

We are to be prepared to march about the 7th. We understand that the 20th Corps and the Army of the Tennessee is going on a big raid several places is surmised as our destination 50 days rations have been prepared or will be. We understand so we think it is the intention to swing clear of Land. All our heavy things that can not be carried on our backs have been packed to be sent to the rear tomorrow morning. . . .

I went to Atlanta last Fryday to view the remains of the Gate City. Gate to Purgatory I should judge by the Looks. most every building is marked either with Bomb-Shells or bullets there and some families yet remaining. it is the most poverty stricken place I have yet been in. Well my opinion of the whole place is so poor that I can say nothing in its favor at all. It, and every other southern City, deserve nothing better than a general destruction from Yankees. We could see where their slave pens and Auction sales had been. the more I see of this miserable country the more I think these Rebels deserve to be severely dealt with, for the high sin they have been guilty of committing in buying and selling their betters. God will bring this Country out of the thicket Yet. . . .

I shall endeavor to Keep right side up with care,

Yours in Love,
Lysander Wheeler

Soldiers made sense of warfare both by describing and by creating stories that might endow it with a higher purpose. This turn to narrative put the suffering that they endured and inflicted within a meaningful larger context. Tales of military violence could hinge on a soldier's own growth or the progress of his cause. The story might just as easily take a more cosmic scope, of puzzling through the mystery of divine intention or registering an emotional response to the allure of patriotism. Whatever the case, soldiers relentlessly attempted to place the mounting carnage within a larger flow of events that might elevate their importance above simple human slaughter.

Henry Berckhoff crafted his stories about soldiering through watercolor sketches rather than words. His visual depiction of combat allowed him to confront war's destructiveness and to display its costs in the bleeding and lifeless figures that appear in his most evocative combat scenes. Berckhoff's narratives are more difficult to "read" than the diaries or letters recorded by other soldiers through verbal description. Berckhoff's reflections did have a point, however, which he conveyed by clustering individual scenes to chart development and plot themes through a narrative sequence. In this way, his clumsy depiction of First Bull Run failed not just because of its unconvincing drawings but because it disrupted the prevailing concern of his first six watercolors, which established the transformation of Manhattan recruits into fully seasoned soldiers. Sketching the regiment's first battle may not have offered a meaningful reflection about that day's fighting and dying if its intent was primarily to show how troops were initiated into military life.

Combat and bloodshed became Berckhoff's central concern in the ten scenes that followed his introductory cluster. This series tracked his regiment's military assignments from the late spring of 1862 through that same fall. "An Attack on the Outposts" (see color insert) marked a transition from the clean camps of German recruits into a world of far greater danger. The Federal scouts and the exploding shells at this picture's margins assured that its focal point was the landscape and the distant mountains. The next five scenes featured similarly carefully rendered landscapes, though in these Berckhoff put troops in the center, showing them in motion toward their most serious fighting of the war. Across this sequence of pictures, the Eighth New York moved across northwestern Virginia, from a snowy Salem, over the Shenandoah and Upper Potomac rivers, down the course of a mountain river, and finally to the banks of the Upper Shenandoah at New Market. The river crossings recorded in these scenes slowed down the troops and allowed Berckhoff the opportunity to craft a perspective outside the very ranks he marched within. When combined with the specific dates, these scenes conveyed that this was not just any march. The tour's primary purpose was to counter the threat that Thomas "Stonewall" Jackson posed in moving Southern troops into the Shenandoah Valley.

In "Blenker's Fatal Fall," Berckhoff showed the danger involved in moving itself (even if the general did not die from this accident, as this scene's title implied). The sense of vulnerability in the other traveling scenes was more remote, but no less real, since over the two months that these sketches document, Stonewall Jackson's Confederates mounted one of the most successful diversionary campaigns in military history. The job of Jackson's men was to relieve pressure from Richmond at a time where an immense Union army was advancing upon the seat of the Confederate government from the southeast. Even before the German Rifles faced a single shot, Jackson had accomplished his objective merely by causing them to pursue a campaign through circuitous mountain passages.

Two months and a day after Berckhoff's Germans crossed the Blue Ridge at Salem, the Eighth New York finally faced a Confederate force in the Shenandoah Valley. In "Battle of Cross Keyes," Berckhoff portrayed a haunting view of the Union disaster there. The attention he gave to graphic wounds on nearly half the soldiers in this picture's foreground was no artistic exaggeration. Casualties in his regiment represented over 40 percent of those engaged at Cross Keys, as 43 men were killed, 134 were wounded, and 43 went unaccounted for. This afternoon marked the regiment's most devastating loss of the war. Such an outcome ended all possibility of Union success in the Valley and gave the Confederates victory over forces that had begun the campaign with a strength ten times their own numbers.

The crushing Union defeat at Cross Keys was balanced, at least in pictorial terms, by Berckhoff's depiction of a Federal charge in the "Skirmish at Haymarket." This Union rout of the Confederates had little military significance, and it did not rise to the level of even a minor battle. Berckhoff seemed to be making a larger point about the need for revenge, however, and he drove this point home by selecting strong compositional echoes between this scene and that of the earlier Cross Keys disaster. While the Union troops moved from right to left in both compositions, the latter picture showed Confederates bleeding and dying. The flaming house at the sketch's center signaled that retribution was directed not just at enemy troops but at the entire Southern rebellion. Civilians no less than soldiers were punished for the suffering that Berckhoff's comrades had endured.

Figure 32. Detail of Henry Berckhoff, "Battle of Cross Keyes 8 June 1862."

The most interesting element of "Skirmish at Haymarket" is the largest Union figure, which appeared closest to the middle of the scene, with a bayonet in his left hand. While this soldier was leading a charge, his gesture also drew attention toward the burning house that marked how this engagement settled the score of the recent Union loss. Showing this ordinary private in this act of pointing was unusual for Berckhoff, who tended to reserve this signal of authority for the officers charged with command. Moreover, the gaze of this charging soldier is cast out of the picture and into the eyes of the viewer, helping him achieve a more intense connection to the audience than in any other figure among Berckhoff's sketches.

All these details raise the possibility that this was not a random soldier. It would certainly be plausible that of the nineteen wartime watercolors, this one allowed Berckhoff to put his own self-portrait in an unusually prominent position. If this were the case, it would be notable, since this dark soldier with a mustache pointed not to where Union soldiers were dying or even to where they were charging. He instead called attention to the dark essence of combat that was meant to inflict terrible punishment upon those enemies who threatened to do the same in return.

After 1865 Berckhoff spent the rest of his career in the U.S. mili-

Figure 33. Detail of Henry Berckhoff, "Skirmish at Haymarket 4 November 1862."

tary. This choice required him to accept the destruction of warfare as a normal part of his life. The matter-of-fact presentation of combat in his 1862 watercolors indicates that this might have been less difficult for him than for other men under arms.

For the great majority of veterans (including all the other surviving penmen of this book), traces of earlier combat stood out more dramatically during the post–Civil War years. Upon returning to the civilian life that these men had temporarily left, they told of victories and defeats that were responsible for the saving of the Union, the destruction of the Confederacy, and the breaking of slavery's bonds. The destructiveness of war mattered to these men on a more personal level as well, and it is in their written testimony that this importance is most clearly conveyed. The terror of combat that had marked their service could be revisited through the written record, if only to take greater satisfaction in the comforts of a hard-won peace.

FOUR

The Union Divided?

In October 1862 George Tillotson bluntly announced to his wife, "I don't feel as patriotic as I did." In addition to his bitter frustration with the progress of the war, the New York sergeant suffered from grave doubts about the recent shift in Union war aims, which now included the emancipation of Confederate slaves. Facing two more years of his army commitment, Tillotson used the privacy of a letter to offer a stunning admission. He put it simply, declaring that he had "rather see the Union divide than have the war last the remainder of my term."

A similarly dark mood informed Henry Berckhoff's sketch of a rain-drenched camp two months later, when despair had become even more pronounced through the Union rank and file. "Bivouac at Dumfries" pictured soldiers huddled inside a tent surrounded by smoke and oblivious of a sharp bolt of lightning, which in a battle scene might have represented an exploding shell. More wood was on its way, assuring that the discussions around the fires would continue, at least until it came time to relieve the lone picket on the picture's bottom left-hand corner. What the soldiers talked about was less important to the scene than the tense uncertainty and anxiety throughout. This composition furnished a stark contrast with the sun-bathed scenes of hope and promise Berckhoff had offered in camp scenes a year earlier. Those seemed to have been drawn during a different, more innocent war.

Figure 34. Detail of Henry Berckhoff, "Bivouac at Dumfries 13 December 1862."

From late 1862 through the first half of the following year the atmosphere in Northern armies was heavy with frustration, as a political storm threatened to stymie a Union effort ending its second year of active campaigning. Following a string of failed Federal advances toward the Rebel capital at Richmond the previous summer, Confederate independence appeared ever more likely. Meanwhile, the war was having a larger impact than many had expected upon Northern society. As military recruiting was ratcheted up to meet ever-greater manpower needs, the male work force was drawn away from communities that suddenly realized that the North, no less than the South, was being transformed by a war that might stretch on indefinitely. Such anxieties were most clear in the shifting tone of Northern correspondence, which offered the same sharp contrast as could be seen between Berckhoff's pictures from the beginning of and the end of 1862.

Letters that had earlier sounded themes of patriotic enthusiasm gave way to those that calculated whether peace was preferable to disunion. This was an ominous sign for those on the home front who received a steady stream of reports from the troops. Correspondence between soldiers and civilians linked realms that were united by their common fixation on how much more it would take to preserve the Union. When soldiers' private notes took up questions of army morale and the challenge of enemies, readers paid special attention. There seemed to be an inherent truthfulness to such soldier testimony, especially when compared with claims made for the troops by a self-interested press or by squabbling politicians. George Tillotson responded to such civilian commentary with impatience. "If the folks at the north find out what we soldiers think and talk among ourselves," he instructed his family, "we shall have to write it ourselves."

Union soldiers, like their Confederate counterparts, expressed their frustrations with remarkably few inhibitions. The frankness of a soldier's pen during the Civil War resulted from how military mail was processed during the 1860s. In later wars official censors monitored the flow of information, paying attention to letters that might affect morale while also policing the release of military secrets or facts that might be used by the enemy. Without such impediments, Civil War soldiers addressed contentious issues regularly, and their civilian correspondents encouraged the dialogues. Both sides of these exchanges knew that victory depended on what soldiers believed about how the war might be won.

Three issues stood out among soldiers' complaints during that dark winter: the military stalemate in Virginia, the incapacity of generals to wage an effective campaign, and Lincoln's preliminary Emancipation Proclamation, which he issued on September 19, 1862. The first two of these had been building for some time and persisted in some form until the victories of early July 1863. Lincoln's most sweeping antislavery measure had been planned for several months, but it was delayed to avoid the appearance of being fashioned as an act of desperation. Only after the Federal victory at Antietam, Maryland, did he take the step that reframed the Union cause and accelerated the collapse of the centuries-old institution of slavery.

Tillotson objected to black freedom less because of his personal views than because he feared what Lincoln's initiative would mean for continued military setbacks. The following two letters explained his belief that a crusade against slavery would only increase Confederate determination to fight on. Along with his comments came his sense of near disgust with the commanders who had not yet made full use of their superiority in resources and in men.

In camp seven miles from Harpers Ferry and 1 ½ mile
from the Potomac River in Maryland
September 24th, 1862

My Dear Wife,

. . . We have just got news that the president has issued a proclamation freeing all the slaves on the first of January. It may be for the best but stil my hopes (if I had any) of a speedy termination of the war is thereby nocked in head for I know enough of the southern spirit so that I think that they will fight for the institution of slavery even to extermination. . . .

Ever your loveing Husband,
George W. Tillotson

Pleasant Valley, MD
October 24, 1862

My Dear Wife,

. . . I have lost confidence in most of the head officers, for I don't believe they want the war to end, and further, in the way things are going, it will never end, by fighting. I am not alone in this opinion, for it is one generally, and openly expressed throughout the ranks, except by some of the new troops, who have not forgotten the old home idea, that the South is a going to be scared to death by a presidents proclamation, or a call for a few hundred thousand more men, but by the time they have fully seen the elephant, the idea of scare, like that of starve, and nothing to fight with, will "play out."

Yours,
George W. Tillotson

The preliminary Emancipation Proclamation did not free "all the slaves," as Tillotson declared. In fact both this measure and the final Emancipation Proclamation (issued according to schedule on January 1, 1863) explicitly excluded slaves in the border states of Kentucky, Maryland, and Missouri, and in all other areas under Union control.

Lincoln and his cabinet produced a narrowly tailored policy so they might present freedom as a necessary war measure, not as a broad attack upon valuable human property. Complete emancipation had to wait until two years later, when the Thirteenth Amendment to the U.S. Constitution was enacted by both Congress and the required number of states.

While Lincoln was deliberately cautious in limiting his endorsement of abolition, his action still marked a decisive turning point in the war. Earlier the president had followed the lead of Congress, which in 1861 resolved by large majorities that the war would restore the Union without overturning slavery. The movement of armies, the actions of slaves themselves, the press of diplomacy, and even Lincoln's notion of divine intentions slowly changed the calculus. Soldiers played a part in this process by welcoming fugitives into their midst, allowing them to work for wages, and protecting them from reenslavement. The number of African-American contrabands (the term used to describe wartime fugitives) steadily increased, assuring that there would be no turning back from a war that would end slavery as decisively as it would suppress rebellion. Under these circumstances, the Union army could hardly avoid overseeing a social revolution at the very time that it tallied battlefield victories and losses.

Many of those unhappy with Lincoln's leadership, his emancipation policy, or his lack of success in gaining victories rallied to George McClellan, the Democratic general who commanded the Army of the Potomac for much of 1862. This "young Napoleon" had already cultivated soldier loyalty in the East and become an iconic figurehead of a "nonrevolutionary" war that would keep clear of the politics of slavery. His popularity with troops was evident to those who received letters at home. David Smith's family followed the action by reading from stationery that explicitly linked the New Jersey general to George Washington, the ultimate "Hero of the Past." When Lincoln removed the "Hero of the Present" from command in November 1862, Democrats were predictably outraged. A rivalry between the two men escalated until the 1864 presidential election allowed voters to make a direct choice between the two alternatives they and their parties presented.

A major military clash that occurred the week before Christmas

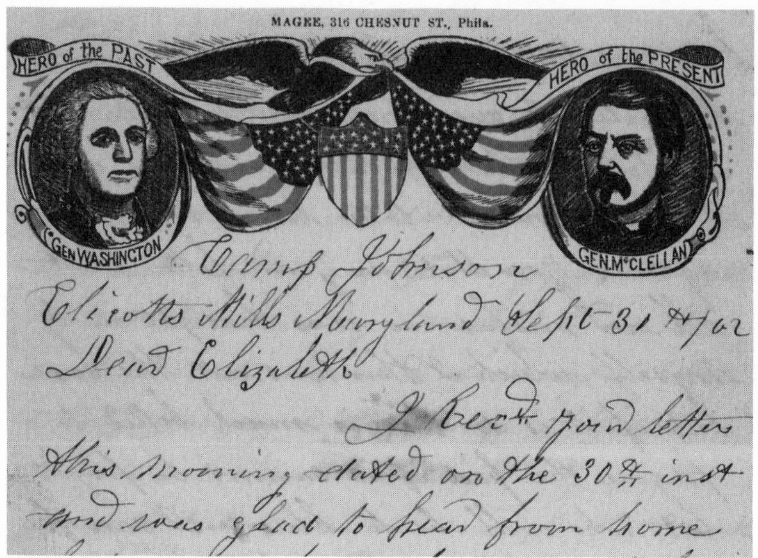

MAGEE, 316 CHESNUT ST., Phila.

HERO of the PAST

HERO of the PRESENT

GEN WASHINGTON

GEN. McCLELLAN

Camp Johnson
Eliotts Mills Maryland Sept 31st /62
Dear Elizabeth
I Recd your letter
this morning dated on the 30th inst
and was glad to hear from home

Figure 35. David V. M. Smith to his wife, Elizabeth, September 30, 1862.

1862 deepened the political disaffection among Union troops and led to even greater despair in soldier correspondence. A standoff had begun when the Federal army crossed the Rappahannock River in order to secure Fredericksburg, Virginia. Robert E. Lee's Confederates, who were in full control of the heights above this small town, turned back the assault that the Union general Ambrose Burnside ordered on December 17, 1862, achieving one of the most lopsided victories of the war. The humiliating rout assured that Northern troops would take a sour mood into their winter quarters, where soldiers had time to discuss their grievances and read attacks leveled against the administration by Democratic newspapers.

Soldiers' letters were filled with complaints that civilians willfully misunderstood the challenges they faced. They were especially frustrated by pro-Lincoln newspapers that inflated every scrap of good news as a means of rallying civilian enthusiasm. Sensational headlines about Union military exploits did not accord with the reality as seen firsthand by the rank and file. The sketcher of the Forty-fourth Massa-

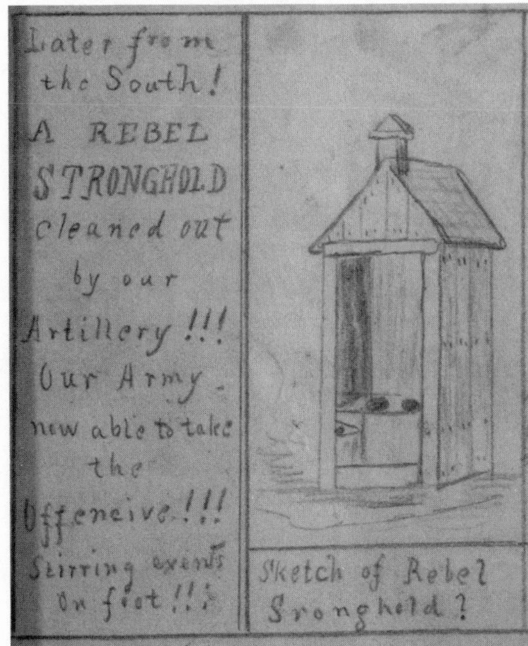

Figure 36. "Gorge"'s view of war news, winter of 1862–63.

chusetts humorously pointed out the gap between the truth and the inflated boasting of the press when he depicted a captured outhouse in one of his several satirical sketches.

In early January 1863, even the weather seemed to conspire against Union progress, as David Smith explained in the following description of the army's ill-fated Mud March. Smith's discussion of Burnside, McClellan's immediate successor, and of Joseph Hooker, who took command after the Fredericksburg debacle, further showed the dispirited state of the largest Union army. The Union's quest for an eastern general who knew how to win decisively would continue.

Camp near Falmouth Va
January 30th, 1863

Dear Elizabeth and Children,

. . . Some of our guns & pontoons lay down toward the River yet fast in the mud & will until it gets better weather than it has been since the storm commenced on last Tuesday night—it began to snow & continued on until Thursday morning as if heaven & earth was coming together. yesterday the snow was 12 or 15 inches deep with the mud about as deep under it. . . .

I don't think that our army will ever do anything any more as they appear to be all split to peaces on their leaders & Discouraged. I was at a Grand Review by Genl Burnside & I suppose there was from 30 to 50,000 men present Some Brigades would make everything ring when Burnsides rode past others would kiss at him others would not notice him at all. So he had to appoint some of his staff to order them to their duty & when it came to give 3 cheers for the Genl a Brigade of 2 or 3000 men would not make as much noise as you have heard at the school house over the Election of an overseer of the Roads of some other officer of the township. So we suppose that he Burnsides has got Discouraged for he has Resigned. . . .

it is now Rumored that General Hooker has taken the command of the army. if So he will find as great a split as Burnsides did & I don't think there is a man alive that will suit as Commander. I do not know what we are going to do or where we are going to. one thing is certain that is we cannot advance before next April or May and most of the men & officers think that it will be settled that time by some other way than fighting and I don't think it can ever be done by fighting. . . .

I must now Close as the mail is about to leave so no more at present but I remain you affect. Husband & Father,

D. V. M. Smith

The danger of tepid cheers was that they might develop into active insubordination. In the first of the following two letters, George Tillotson reported how mass mutiny seemed possible after the Fredericksburg setback. The second linked his own frustrations to disillusionment throughout the rank and file. The apologetic tone of this letter's conclusion no doubt came after Tillotson's views generated criticism from those at home.

Camp opposite Fredericksburg
January 19th, 63

Dear Wife,

. . . The soldiers I guess are full as badly discouraged as anybody at home is. I hear this morning that we have a little bit of mutiny in our brigade. The 103rd regt NYV last night burnt up all their cartridges. They say there ant an officer in the regiment that has got his commission and they declare they wont lead them into a fight. I wish the whole army of the Potomac would mutiny and leave for home. i'd go in a minute. Talk about calling for more troops I too hope they will and when they see how that works Maybe they will think best to settle somehow. . . .

Your own,
Geo. W. Tillotson

February 5th, 63
Camp opposite Fredericksburg

My Dear Wife,

. . . I would have you know that I am not the only one in these digins whose patriotism has cooled down so that we can look at the matter as it stands, and count the cost also. And as I count it has cost now in treasure more than I would give for the whole south to say nothing of the blood and misery. Now in all reason isn't it better to let that go and be lost rather than spend twice or three times as much more and then not be any better off but just the cost out, and be the worse off by haveing a bankrupt government and ourselves be the worst taxed slaves that the world affords. And even could the south be whipped back into the Union (which I cant see) what kind of union do you suppose it would be? Just no union at all so far as union in feeling is concerned. I believe if we ever get them back into the union, that we shall soon be sick enough of them to wish them out again. But enough, you will probably conclude with Ed that I am a Rebel. . . .

Accept my love and a kiss. From your own,
George W. Tillotson

Soldiers in the Union's western armies were generally more confident than their counterparts in the Army of the Potomac. Over the course of 1862 they had worked to extend Union control over nearly all of Kentucky, much of Missouri, a good part of Tennessee, and a strategically important slice of Louisiana. Such achievements did not offset the political disaffection of some western Democrats, however, who feared a threat to the traditionally Jacksonian mixture of small, decentralized government and a populist strain of white supremacy. From the perspective of many (though by no means all) Democrats, Lincoln's Emancipation Proclamation was the latest assault of "puritanical" abolitionism. The midwestern opposition to black freedom resonated especially strongly among immigrants, Catholics, and those small farmers from the rural areas of the Ohio Valley.

Late in 1862 Hillory Shifflet expressed his disgust with emancipation by imagining Lincoln "in hell and a negro tide to him." This fantasy indicated both his Democratic principles and his lingering sympathy (as a native Kentuckian) for Southern society. Letters exchanged between Shifflet and his wife, who had also been born in Kentucky, produced an agreement that the family would relocate southward after the war concluded. "If I ever live to git to Ohio I wonte stay two weeks," Shifflet wrote, since "all or half of the state is negro wersherpers." The fight he had been initially eager to join had been corrupted by antislavery zealots.

Shifflet's racist hostility, like that of many Democrats, was heightened by class resentments against those who "mis the war and git others to do the fighting for them." His family's dire circumstances meant that small difficulties like a delay in regimental pay had immediate consequences for day-to-day existence. Letters from his wife informed him that she was working during the harvest of 1862 in the tobacco fields alongside the other field hands, who were mostly men. Shifflet blamed his family's humiliating circumstances on antislavery Republicans, whose rhetoric about freeing slaves stung all the more because of its contrast with the party's apparent disregard of poor white families in both the North and the South. The following letter touched briefly on Lincoln's policies before Shifflet described how fellow soldiers were inflicting overly harsh measures upon defenseless Southern civilians. The lines between enemies and friends were blurred by the couple's shared Southern sympathies.

February the 13th, 1863
Camp Sill Tennessee

Dear Wife

. . . I hav bin out with the forage teemes today me and Sahue McKelvy went with Ean McDanel he is driven a teem and he is as tired as I am of the war. our Regiment has to dwo all the hardships. I had drother bee at home a working for 25 sense a day and borde my Self than to bee in the war. but this onholy war wood a bin over if oald Lincoln wood a let the negros alone. I wish he had forty the blackest negroes in the South tide to him. hit is a Shocking Sight to see how the soldiers starvs the farmers. tha take everthing before them. I saw them to day goin to a hous and take ever thing tha cood lay thaer hands on and then even for the chickens out adoors and the worst of all hit was a poor widow woman with fore little children, I was mity sorry for her She beg them to not take her things for her little Children wood Starve if tha took her provishion but tha went a head and took. I hav saw a heepe such cases as that tell I am tired out of such doings. I hante got nothing to right but if I was at home I cood tell you a heepe such things as I hav seen. . . .

Mima I hav no candle tonight & I will hav to quit. I will git pade aMunday and I will send you a letter Mima. I hante got no postedg stamps to put on my letters nor cant git none and I am sorry for hit but I cant help hit. Right as soon as you can.

Hillory Shifflet

In writing to his family in northern Illinois, Lysander Wheeler displayed none of the political anger that consumed Shifflet. Wheeler's correspondence was nonetheless filled with accusations that Republicans had not done enough to win the war effectively and that voters should punish them as a result. Late in 1862 Wheeler discussed the party system as a self-regulating mechanism that shifted power into new hands when events took a turn for the worse. The letter indicated that he was open to compromise with the Confederates and was willing to consider nonmilitary means of luring white Southerners back into the Union.

Scottsville [Ky.]
Thursday Afternoon
Nov. 13th 1862

Dear Parents and Sister,

. . . We hear the Democrats have carried the day generally in the North it is pretty generally liked by every one that I have heard express an opinion on the subject. They think that it will be apt to drive the Republicans into doing something for some body else's benefit besides their own pockets and if they don't close this thing out before the democrats come to power they may see a compromise made with the South which they won't like so well and I see the North are coming to it fast in spite of everything. So the next Congress had better pitch in. They say at the North that the Soldiers wouldn't vote for a compromise. It is just like this if they could go ahead it would be all right but under the present rule of things, they would to a man vote for a compromise to-morrow. That is what I think I have heard hundred if not thousands say and have never heard any say otherwise yet from Captains down. . . .

Your son and brother, Ever in respect,
L. Wheeler

As partisan opposition to Lincoln mounted during the winter of 1862–63, two distinct wings of the Democratic party emerged. War Democrats supported the vigorous military assault upon the Confederacy while protesting Republican encroachments on white supremacy and decentralized government. Their self-consciously conservative slogan—"The Union as it was, the Constitution as it is"— emphasized the party's pledge to restore the antebellum Republic. The Peace Democrats were far more controversial in demanding a cease-fire and in welcoming open-ended compromises that many assumed would lead to two separate American republics. At times this faction even suggested that Confederate independence was preferable to a Union governed by what they called the Lincoln tyranny. Such rhetoric gave Republicans an opening, which they used to link these so-called Copperheads to the entire Democratic Party. The onus of treason associated with notoriously antiwar figures like Clement Vallandigham of Ohio and New Yorkers Ben and Fernando Wood gradually discredited all of Lincoln's political opponents.

The stance of Peace Democrats outraged many soldiers, whose letters explain how such opposition represented a personal affront to those in uniform. In the spring of 1863 new Democratic majorities in the Illinois and Indiana legislatures sparked a backlash from the troops when they suggested that the states' regiments might be withdrawn from military campaigns that seemed to be faltering. In an episode that the historian Mark Neely has dubbed the revolt of the Illinois line, dozens of regiments publicly threatened to march on the state capital of Springfield rather than allow themselves to be taken out of the action. Neither James K. Magie nor Lysander Wheeler participated in this threatened coup d'état, but both men were touched by its underlying spirit. Wheeler turned from his earlier flirtation with the Democrats to a series of complaints about "Copperhead disloyalty."

Magie's faith in the Republican administration was never in doubt. As the absentee editor of his hometown party newspaper he rallied enthusiasm for Lincoln's most recent measures, arguing that these would win the war and restore America's standing as the world's greatest Republic. His party could take pride in implementing an ambitious agenda that looked past the war by laying the basis for a truly national Union. Magie's confidence in the Republican vision of national economic and political strength was bolstered by the reaction of the troops, who were increasingly hostile to Democratic intrigue, which seemed to border on treason. "When the soldiers come home," he wrote late in the spring of 1863, "they will carry the whole country" for Lincoln. His mounting optimism about soldiers' devotion to the president was a sign that the long winter of discontent was nearing an end. In discussing the improving state of affairs, Magie turned away from questions of Northern resolve and took up the mounting indications of Confederate weakness.

Franklin Tenn.
March 20, '63

My dearest love,

. . . I think I shall try and get a furlough to come home in May or June if the war should not close before that time. There seems to be considerable confidence of late in the army that the war will not continue through the summer. I really hope that it will not. The rebels are in a deplorable condition and in some localities are actually starving to death. . . . We are taking a few prisoners every day and sometimes we lose a few. Yesterday we lost 33 men who were out on a scout, but we took about the same number. Those that we take give a sorry picture of matters in rebeldom. They are ragged, hungry, and dirty. . . .

Please continue to write often and much oblige
your ever affectionate husband,
James K. Magie

The nineteenth century's chaotic election calendar gave voters the chance to register the ebb and flow of party preference through an unending series of state contests. Democrats capitalized on mounting discontent in the fall of 1862, which saw victories in Shifflet's Ohio, Tillotson's New York, Smith's New Jersey, and several other states. A round of elections the following spring showed improving Republican fortunes. This period witnessed the first state-level experiments with soldier absentee ballots, one of the war's major political innovations. Republicans sensed that they had the most to gain from soldier voting and consequently took the lead in enacting new legislation to allow voting in army camps. They were proved right in April 1863 during their successful campaign for a new member of the Wisconsin Supreme Court. The twenty-eight-hundred-vote victory of the Republican candidate would have been a forty-nine-hundred-vote deficit without the tally of soldiers, who voted for Lincoln's party by a margin of eight to one.

While soldiers cast their ballots from the front, they also used their pens to influence the political commitments of friends and family at home. Shortly before the Wisconsin Supreme Court election, Dolphus Damuth heard rumors about his brother's politics that caused him to write the following angry letter. Cajoling family members to vote Republican usually did not involve dire threats like those made by Damuth. Troops' resolve to monitor loyalties within their immediate circle of correspondence became increasingly common, however. Such actions showed how soldiers were coming to consider all Democrats—whether identified with the peace or the war factions—as traitors to the cause they defended with their lives.

March 17th / 63

Bro. John,

. . . Do you belong to the Democratic Club if you do I want to know it. I hope you don't, I had rather See You in the Rebel army than in Krebs Hall* to a meeting of that crew. I understand the Copperheads are drilling in the north. I wish the Gov. of our State would call home a few of us and let us go at them. I would shoot my own brother as soon as I would a Snake if I should see him in the ranks of such a god forsaken set of trators. it makes me mad to think of it and thear is just this about it. I wont write or do I want to hear from any ones that does and any one that writs to me that belongs to that tribe I shall take it that they mean to insult me. This war has got to be ended by fighting and thear can be but two parties engaged in it Patriots & Trators. feel glad I enlisted, I feel proud that I belong to the Union army. If I live through it, it will be Something to think of in after years. if I die it will be in the best cause man ever died in. . . .

John, I have wrote this in a great hurry but I guess you can read it.

From Dolph Damuth

Saving the Union ultimately depended on successful military campaigning, which began in earnest when Federal armies broke their winter camps in the spring of 1863. Commanders of the eastern armies regrouped and made a concerted effort to raise soldiers' dismal morale and to increase their depleted numbers. This internal rejuvenation allowed the army to survive another major setback at Chancellorsville in

*This may have been the local headquarters of the Democratic Party in Fort Atkinson, Wisconsin.

Eastern Front, 1862–1863

PENNSYLVANIA

Lee's Second Northern Advance

Gettysburg
July 2–4, 1863

Antietam
September 17, 1862

Frémont's Pursuit of Jackson, 1862

MARYLAND

WEST VIRGINIA (1863)

Winchester

Shenandoah Valley

Lee's First Northern Advance

Washington, D.C.

Second Bull Run
August 29–30, 1862

Union

Cross Keys
June 8, 1862

Chancellorsville
May 2–6, 1863

Fredericksburg
December 13, 1862

Chespeake Bay

Jackson's Valley Diversion, 1862

Seven Days' Battles
June 25–July 1, 1862

Richmond

VIRGINIA

Peninsula Campaign

Union troop movement

Confederate troop movement

0 Miles *50*

0 Kilometers *50*

May and to ready itself for what would be its biggest challenge, to stop Robert E. Lee's second invasion of the North in late June. Confederates hoped that their midsummer raid into Pennsylvania would widen Northern divisions and thereby weaken support for the war. Their decision produced a Union victory at Gettysburg that marked the end of what had been a prolonged period of Northern despair.

In the west, General Ulysses S. Grant set his sights on completing Federal control of the Mississippi River, which was a priority for midwestern communities that depended on river-borne trade. Grant's series of logistical and strategic initiatives exposed the vulnerability of Vicksburg, the last and most stubborn Confederate western stronghold. After a series of probes Grant ordered a Federal flotilla to run past Southern defenses in mid-April. This dramatic move allowed his army to circle the city and, after achieving a major victory at the Battle of Champion's Hill, begin a lengthy siege of Vicksburg from the rear. Northern civilians yearned for a quicker assault and expressed impatience with what they took to be yet one more stalemate. Yet this time, unlike a few months earlier, soldiers sensed that prospects were far better than the press reported. Their confidence was vindicated on Independence Day, as Dolphus Damuth enthusiastically reported in a note to his sister written the following morning.

The victories at Gettysburg and Vicksburg caused Union spirits to soar and Northern letters to take a more hopeful note. These military successes and the confidence they inspired strengthened Union cohesion, largely to the detriment of the Democratic Party. Politically uncommitted soldiers like Lysander Wheeler responded to this rush of good news by putting the defeat of Robert E. Lee at Gettysburg within a still-larger context. He found a silver lining in the invasion of southern Indiana by the Confederate raider John Hunt Morgan, noting that this area of the Ohio River Valley was associated with Copperheads, who seemed to be getting what they deserved with the arrival of Southern arms. Morgan's raid ended in disaster in late July, when a fragment of his original force retreated to Tennessee. During the same period General William Rosecrans (a leader the troops called Rosy) was in the process of transferring Wheeler's regiment and the rest of the Army of the Cumberland toward Chattanooga, establishing yet one more prong of a coordinated Union advance. Wheeler's discussion of the situ-

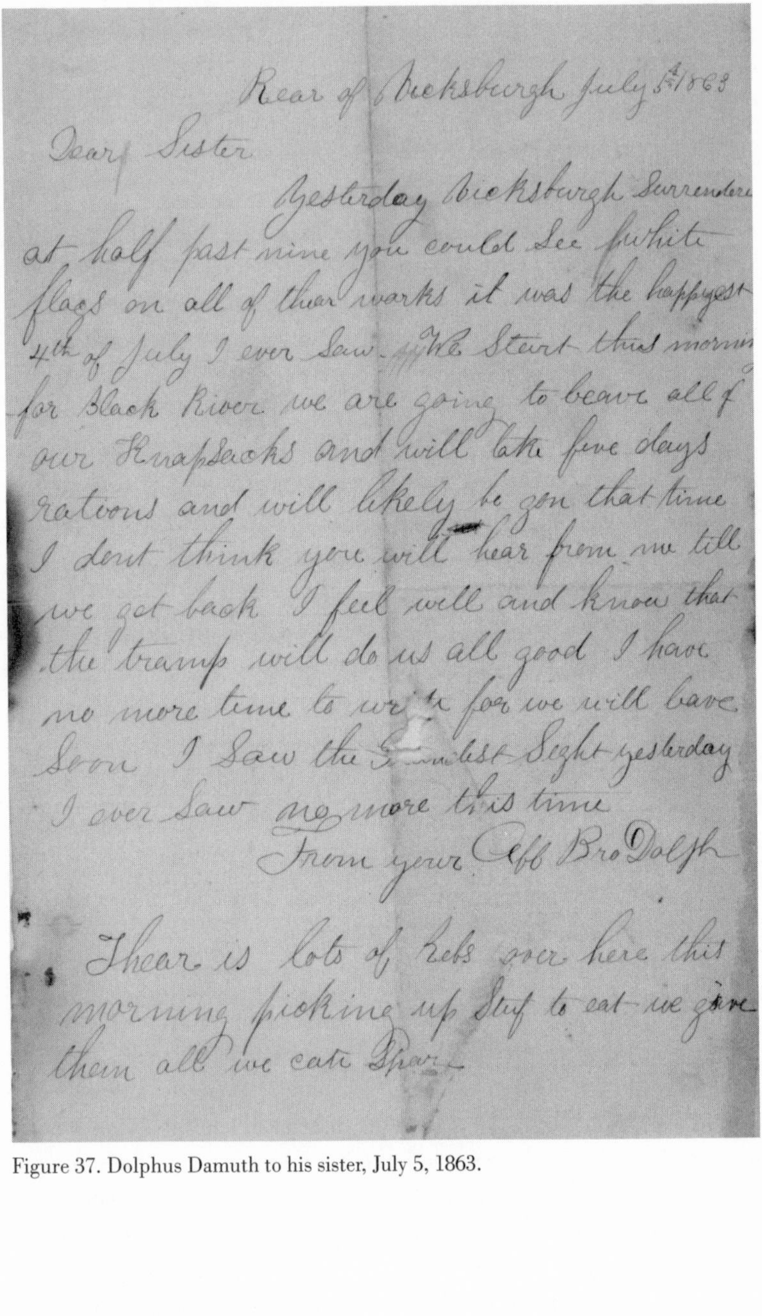

Rear of Vicksburgh July 5th 1863

Dear Sister

Yesterday Vicksburgh Surrendered at half past nine you could See the white flags on all of thear works it was the happyest 4th of July I ever Saw We Start this morning for Black River we are going to leave all of our Knapsacks and will take five days rations and will likely be gon that time I dont think you will hear from me till we get back I feel well and know that the tramp will do us all good I have no more time to write for we will leave Soon I Saw the Grandest Sight yesterday I ever Saw no more this time

From your Aff Bro Dolph

Thear is lots of Rebs over here this morning picking up Stuf to eat we give them all we can Spare

Figure 37. Dolphus Damuth to his sister, July 5, 1863.

ation indicated that his entire family had a common understanding of who was furthering the cause and who was hampering it.

July 12th [1863]
Murfreesboro

Dear Parents, Brother & Sister:

. . . I read every word you wrote me with great interest and care. The many words of encouragement which it contains, etc. . . .

We hear that Mr. Morgan is up in Indiana among the natives all right if they can stand it we certainly can and wish he would Massacre some of those copperheads and then get massacred himself and all his crew. Lee's fate was a just one. . . . Hurrah for the fall of Vicksburg (I guess it's done gone up) and 3 times 3 for our Gallant Rosecrans whose Headquarters are at Chattanooga and Hind Quarters at Murfreesboro. Our best wishes is to go and be with him. I hope the Fatherless army of the Potomac* has at last found a worthy leader Half as good at least as ours (Rosy). We think the dawn of a brighter day is just beginning to appear above the Horizon. Action is the word and this war will soon be played out. It is the best thing ever happened. The invasion of the North by the Rebels. The war would close quicker if they penetrated way up to Chicago. The Northern Copperhead would get waked up. . . .

Lysander

The military successes that boosted Northern morale did not remove all the political divisions within the Union. Manpower needs remained a leading cause of internal frictions, especially after efforts had failed to encourage volunteering with bounties and the threats of a wider draft. By midsummer 1863 officials had begun to implement the Enrollment Act, which required states that had not met established

*George Gordon Meade had been appointed commander of the Army of the Potomac in time to lead it at Gettysburg, though there was a popular perception that his position would not be permanent. Meade retained titular command even after U. S. Grant (the true "head" of eastern armies) came to Virginia as a lieutenant general in the spring of 1864.

volunteering rates to institute conscription. This law included a provision for commutation, which allowed those drafted to purchase an exemption from service. Though this provision was successfully assailed as a sop to the wealthy, it was not implemented along strict class lines. Compared with the Confederate policy of substitution (which required a draftee to hire a replacement at a price mutually agreed upon), commutation was within the financial means of many Northerners of modest incomes. Workingmen joined draft insurance societies as a means of pooling their resources and were among the main beneficiaries of the commutation provision.

New York City was expected to be the site of draft resistance because of both its long-standing Southern ties and its more recent role as a hotbed of anti-Lincoln sentiment. Few, however, predicted the chaos that erupted in mid-July, when one of the largest urban riots in American history broke out across the city. As authorities lost control of Manhattan, it became clear that both racial hostility and charges of class favoritism had ignited deep political passions. While much of the antidraft violence was directed against the city's wealthy and the Republican Party, it reached its most lethal intensity when directed against black New Yorkers.

The New York draft riots furthered the political split between soldiers and civilians. Copperheads stoked the defiance of potential soldiers at the very time that enlisted men longed for more manpower to complete the war. Despite their differing political views, George Tillotson, Hillory Shifflet, James Magie, and Dolphus Damuth expressed their strong support for conscription in letters to their families during the summer of 1863. Charles Morey of Vermont did not address the issue explicitly, and he continued to favor McClellan. But his short tour of duty in the late summer of 1863 showed that he too was willing to take part in the compulsory enlistment of unwilling soldiers. After making a two-week show of force in New York City's Washington Square, Morey's unit traveled to Poughkeepsie, where he wrote the following diary entries. His records show the determination of Union authorities to assure that as the draft proceeded in smaller cities, there would be none of the violence that had swept Manhattan in July.

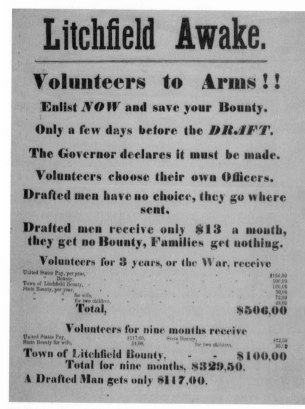

Litchfield Awake.

Volunteers to Arms!!

Enlist *NOW* and save your Bounty.

Only a few days before the *DRAFT*.

The Governor declares it must be made.

Volunteers choose their own Officers.

Drafted men have no choice, they go where sent.

Drafted men receive only $13 a month, they get no Bounty, Families get nothing.

Volunteers for 3 years, or the War, receive

United States Pay, per year,	$156,00
" Bounty,	100,00
Town of Litchfield Bounty,	100,00
State Bounty, per year,	30,00
" " for wife,	72,00
" " for two children,	48,00
Total,	**$506,00**

Volunteers for nine months receive

United States Pay,	$117,00.	State Bounty,	$22,50
State Bounty for wife,	54,00.	" for two children.	36,00

Town of Litchfield Bounty, - - $100,00

Total for nine months, $329,50.

A Drafted Man gets only $117,00.

Figure 38. Union recruiting broadside, 1863.

[September 1863]

Monday 7. Nothing of importance aside from the draft in the city going on everything passed off quietly no riots and no disturbance. Dress parade at 5 P.M.

Tuesday 8. The draft still continues in this district without trouble. There are two companies of our regiment on duty in the city. We have company drill in A.M. and Battalion drill and Dress parade at P.M. Wrote to Cousin Emma.

Wednesday 9. The draft still continues without any disturbance and the best feeling is exhibited by the people. Visited the town this P.M. had my moustache shaved off.

Thursday 10. Very Pleasant weather and we are enjoying ourselves greatly here. A great many people come out daily to see us drill and our Dress Parade. Went to town this evening.

The year 1863 ended far differently than the previous year had, when Northern confidence had been shaken by the Fredericksburg setback and Confederate independence had appeared likely. Elections held in Ohio and Pennsylvania during the fall of 1863 marked the continuing political resurgence of the Republican Party, which by having weathered its earlier difficulties could look toward what reconstruction of the Union might entail. Lincoln's Gettysburg Address that same November offered soldiers an eloquent assurance that both past and future sacrifices would not be made in vain. Though the occasion involved the dedication of a cemetery, Lincoln hailed a "new birth of freedom" as the country's most important goal.

Even those unmoved by the eloquence of "Father Abraham" tended to respect the president's consistent efforts to restore Federal authority by armed force. George Tillotson expressed his own outlook in a letter written from Charleston's outer defenses. While his politics were still relatively noncommittal, there was far less anger at leaders than had been true twelve months earlier.

Folly Island
Nov 21st, 1863

My Dear Wife,

Your letter of the 4th I received two or three days ago and also the Tribune of the 31st ult. I hope your dreams will come to pass some of these days before long. The Captain I believe has promised the next furlough to Hank Talmage. . . .

But I have another hope (which still may turn out a disappointment) of getting home this winter. It has been determined on, and approved by Gen. Gilmore, to send details out of each regiment (the N.Y. regiments at any rate) home to recruit. For the regiment in our brigade are to be sent a captain and three or four enlisted men from each company. The details are not made yet and it is not certain that the order will not be countermanded, so that none will go. And besides I aint certain of being one of the luckey ones if they do. I asked Capt Lewis for the privaleg of being detailed for one, but he said he hadn't made up his mind yet who to detail. So you see I don't know yet but am only hopeing and wishing. No I don't suppose for a moment that any soldier would go home and vote a Copperhead ticket, and on the other hand, I wouldn't vote a republican ticket just merely because it was republican but I should most assuredly vote for the Union, and those that would maintain it, let the principle appear under any name whatsoever. . . .

Your most affectionate husband
G. W. Tillotson

After a relatively quiet winter the third year of campaigning opened in the spring of 1864 with high expectations. The Union's manpower advantage was supplemented by black troops, while its military fortunes were entrusted to Ulysses S. Grant, whose string of victories at Fort Donelson, Vicksburg, and Chattanooga culminated in his appointment as lieutenant general. Grant's fighting spirit filtered down to his troops, who sensed that a victory might be won that spring. The troops' rise in morale was quickly transferred through the mail to civilians at home. Just before commencing the Overland campaign in Virginia, Charles Morey expressed a sense of guarded optimism in a letter sent to his mother in Vermont.

Headquarters Second Vermont Infantry, Sixth Corps
May 3rd, 1864

My Dear Mother,

As we are about to march I write you a few lines to let you know that my health never was better than now and that I am confident of success for Gen. Grant has been very busy arranging his plans and I hope and pray that he will not meet with a disaster. I have been on many campaigns and never received a scratch but we know not what a day may bring forth. Let us trust the event in the hands of Him who rules the raging battle as well as the quiet sunshine and let us pray that God may grant that this campaign may end this Hydra headed rebellion and cause the people of the south to see the error of thier ways and return to thier aleigence. Never did this army move when it was in better condition or spirits than at present and all seem to be quite confident of success. . . .

Accept much love from your son,
C. C. Morey

P.S. We move tomorrow morning at 4 o'clock with 6 days rations.

When Morey wrote this letter, Grant's plans for a coordinated offensive had already begun to fray. William T. Sherman's army was advancing more slowly than expected into northern Georgia, in part because he was deprived of troops taken by General Nathaniel Banks on an ill-advised campaign up the Red River in northern Louisiana. In the following letter Dolphus Damuth described what a difficult time he and the other soldiers under Banks had in this remote frontier area. His account focused on the decisive turning point at Sabine Crossroads, where General Richard Taylor's twelve thousand Confederate troops outflanked the roughly twenty-eight thousand Union soldiers and forced them to undertake a chaotic and costly retreat. There were more than twenty-two hundred Federal casualties in the clash, including several friends of the Damuth family. Dolphus provided telling details to his sister, but he wanted her to save any press reports that might give him a sense of the larger picture.

Grand Encore
April 15, 1864

Dear Sister,

As we have got our fortification all done and now consider our Selves perfectly safe, I will Spend a little time in writing to you. I will tell you a little Something of the fighting and marching we have done for the last few days before we came here. . . .

We formed in line of Battle in a very rough place. . . . We marched in line till we came to a fence and the Balls began to fly. we could See the rebs run across the field into the woods beyond. Fred & Charlie were killed thear and all the men we had wounded were shot thear. The Major ordered us to fall back a

Private Henry Berckhoff's Watercolor War

Like other Civil War soldiers, United States private Henry Berckhoff took up his pen to pass the time, to record his impressions, and to share his firsthand experiences of army service with others. This young immigrant began his depiction of infantry life during his two-year enlistment in the New York City "German Rifles." Some time after his unit disbanded in the spring of 1863, he selected the most compelling of his wartime ink sketches, finished these in watercolor, mounted them on stock paper, provided proper titles for each, and arranged them in a portfolio for safekeeping. The nineteen plates featured in the following pages reproduce the end result of his meticulous work.

The first seven compositions show recruits moving from the streets of New York to the Virginia front, where a brief taste of combat disrupted their establishment and defense of encampments. The next six pictures follow these fighters through the spring and early summer of 1862 as they marched, and marched, and marched, and marched, until they were badly beaten by Stonewall Jackson's Confederate troops in the Shenandoah Valley. The final six watercolors move from three successive combat scenes through the regiment's final winter routines into a closing view of troops happy to be "Home ward bound."

Marching to the seat of war
27 May 1861

Bivouac on the Potomac river
near Alexandria Va.
10 July 1861.

Gen. Blenker
at the close of the battle of Bull Run
21 July 1861.

Camp
at Roach's mill
August 1861.

Building Fort Blenker
September 1864

Morningscene
at Camp Hunter's Chappel
October 1861.

Attack on the Outposts near
Annandale Va.
5 December 1861

Gen. Blenker's fatal fall
at Salem
7 April 1862.

Crossing the Shenandoah river
on pontoons at Berryville
17 April 1862

Passing the hanging rocks gap
near Romney
3 May 1862.

Crossing the upper Potomac
near Franklin
13 May 1862.

Bridge building at New Market
5 June 1862.

battle of Cross Keyes
8 June 1862.

Battle on Manassas plains
2d Bull Run
29 August 1862

Skirmish at Haymarket
4 November 1862.

#16

Cavalry skirmish near
Aldie 28 November 1862

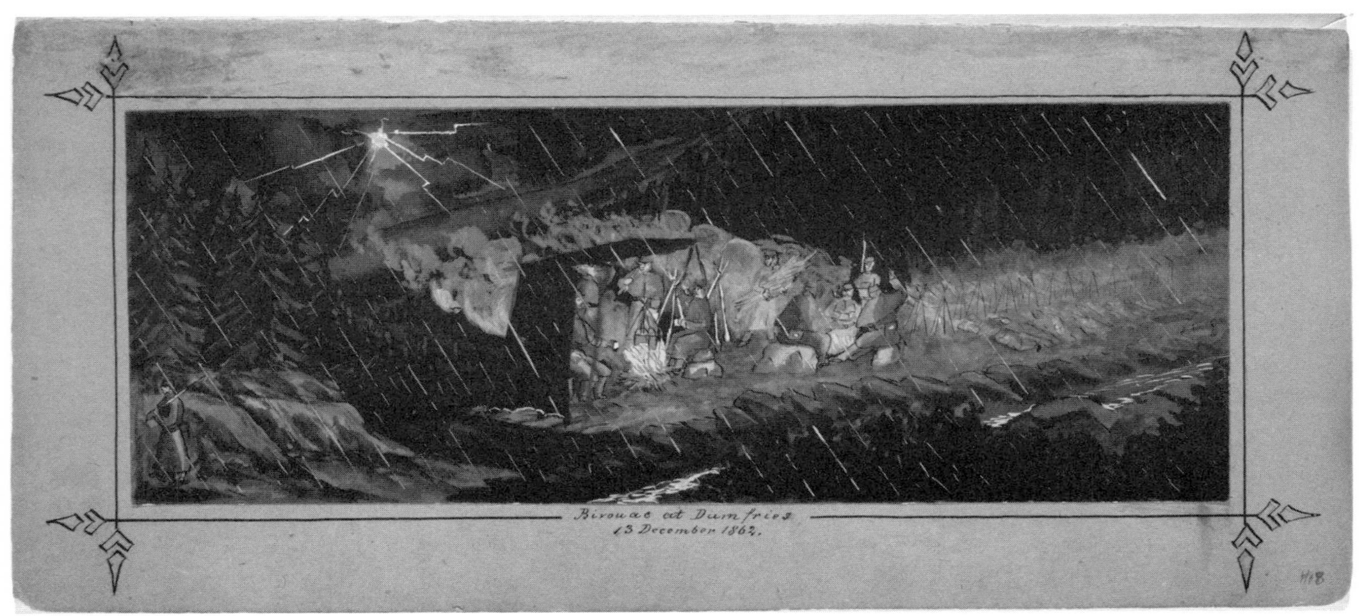

Bivouac at Dumfries
13 December 1862.

118

Rail Road guard near Brooks Station
Februar 1863.

Home ward bound.
Hop's Landing on the Aquia creek
May 3. 1863

little. I got the Co. back as well as I could, thear is where I first missed Capt. I knew he was either killed or wounded or he would be with us. I asked the Major whear he was. he said he was wounded and gon to the rear. We stood our ground tell we saw thear was no use. The Rebs had flanked us. we fell back about 30 rods and made another Stand. Then our Co was all thear that was not killed or wounded we gave three cheers for the Flag, and the Sound had hardly died away before they were on us in overwhelming numbers. They fixed at our Co. but Shot over. If they had not we should all fell then. The retreat began. every man for himself. my gun was shot through the Stock and Spiled. I through it and my knapsack and lost every thing. The Balls came thicker than they had before. Men fell dead all around me and I thought my turn would come next. I could See the Rebs and hear them say, Stop you Yankee Sons of Bitches, Surrender you dogs. but we kept on as fast as our legs would carry us. The Cavalry, Infantry, and trains was all mixed up together. The brush was so thick we couldn't go on the side of the road. Men was knocked down by horses running against them and run over by the teams. It was a horrible sight to See. . . . I got hold of a horses tail and she jerked me a mile that way very quick. The boys laughed when I told them of it but thought it a good way. . . .

Most everyone thinks that Banks has Shown very poor Generalship in this fight. You will hear all about it in the newspapers and I wish you would keep the papers that has anything about it in. I don't know what will be the next move, but I am sure that as long as we are here thear is not much danger of an attack from the Rebs. I wish they would try us on once more, we would give them all they want. . . .

I must close for they are packing up the mail,

Yours Truly, Dolph

Grant's Virginia operations against Lee also proved harder than originally expected, even if it was led by a far more accomplished general than Nathaniel Banks. The 1864 Overland campaign began with the inconclusive Battle of the Wilderness, where dense undergrowth required close-range fighting that set the tone for the following bloody six weeks of nearly constant combat. In the following letter, Charles Morey told of the death of his company's captain, whose vacated position Morey himself soon filled. As the woods began to burn near the conclusion of the battle, many of the wounded chose to kill themselves rather than be consumed in flames. A few days later the clash at Spotsylvania's Bloody Angle gave troops a still more horrific experience. Throughout nearly the entire rainy, cold day of May 12, Federal troops tried and failed to push beyond the Confederate entrenchment they had captured at dawn. Separated from his enemies by only a few feet for several hours, Morey experienced the fiercest combat of his entire four years of service. In little over a week his regiment of 700 men suffered a total of 471 casualties. Such bloodletting tarnished Grant's reputation in the press, though soldiers like Morey wanted to reassure their families that he was still the right man to lead them to victory.

Headquarters Second Vermont Infantry, Sixth Corps
May 13th, 1864

Dear Parents

It is with gratitude to God that I am permitted to write you a few lines once more. I don't know what to say first but will say praise God for his goodness in sparing my life while so many of our brave comrads have fallen victims to the enemy's shots, we have been under fire for the past nine days and now as I write the picket are skirmishing with the enemy. The 5th of this month we were heavily engaged our loss was heavy on the 6th we were engaged again and Capt. Bixby was killed. Yesterday we were terribly engaged we charged on the enemy's works but they would not leave and we fought with them on one side of the parapet and we on the other for nine long hours. our loss was terrible. we have only 16 Enlisted men with us in the company this morning but some more will come in who got separated from us in the fight. but this is not all the fighting we have done we made another charge on the enemy's works drove them out but could not hold them and were obliged to retreat. Yesterday there was a spent ball hit me on my leg but did not disable me. I think Gen Grant intends to win. Praise God for his kindness and accept a great deal of love from your son in the army. write soon, we have not had any mail since we started. Shurb is well Lt. Hayward is well Sgt. Allen was wounded in arm. write soon.

C. C. Morey

After these setbacks Grant famously resolved to "fight it out on this line if it takes all summer." Yet determination alone was insufficient, and after the Union's costly assault on Confederate trenches at Cold Harbor produced another seven thousand casualties, Grant swung his troops south of Richmond to move against the railroad center of Petersburg. Lee's entrenched Confederates successfully protected the city, and a siege resulted that once more caused the Northern public to fear a military stalemate. Over the course of six weeks the Army of the Potomac had suffered the loss of approximately sixty-four thousand men.

The hard fighting in Virginia led during the summer of 1864 to a second crisis of Northern confidence, which differed in important ways from the challenges faced during the winter of 1862–63. The political stakes were much higher, since Lincoln himself, and not merely his party, stood for reelection this time around. A rejection of the country's commander in chief in the November vote would mean a fundamental change in war aims and perhaps a peace treaty with an independent Confederacy. Democrats chose George B. McClellan as their presidential nominee, in part because his military service seemed a way to blunt questions about the party's loyalty. They also adopted patriotic symbols and anniversaries in an effort to associate their own efforts with earlier American history. William Woodlin noted this strategy in a diary he kept while serving in the Petersburg trenches. The actual date of the Democratic Convention was in fact slightly later than the initial reports indicated.

Soldiers who supported McClellan argued that he would match the Republicans in his determination to wage war against the Confederacy. Charles Morey expressed this opinion in the following correspondence with his mother, though he stopped short of indicating exactly how he would vote. He composed the letter after receiving a minor injury outside Petersburg, which was the first wound he had suffered that needed medical attention. On election day his regiment was among the few New England units to favor the Democratic candidate.

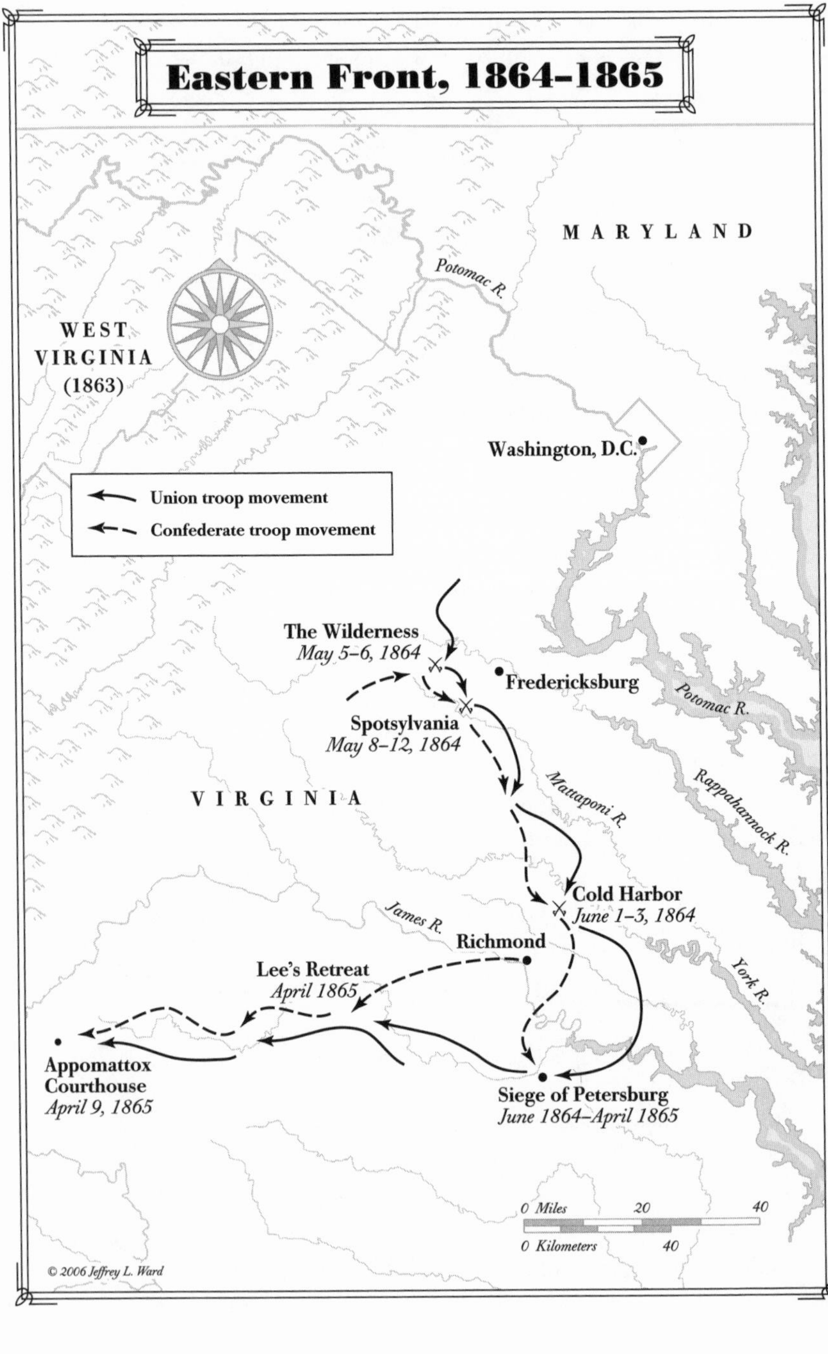

Eastern Front, 1864–1865

MARYLAND
Potomac R.
WEST VIRGINIA (1863)
Washington, D.C.
Union troop movement
Confederate troop movement
The Wilderness
May 5–6, 1864
Fredericksburg
Potomac R.
Spotsylvania
May 8–12, 1864
VIRGINIA
Mattaponi R.
Rappahannock R.
Cold Harbor
June 1–3, 1864
James R.
Richmond
Lee's Retreat
April 1865
York R.
Appomattox Courthouse
April 9, 1865
Siege of Petersburg
June 1864–April 1865
0 Miles 20 40
0 Kilometers 40

Ward 11 Camden St. Hospital
Baltimore, Md.
Sept 1st, 1864

Dear Mother

Your very kind letter is just received. it is the first one I have received since being wounded. I have just written to Sister Hattie, and will enclose this note with her letter. I am happy to state I am getting on nicely and hope to be well in a few days.

The news is this morning that Gen. McClellan is nominated for the next Presidency. I must say that those copperheads who cry peace! peace! on any terms and expect to see it on any other condition than honorably to the United States will be mistaken if he should be elected. I think that the Republican party need not be alarmed even if he should carry the day and be the next President for if I mistake not he is in favour of a vigerous prosecution of the war and he will prosecute it I think to the bitter end, but we do not know yet who will be chosen therefore will wait and watch.

Your son, C. C. Morey.

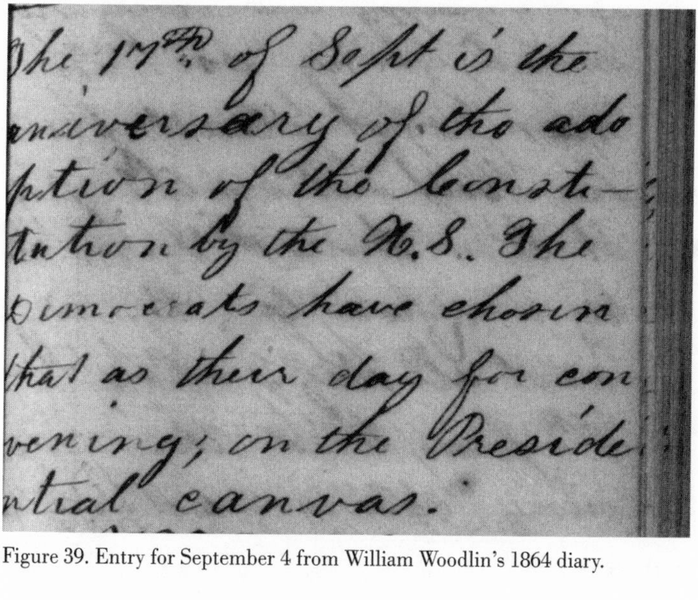
he 17th of Sept is the
nniversary of the ado
ption of the Consti-
tution by the U.S. The
Democrats have chosen
hat as their day for con
vening; on the Preside
ntial canvas.

Figure 39. Entry for September 4 from William Woodlin's 1864 diary.

During the excitement of this election season Lysander Wheeler kept his thoughts focused on the ultimate objective of military victory. In mid-August letters home expressed his soldierly determination to fight as long as it took to vanquish the Confederacy. "Discouraged is no longer a word that makes sense in the army," he insisted. The next month, as military fortunes brightened, stoicism was replaced by confidence. Wheeler now looked forward to Lincoln's victory, though he did so with little avowed partisanship. He trusted the Republican Party but had an even deeper faith in the resolve of William T. Sherman.

September 14, 1864
Camp 105th Ill.
Chattahoochie River, Ga.

Dear Parents, Bro., and Sister:

. . . you spoke of its being 2 yrs and over since we started for the field that's whats the matter. We surely hoped it would be crushed out by this time. But the present light don't show such to be the Case however. all goes favorable or would if the North but showed an undivided front; if there had never been a Copperhead in the North this war would have been closed ere this. I am heartily glad the Republican Party has stood up fair and square to the rack. I hope they will thus continue and be finally successful in Electing Abe & Andy. should fate Decree the Election of McClellan and a Dishonorable Compromise be effected why it is not mine, or your fault if we do all in our power to prevent it. that is all that is required of us. To do our own part well. To clear our own skirts from slavery, first and if Disloyalty at the ballot Box comes ahead for the time. Why we must evidently stand it and try again. . . .

General Sherman says he intends to stand by us always. Grant had better look out or he will be out rivalled. I think neither of them intend to be rivals, however. The Army this Day is better united than ever. Martha, in both of your letters still you feel that same anxiety with mother and the rest for my welfare. Well we must go on hoping always for the best and that this war will end in Righteousness. I know if you sometimes wish its close otherwise it is because you think it will be better for me. that is the only reason for when Arnold Comes around with this Copperhead talk immediately there is a flash in the Pan. . . .

I don't know whether I should have enjoyed a visit with Ed if he had commenced with me about their miserable peace party convention. I suppose this country will be always more or less cut up in Politics as for me I'm sick of political papers. . . . if men would vote without quarrelling over it, it would [be] another thing. To say nothing about fighting between Elections. . . .

My best wishes to each one of you at home. hoping the time may come when we meet in peace, soon and war ended.

Your Son & Brother,
Lysander

The Democrats struggled during the autumn to bring their war and peace wings together. This was a difficult challenge, despite the broad party support for McClellan. The key moment came at the Chicago convention, where delegates adopted a party platform that lamented the "four years of failure to restore the Union by the experiment of war." The suggested alternative was a cease-fire to permit negotiations with the enemy. What was intended to be a slap at Lincoln's failure as president was taken by most soldiers as a slur on their own valor and an attempt to jeopardize their service and the sacrifice of their dead comrades. McClellan sensed the damage by insisting in reply that peace could come only after the Union itself was assured.

The confusion about the Democratic Party's priorities cast a shadow over its political prospects at a time when politics became an ever more important theme of soldiers' correspondence. Within armies that had become a key base of Republican support came a regular effort to belittle McClellan's attempt to balance the two distinct wings of his party. In the following letter, Dolphus Damuth continued his effort to sway civilian votes toward Lincoln. He insisted that his family and their Democratic friends not just consider the merits of McClellan the man but ponder the party that hoped to elevate him to the country's highest office. He claimed that his own views were shared by all truly loyal soldiers and lashed out at the opposition newspapers that his family apparently continued to read.

St. Charles, Ark.
Oct. 1, 1864

Dear Sister,

. . . You wanted to know what I thought of McClellan. I like him well enough, but the party that nominated him and the platform that he stands on I despise and we can't expect any more of him than the men who nominated him and support him. Do you suppose you can make a soldier believe that an armistice would be right. The sneaks would give the Rebs all we have gained in the last three years. If the Union was worthy saving in the first place it is worth it now. I would ask Pa or any other man that pretends to know anything what Lincoln has done that any Union man that loves his country can find fault with. Let them look at his past life and see if he could have done better in any instance, then why not support him. I intend to say that any man that votes against him and for McClellan votes against his country and right and favors the Rebels and treason. The good book says the sin of ignorance is to be winked at. We should look at the way some vote in the same way. There are a great many men that know no better. Some are as foolish as to think if we can defeat Lincoln the war will end right away. But I think the election of Lincoln will do more toward ending the war than any victory of our armies since the war began. I hope no one that has sons or brothers in the army will do them so great an injustice as to vote for McClellan with the expectation of shortening their term of service in the army and any one that does it I will remember as long as I live. If you would burn that Copperhead Patriot* up and take a paper that pretend to tell the truth, you would think different from what you do. I have not heard Sam Say a word about politics in six weeks. I am quite sure that he will not vote this fall for any one. I think we have but one man in our Co that will vote for McC. and he is an ignorant Irishman. Do you think you will understand by what I have written what I think?

I will close for this time for I have written all I can think of,

Yours as ever, Dolph

*The *Patriot* was the main Democratic Party newspaper of Madison, Wisconsin, and one of the most important in the state.

Damuth's letter, like those from other Republican soldiers, had taken on a more confident tone, especially when compared with the angry threats made the year before to his wayward brother. The reason for such optimism was the battlefield successes won in Georgia. Sherman's capture of Atlanta in early September ended an approach toward that city that had begun in the spring. Like the surrender of Vicksburg in the summer of 1863, this Union achievement was both a key logistical victory and an important symbolic turning point. By occupying a vital railroad center, Federal forces had the means to squeeze areas that had thus far been beyond the direct impact of war. By doing so at the height of a political campaign, Atlanta's fall all but assured the future of the Republican president and, by extension, the future of an undivided Union. By the state elections of October 1864 the political drift was clear. Republicans won another set of contests in Ohio and Pennsylvania and even carried Indiana, usually a Democratic bastion. In a Maryland referendum on emancipation, soldiers provided the winning margin for abolishing slavery, an institution as old as the state itself.

In early November Lysander Wheeler awaited the final election news all but certain of Lincoln's victory. He knew that there was still a campaign to be waged beyond Atlanta and beyond politics. A new assignment would soon take him in the direction of Savannah, and he wanted his family to know he and the rest of the army were ready to put political campaigning behind them and get back to the business of making war on the enemy.

> Chattahoochie Bridge
> Wednesday morning Nov. 9th, [1864]
>
> I thought I would send you a few lines this morning as the mail is going out at 11 A.M. (It does not go out every day). . . .
>
> We were intending to leave here to-morrow morning early, but how it will be now I cannot tell. This morning about 2 hours ago there was heard heavy Cannonading at Atlanta which continued an hour or so good and strong. at first we did not know but the wires had brought down some Extraordinary good news of the Election and they were firing salutes but we soon changed our minds from the manner in which they were fired and we

were right for Rebel General Wheeler* has been making an attack on the City and must have met with a repulse. We have no particulars therefore I can not tell anything as yet. Our boys had on their Cartridge boxes Determined to be ready if he calls around. We have no news yet from the Election. The wires were down this morning between here and Atlanta. . . . We are very anxious to hear of Old Abe's re-election. . . .

Yours in Love,
Lysander Wheeler

Throughout this final season of wartime politics George Tillotson remained relatively indifferent, though some of the grievances of two years earlier were still evident. The following offhanded comment to his wife early in the campaign showed that he too had come to support Lincoln's reelection and was now directing his anger toward the Democrats.

Fort Powhattan
Sept 21th, 1864

Dear Wife,

. . . You may as well let the Copperheads croak for you know the old saying is that "every dog will have his day" and I think that their "dog star" will set about the 8th of November, for as near as I can judge the Soldiers will be a great help in Making them loose their "all" if they "stake it on McClellan." . . . the truth is an honest Secessionist is not one tenth part as Mean as a sneaking Copperhead. . . .

Hopeing to hear from you soon and e'er long to see you also I remain as ever,

Your Most Affectionate Husband,
George W. Tillotson

*General Joseph Wheeler (not related to Lysander) had become the ranking Confederate cavalry leader by the late spring of 1864. After Atlanta's fall, his mounted troops were the only Rebel force to oppose Sherman's army.

It is easy enough to understand why politics all but disappeared from Tillotson's last letters home. As his three-year commitment drew near an end, his return to civilian life crowded out every other issue in correspondence with his wife and children. On November 8, 1864, the New York sergeant was en route from Virginia to his home, ready to rejoin civilian life. He was certainly aware that other issues were being decided that same day. Brunt, Damuth, Magie, and Wheeler each cast ballots for Lincoln on the first Tuesday of November, while Woodlin (who as a black man lacked the right to vote) would have voted Republican if he had had the chance. Berckhoff and Morey may or may not have voted for McClellan, the candidate that Shifflet and Smith would likely have backed had they still been alive. As a whole, three-quarters of Union troops supported Lincoln, who won the clear electoral mandate denied him four years earlier.

Two days after Lincoln was reelected with 55 percent of the vote, Tillotson reached his final destination in central New York and was mustered out of the service. As he had imagined during the darkest period of the war, his term had expired before the Union was restored. As

Figure 40. Soldier voting in 1864 presidential election, as depicted by *Frank Leslie's Illustrated Newspaper.*

he left the army for good, it seemed increasingly clear that Federal victory was only a matter of time. Northern soldiers were united by faith in this war, if still not completely of one mind in their politics. The military resolve was enough, however, to do what was needed to end the Confederate rebellion.

FIVE

The Fading Gray

When 1862 opened, it was Confederates who found the most cause for optimism about the future. The Louisiana private and diarist William Clegg marked his first New Year's Day under arms by reflecting upon the recent past and imagining the South's glorious destiny. Over the course of twelve pages, Clegg reflected about the prospects of his cause in glowing terms. What was his wartime diary's longest single entry contrasted the Confederate Republic with a Republican-dominated Union whose best days were in the past.

> 1862 January 1st Out of the old government a new one has been formed, all its parts put into active & vigorous operation. Never has there been in so short a time such an one formed so perfect in all its parts, and founded on so sure a basis. A large army of half a million has been raised, clothed & fed and this without one cent to begin with. So far the omens seem to be good for the success of our new government, and the people of it are more united than ever and determined to resist to the bitter end.
>
> There has been quite a change in the old US govm't. The masses are wild with fanaticism and urged on by still more fanatic leaders. The Federal constitution once held sacred & binding, has been violated more openly and flagrantly than ever.

Figure 41. Photograph of William Clegg.

An army has been raised by the Pres. without the authority of congress. The habeas corpus act suspended. Citizens imprisoned by military authority without charge, or hope of trial, ladies subjected to injuries & insults entirely unbecoming a civilized nation. These and other acts have been performed, not only disgraceful & dishonorable, but proofs of the imbecility of the government. So far the aspect of affairs in the North seem fast tending to a military despotism & whether they avoid it or not the govm't will never command the respect with nations it did before the rupture.

The South as yet has acted entirely upon the defensive. The

> plunder seeking Vandals of the North have been met at every point on land with success and our home and firesides have been defended from devastation and their polluting touches. Our Arms have been victorious at the battles of Bethel, Bull Run, Manassas, Springfield, Oak Hill, Lexington, Carnifax Ferry, Belmont & in other less engagements.
>
> The enemy in all as yet accomplished little more than the capture of two small seacoast batteries at Forts Hatteras & Port Royal. This is doing but little after one year has expired when the people of the North had made the discovery that the Southerners were terribly in earnest. . . .
>
> We are now entering upon a new year what it may bring forth mortals know not but God still being our helper, although we may sustain reverses we will at last be victorious. Our ship of state has been launched. Though upon a troubled sea, we have a brave & skillful pilot and with Jeff Davis at the helm we may expect to weather the storm & ride safely into the haven of peace & prosperity.

Over the first month and a half of 1862 this apparently rosy situation took a turn for the worse. As the Union navy increased its dominance of the south Atlantic coast and western armies pushed into the interior of Tennessee, Clegg's writing predictably took on a gloomier tone. He somberly recorded a major Confederate loss at Roanoke Island, the death of General Felix Zollicoffer at Cumberland Gap, and the biggest disaster of all, the Confederate evacuation of Fort Donelson, which he insisted (with a nod to ancient Greece) "should have been our Thermopylae." These setbacks were deeply discouraging to partisans of Southern independence. Clegg's spirits lagged, though he kept faith that the new government would win what now seemed likely to be a difficult war.

> 18th Feb 1862 To day our government assumes a permanent form and the Provisional Constitution has passed into history. . . . Great are the responsibilities of this Congress and the men composing it upon whom our country has reposed the ut-

> most confidence & showered the highest honors, are to call into play their brightest faculties. Not only the fate of this Nation depends upon their deliberations, but the preservation of republican liberty rests, perhaps, solely on their labors. Not only the representatives by their energy, and vigorous actions are to give force to the Gov't. but the whole heart of the people must be inlisted. We are entering on a high and peerless enterprise. A brilliant or a fearfully dark future lies immediately before us. Victory or worse than death is close at hand—shall we be free or the mere vassals of an insolent foe? Shall our flag wave in its defence, or shall its folds, as it trails in the dust yield to the insults of an enemy who in lowering it subjugates us!!

Clegg's entries conveyed both the potential of Confederate patriotism and the forces that were to undermine Southern morale as the war progressed. Despite the new government's youth, many initially agreed with Clegg that Southern nationhood was a "high and peerless enterprise" worthy of support from "the whole heart of the people." More soldiers rallied to the new Rebel flag during the first year of war than could be effectively put under arms. Broadsides issued by individual state governors helped draw forth this vigorous response by calling for the defense of Southern homes, the preservation of American republicanism, and the vindication of slave society. Over time such themes were embraced with varying degrees of enthusiasm by soldiers within the Confederate military. A considerable number of true believers in the ranks fought to the bitter end and surrendered only when all chances of success had been crushed. For others, enthusiasm waned well before the final defeat, especially as their families suffered from Union occupation or demands made on their property by the Confederate army itself. Disaffection became a particular problem among nonslaveholding Southerners who made up the rank and file of the major armies.

As Clegg's spirits lagged, he simply quit writing. There would not be a second patriotic diary once he finished the first in the closing months of 1862. A journal he produced during the last two years of the war was largely an account of official affairs, containing hardly any of the introspection that marked entries made in his first diary. For a

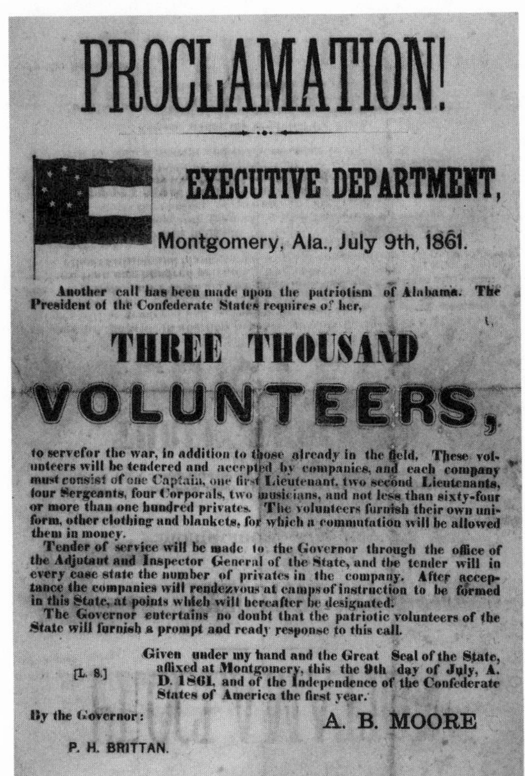

PROCLAMATION!

EXECUTIVE DEPARTMENT,

Montgomery, Ala., July 9th, 1861.

Another call has been made upon the patriotism of Alabama. The President of the Confederate States requires of her,

THREE THOUSAND

VOLUNTEERS,

to servefor the war, in addition to those already in the field. These volunteers will be tendered and accepted by companies, and each company must consist of one Captain, one first Lieutenant, two second Lieutenants, four Sergeants, four Corporals, two musicians, and not less than sixty-four or more than one hundred privates. The volunteers furnish their own uniform, other clothing and blankets, for which a commutation will be allowed them in money.

Tender of service will be made to the Governor through the office of the Adjutant and Inspector General of the State, and the tender will in every case state the number of privates in the company. After acceptance the companies will rendezvous at camps of instruction to be formed in this State, at points which will hereafter be designated.

The Governor entertains no doubt that the patriotic volunteers of the State will furnish a prompt and ready response to this call.

[L. S.] Given under my hand and the Great Seal of the State, affixed at Montgomery, this the 9th day of July, A. D. 1861, and of the Independence of the Confederate States of America the first year.

By the Governor: A. B. MOORE

P. H. BRITTAN.

Figure 42. Confederate Recruiting broadside issued by Alabama Governor A. B. Moore, 1861.

sense of how common Southern soldiers responded to the ebb and flow of Confederate fortunes, we must turn to the stream of letters that the other penmen managed, despite the postal difficulties, to compose through the early part of 1865. Collectively, this correspondence showed that Rebel soldiers were comparatively more deprived than their Union counterparts. Their bad food was worse and less regular. Government-issued provisions like shoes and medicine were far more likely to fall short of the troops' basic needs. Requests for additional help from home took an accordingly more desperate tone.

Southerners' letters demonstrate that there were important differences of kind as well as degree separating the experience of Confederate and Federal infantries. Such distinctions had a marked impact on the written record that was sent through the Southern wartime mail. Confederate soldiers fought against an army intent on occupying enemy territory. How Epperly, Hutson, Tate, and Ward responded to this armed invasion of the Confederacy played an even more important role in the outcome of the war than the letters sent home by their Northern counterparts. Correspondents in the Federal armies might discuss how the Lincoln administration and its conduct of the war might or might not be worthy of support. Confederate letter writers addressed more basic issues of loyalty, and these would have a direct impact on whether the cause would be sustained. Some discussed opportunities for soldiers to desert the army so that home and family could be protected against hostile outsiders. Others addressed whether civilians should take the Federal loyalty oath or remove themselves beyond the reach of Union officials. The war put a strain not just on individual soldiers but on their relationships with family members when there was basic disagreement about such issues.

The spring of 1862 marked a crisis for the Confederacy not simply because of significant Union advances and Federal occupation of such crucial cities as New Orleans and Nashville. A manpower shortage loomed as a result of the imminent expiration of the twelve-month commitment made by the bulk of early Confederate recruits. Realizing that thousands of enlistments were set to expire, Confederate authorities in Richmond responded by implementing a new conscription policy that would keep the army intact. While the draft staved off collapse and certainly prolonged the war, it planted the seeds for ongoing conflict within the Confederacy. The idea of compulsory service itself was objectionable in a political culture that emphasized free volunteering and a citizen soldiery. Yet the most poisonous aspect of the measure was its system of exemptions; its perceived tilt toward the interests of slaveholders drew accusations of class bias.

Jeremiah Tate of Alabama was a reliable Confederate patriot throughout nearly all the war. Yet as the following letter to his sister suggests, he and his fellow soldiers still experienced a sense of betrayal when they learned of the looming Confederate draft. He addressed the topic while preparing a defense against George B. McClellan's massive Peninsula campaign, then in its early stages.

Yorktown Va
April the 23, 1862

Dear Sister,

. . . Thare is a grate excitement in regard to the Conscript Law that was recently past by Congress to keep all the Twelve months volenteers two years longer. It appears that we will never git to see home again. I thinke the soldiers will rebell against it as soon as this battle is over, evry man to a man is willing to stay that long but so soon as it is terminated and our time expires you will hear of sum goine home. it is said that sum has laid down their guns and say they wont fight. they say if Congress had of ast them to of staid two or five months they wood of did it freely but they cannot bare the ide of being prest for two years. I am going to work evry plan I no to git to cum home a month or two this sumer if I cant do other wise I will git a sick and cum home an find long enough to see my sweethart. . . .

you must do the best you can til I cum for I no not when that will be as I have a very hard master but I can assure you that I will be thare as soon as I can git off, I never wanted to see home half as bad in my life nothing woud afford me more pleasure on earth than to view that happy place once more. . . .

Nothing more but remains yours til we meet again,
J. M. Tate

The Confederate draft not only retained those already in the army but made soldiers of those unlikely to enlist on their own. Marion Epperly of Floyd County, Virginia, was among the reluctant soldiers brought under arms during the spring of 1862. Epperly began the following three letters while in the Virginia militia, which the state had already begun to fill with unwilling recruits. He and his wife both realized that volunteering for the Confederate army (and thus relinquishing his position in the militia) would seal his fate for at least the next three years. Yet inaction was a gamble too since conscripts lost any chance to select their specific assignments and thus risked separation from friends and neighbors. Epperly chose delay, and soon after Congress had implemented the draft on April 16, 1862, he found himself drilled into an artillery company where he spent the next fourteen very unhappy months.

Camp Winder
April 9th, 1862

Dear wife,

. . . you wrote to me not to Vollantear.* . . . I havet Vollanteered yet and I dont think I shal til I see further into matters than I doo now. . . . wee ar al more confused here than wee was when wee was at home for the reason wee don't no what ma be the best for us to doo to Vollanteer or to stay whair wee ar. it is a hard thing to deside for the best in the future. Wee don't know one day what another ma bring forth. I don't see no chans for us to get home soon but sometimes the darkest hours is just befor day. . . .

I Reamin your Tru husband til Death,
C. M. Epperly

April 22, 1862
Ginarl Steward's ecampment, 5 miles of Yorktown

My Dear Wife,

. . . We ar detatched to Ginerl Stuards Hors Artilary. Under Captain Pelham. . . . we have all of our napsacks hauld in the bagage Wagon an wee ar to have horses to ride when on a march. but all this I had much rather be in the northwest in Trigs Regiment than to be here and live on bred and water all tho wee ma com out better here in the end than wee would thair. . . .

I dont no how long wee will remain here nor how long wee will haf to stay in this company. wee ma half to stay during the war and wee ma go off soon. wee are just Monday detatched to this Brigade an far no surtain time. ther is a bout one hundrid an Twenty thousands here now if the fight dus com off it will be a sarrious time. . . .

*The question at hand was whether Epperly would willingly leave the Virginia militia to enlist voluntarily as a Confederate soldier.

I will no doubt half to go throo a maney a hard ship befor this war coms to a close but I think god will give me Strength to go throo all that ma be put a pon me. . . .

C. M. Epperly

James Sity Co. Va.
April 27th / 62

My Dear Wife,

. . . I am sarrow to write to you that I expect wee ar bound for the war unless the nort draws som of ther forses that wee wont half to keep so many men in the field an if they doo that wee ma get home in the cors of 3 or 4 month if it is the will of god to spar us. . . .

you dont no half the harrows of this war an the destruckshon of things without you was here one moment you could see onuff to Satisfy your mind that war is one of the most distressing things that man ever had to contend with. . . .

I don't like this Survis very well in fact ther hant any of our men that dus. all tho it ma be the best for us this company hant taken in clos contact like an infantry Company wee haf to fight when the enemy is a long distant off wee have been draged here an will half to bar with it the best wee can. I would give fifty dollars to get to vollanteer an go whar I want too If I could get to go.

C. M. Epperly

The strengthening of Confederate armies in the spring of 1862 was followed by a string of Southern victories, which in most cases increased soldiers' morale. By late June Stonewall Jackson's Valley campaign and a series of battles around Richmond forced the hundred thousand troops in the Union's Army of the Potomac to end the Peninsula campaign. By the fall of that year momentum had shifted toward the Confederates, who launched coordinated thrusts into Maryland and Kentucky, though these were turned back at the bloody battles of Perryville and Antietam. On the heels of these invasions came the Battle of Fredericksburg and with it the long winter of Northern despair.

Figure 43. "George"'s view of a Confederate dispatch.

Yet despite its appearance of strength, the Confederacy's fighting spirit was already showing signs of strain, made worse by the fading Southern economy. Northern soldiers were quick to scoff at the South's comparative poverty, as the anonymous Massachusetts sketcher showed in his satire of a Confederate dispatch.

Marion Epperly, for one, was unaffected by the late 1862 rise in Confederate confidence, as he devoted nearly all his letters to his own unhappiness with army life and to his ambivalence toward the cause of an independent South. His scrawled notes addressed the general miseries of soldiering, the unfair policies concerning substitutes and furloughs, and his personal difficulties at Fredericksburg. In the following letter, written shortly after that major Confederate victory, Epperly even contemplated his own death and the prospects of a more comfortable afterlife. Rather than rejoice in improving Southern fortunes, he worried how Confederate troops might inflict harm on his own family at home.

Camp Loids Rappahanoc River 1863
Esecs County Va Jan the 27

My Dear and Well Beloved Wife,

I again have another opportunity of answering your cind letter which cam to hand on the 26 of the presant month which found me well and harty and gave me much pleasure to hear from you and to hear that you was all well. . . .

Dear Mary it seames to me like it would be a pleasure to me to die and leave this wicked wourld if we could go together. But the idy of never seeing you and the Children on erth again I cannot bear. I feel satisfide in mi heart somtimes that I will soon get to com hom and then again all chanses seam to banish away and every thing becoms lonsom and desolate; and I cant hear any thing in camp day nor night but Cursing and swaring and men Cawling on god to dam ther souls: you don't no how wicked som men is. They don't regarde ther maker as much as they would a man at the card table. I pray god will forgive them and they ma at last be saved with all of gods people in heaven whair swaring is never heard: but the songs of the redeemed is heard for ever and ever. Dear Wife you wrote to me if I hadent been Vacsinated to be vacsinated. I have been vacsinated about too weeks ago it taken very nise. mi arm is getting nearly well now. I was very glad to hear that you all had been vacsinated.*

Dear mary if aney of you have aney grain or meet to sell I advise you to sell it befor the Government presses it and takes it from you they wont give as much as you can get you had just as well have the money as others: wee ar yet stil at the same campe wee was at when I written you the other letter. I dont think wee will Stay here much longer at this camp but I cant tel whair wee will go from here: you must write to me as soon as you get this letter and gave me the noos of ould Floyd: If any of the Cavalry comes thair after aney thing you all must charg them as much for things as wee hafte pay here and if you dont watch them they will steal all of your gees and Chickens and Beecomes wheather they have honey in them or not they steal here and I dont sepose them that thair is any better. I tell you they need watching I beleave I have writen you all the noos I have at the

*Soldiers were vaccinated for smallpox by exposure to the scabs of those who had contracted the virus. This was one of the most successful medical policies adopted by Civil War armies, which were far less effective in limiting other contagious diseases.

present tell father and your Mother I will write to them in a few days

I Stil Remain your Tru Husband Til Death.
Write Soon
Very soon.
C. M. Epperly

Most Confederate soldiers had a more positive outlook at the beginning of 1863. Jeremiah Tate and his fellow soldiers under Stonewall Jackson's command largely abandoned earlier thoughts about leaving the army and instead began to bolster the morale of those back home. Tate sent encouraging news to his family in Alabama, who remained beyond the reach of Federal forces. He even tried to share some of the patriotism of the camp by sending home the lyrics to "Bonnie Blue Flag," "Maryland, My Maryland," and "Wait for the Wagon." In the letters that contained these songs, he instructed his family to sing what he realized were among the war's most stirring tunes.

Charles Hutson had enough confidence at the start of 1863 to assert that Confederate independence would be won by July of that year. This prediction seemed to be on track after the Union's inconclusive spring campaigning. The emerging signs of Northern discontent over its draft

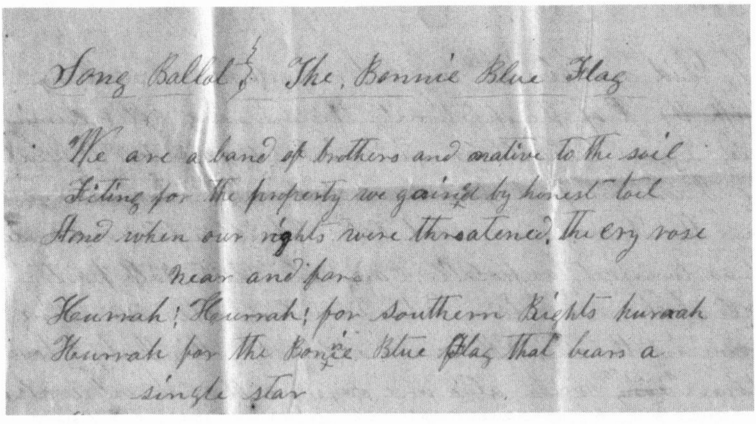

Song Ballot; The Bonnie Blue Flag

We are a band of brothers and native to the soil
Fiting for the property we gained by honest toil
And when our rights were threatened the cry rose
near and far
Hurrah! Hurrah! for Southern Rights hurrah
Hurrah for the Bonie Blue Flag that bears a
single star

Figure 44. Jeremiah Tate's "Bonnie Blue Flag" verses, sent to his sister Mary, February 15, 1863.

were further evidence that a Southern triumph might be near. In the closing days of June, Hutson thus found himself marching with the rest of Robert E. Lee's army north into Pennsylvania. The trip showed Hutson that despite Northern political fractures, the Union still had a decided material advantage. The comparative wealth of the Pennsylvania countryside caught his eye, as the following letter explains to an audience unlikely to receive truthful firsthand accounts elsewhere. Just a short time earlier severe shortages of food had sparked bread riots in a number of Confederate cities.

Bivouac near Chambersburg, Penn.
June 28, 1863 Sunday

My dear Mother,

We crossed the Pennsylvania & Maryland line yesterday morning and traveled about 12 miles into this rich country, bivouacking near this town. . . .

The whole army is now together and striking towards the very heart of Penn. I think we will resume the line of march tomorrow in the direction of Harrisburg, occupy that capital & establish a base of operations. Hooker is behind us and has not caught up yet. This is a grand expedition and I trust will be fruitful of good results to us. This is a rich country and very beautiful—The wheat crops are magnificent and the clover and their other hay fields are the richest I have ever seen. This war seems to have had no effect on these people & they are living in the most luxurious bounty. . . .

The men have cleared some farm yards. This pillaging has been stopped . . . but it is almost impossible to prevent men from taking what they want. The people deserve the treatment—but I object to it as having a bad effect on the morale of the army. . . .

The people . . . are completely subdued & are as polite and civil as possible, deploring the war & longing for peace—I trust our hour of deliverance is at hand and God spiriting us we may conquer a peace this summer—The mail communication is very precarious now—A mail leaves here tomorrow and I send my letter—Do write, carefully direct your letter—Much love to father, Daughter Machie, and the others,

Your loving Son,
Charles J. C. Hutson.

Confederate spirits sank when Lee's Pennsylvania offensive was turned back at Gettysburg on July 4, 1863, and then, on the same day, the entire Army of Mississippi was forced to surrender at Vicksburg. These defeats had political consequences, even though the traditional two-party system was much weaker in the wartime South than in the Union. Southern soldiers usually did not debate the merits of political candidates in letters to civilians; none of the Confederates included in this book addressed the topic in their correspondence. Yet despite this relative lack of popular political engagement, candidates opposing Jefferson Davis and his policies did very well during the Southern elections that were held late in 1863. Davis barely managed to keep a majority of support in the Second Confederate Congress, which began its session in 1864. Only the strong showing of his allies in border state areas under Union control kept him from facing a hostile legislature. Pro-Davis representatives from these areas were primarily elected by Confederate troops since Union occupation prevented significant civilian voting.

When Confederate victory looked probable early in 1863, Hutson looked past the crude conditions of soldiering. During the Pennsylvania campaign he similarly ignored how the crisp stationery and high-quality ink of the opening of the war had given way to the coarse lined paper with barely legible pencil markings that now carried his notes to South Carolina. In the aftermath of defeat at Gettysburg, these stark and growing disparities between Northern comfort and Southern want became ever more apparent.

The following letter from Hutson conveyed his growing concerns about the dwindling value of Confederate money. He realized a depreciated currency meant serious trouble for an upstart government. Financial weakness preceded that summer's military setbacks and contributed to the sense that the Richmond government was unable to sustain itself. Hutson found the preference of some Confederates for Yankee greenbacks an ominous sign, but he did not fault Southern economic policies, choosing instead to argue that unpatriotic greed accounted for the comparative soundness of Union money. His letter joined what was becoming a chorus of complaint about tradesmen, smugglers, and any other Southerners who seemed to value quick riches over the common good. His comments revealed that while class conflicts between planters and nonslaveholders persisted, the strains of war created increasingly widespread tension between all soldiers and civilian profiteers. This new development created an internal enemy common to all Confederate soldiers and produced the equivalent of those Copperheads whom Union troops were collectively speaking out against at the same time.

Near Gordonsville Va
August 11th, 1863

Dear Daughter,

I commenced a letter to you this morning at our camp near Orange C.H., but had not time to finish it and left it in its unfinished state. I received your short note two evenings ago, giving me the good news that clothes were on the way to me. I have not received the bundles which you sent yet—but this is not to be wondered at—I think the mail is a pretty reliable means of transportation: and will expect my bundles when I return to camp. . . .

At Gordonsville and Orange there are stores tolerably full of articles at visionary prices—In fact of late everything has risen

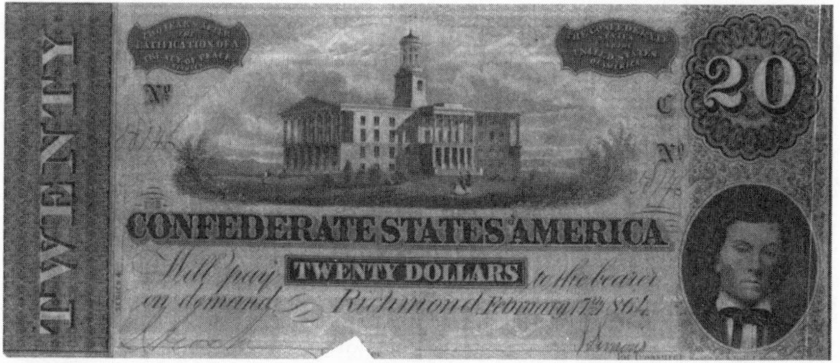

Figure 45. Confederate twenty-dollar bill issued in 1864, amidst spiraling depreciation.

with Gold; and merchants require for their goods an equivalent in Confederate money equal to its equivalent in Gold—i.e. about 10 to 1. The condition of our currency is really melancholy and I sometimes fear it never will be reduced. Men have become accustomed to regard Confederate money in the same light as the Continental money was regarded in olden times—Now in Pennsylvania the Yankee greenbacks were almost as good as specie and are even good in our Confederate land—a reflection upon the earnest patriotism of our speculators and blockade runners who are daily selling their country for paltry money, using the dead bodies of their countrymen and natural friends as stepping stones to great wealth and burying their consciences beneath the dress of sophistry and hypocrisy. I have an utter contempt for such cowardly traitors and believe that righteous vengeance will yet confront them unpleasantly in their pathway. . . .

Love to my cousins—

Believe me
Your affectionate brother,
Charles J. C. Hutson

Marion Epperly had little to say about the military events that transpired during the summer of 1863 since his greatest concern was a much-anticipated trip home and a subsequent transfer to a new regiment. His new position in the Fifty-fourth Virginia Infantry was far more to his liking, not least because it put him back among fellow Floyd County residents who were serving in the western Army of Tennessee. Not long after this reassignment, Epperly and his wife, Mary, began a frank discussion of how he might leave the army for good. Mary tried to steel her husband's courage by explaining in her letter of August 9, 1863, how others from his neighborhood had already fled the army and had then beaten the men who had tried to arrest them for their serious violation of military rules.

Marion responded to his wife a short time later. While he reported that the stream of men coming home was likely to continue, he displayed his own sense of caution by resolving to follow others' lead.

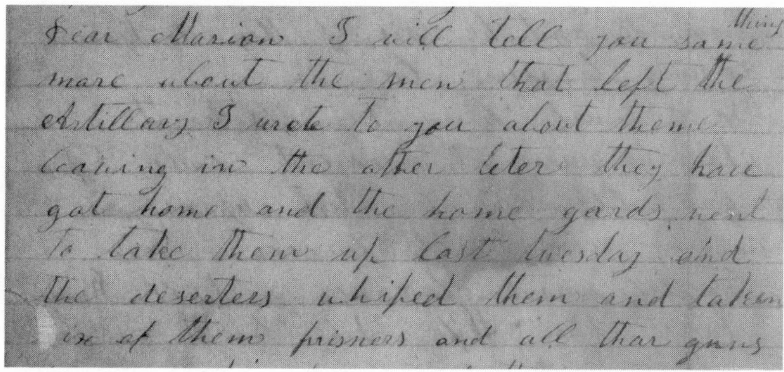
Dear Marion I will tell you same
mare about the men that left the
Artillary I wrote to you about theme
leaving in the other leter they have
got home and the home gards went
to take them up last tuesday and
the deserters whiped them and taken
six of them prisners and all thar guns

Figure 46. Mary Epperly to her husband, Marion, August 9, 1863.

Camp New Bells Bridge, Tenn
Aug the 14 / 63

Dear Wife,

. . . I dont hear no noos much here at this time. Times is very dull an sad here the soulders is getting verry tired of this war they ar leaving the armey dailey. I hope they will soon all get home. this Regt numbers now a little over six hundred and I supose ther has been fuer men left out of this than eney. Som of our oncst nabors is on thair way hom now if they hant thair all redy an others will follow befor long if times don't soon change. I will wait a while yet an if every boddy else comes hom I will com too. I don't beleave in staying with the smallist crowd I think Session* is amost dide out. I beleave it would a been a grate thing for us if it never had been a live. . . .

Farwell for awhile,
C. M. Epperly

In September Epperly did make an unauthorized trip home to his wife and two young children, and he remained there for more than a month. Despite his wife's hope that he would stay permanently, Epperly rejoined his unit in Chattanooga and subjected himself to twenty

*Here Epperly means "secession," referring in general terms to the entire disunion movement.

days in the guardhouse for violating military regulations. Once he completed this sentence, he insisted that seeing family and friends back in Floyd County had been worth this relatively light punishment. Had his return not been voluntary, his sentence would surely have been far more severe.

The Alabama sharpshooter Jeremiah Tate also missed home in the fall of 1863, and his fears for his family's safety were intensified by the proximity of Union troops to his home. How he might return temporarily became a running theme in his letters; at one point he even jokingly asked his mother to select a wife for him, so he could use a wedding as an excuse for a furlough. But Tate's attitude toward the civilians back in Pickensville was beginning to be marked by his own suspicions about civilians' resolve under the pressures of Federal invasion and occupation. Speaking out against the mounting defeatism of the home front, Tate offered a harsh remedy for those who were backing down from their initial enthusiasm for the Confederacy.

Camp near Orange CH
Sept the 12th 1863

Dear sister Mary,

. . . I never want to leave Virginia to reinforce any army except alabama, and at the presant state of affairs I am not very anxious to go thare. I never want to fight for any set of men that when a little discouraged or meet with misfortions and are defeated in a few instances to crie out for reconstruction of the Union or peace on any terms, sum have throne down there arms and are now skulking around home and sware that they do not intend to fight any more, those men was the first to cry out seceshion and to ware the cockade on thare hats in 1860 and say that we can whip them out in a few days. Cum boy rush to the battle field, I will go fight bleed and die with you. Wher are those men today skulking around there homes and planning sum skeem to give the conscripting officer the slip, or with sumthing liken to a hand stick in there hands hoping round with war rumatism crying out for reconstruction of the union, are willin to sacrifice evry thing they possess rather than march to the battle field. Such men should be treated as trators and delt with according. They should not be tolerated by southern people, they shood be delt with as General Lee treats his deserted. tie them to a stake and shoot them til they are ded. . . .

J. M. Tate

Public execution of deserters was meant to warn soldiers about the dire consequences of leaving the ranks and to convince them to stay in the army at all costs. If comments in letters home were any indication, this strategy worked, even if there was a wide range of opinions about whether such punishments were just. While many considered such stern action perfectly acceptable, Marion Epperly, whose perspective was shaped by his own unauthorized leave, condemned it as a ruthless act of murder. After witnessing the execution of fourteen North Carolina soldiers in the spring of 1864, Epperly called those responsible "wicked" and their actions "too cruel for mortal man to behold." Even so, the spectacle of such a deeply dishonorable death caused him to abandon future plans for another trip home. He continued to seek furloughs from his commanding officers, though these were consistently denied.

Charles Hutson took a direct part in the effort to stem Confederate desertion, as he explained in a letter he wrote to his father in November 1863. Implementing the draft was supposedly the responsibility of civilian agencies in the War Department, though military commanders often used their own forces to help round up those absent without leave. In doing so, they began a series of campaigns directed not against enemies in the Federal army but against Confederate men and the women who supported them.

Bivouac 1st Regt. S.C. Vols.
Between Sperryville and Little Washington
November 7th, 1863
Saturday

My dear Father,

I have been regretting ever since we left the main army that I could not have written to you all before our unexpected move, in order to relieve you of any anxiety concerning me. . . .

It seems that the mountains have become a resort for all of

the deserters & delinquents of our army and Gen. Lee has thought it expedient to send a select party from his army to arrest these traitors to their country and relieve the inhabitants of the mountains from their continued depredations. The 1st So Ca of Hill's Corps & 12th Ga. of Ewell's were selected by Gen Lee for this duty and left Brandy on Monday last, under command of Col. Miller of Ga. The purpose of the expedition was a secret in the army & we ourselves were ignorant of our business until we reached the mountains. We arrived at Chesters' Gap between Flint Hill and Front Royal on Tuesday night when our force divided, the Ga. Regiment proceeding over into the Valley in order to "hunt" deserters & conscripts on the further side of the Blue Ridge while our Regiment attended to a similar duty on this side. We have been steadily at the work ever since our arrival, moving from place to place and "skirmishing" the mountains as we go along. We have collected up to this point about 30 conscripts & deserters & they continue to come in to the charge of our guard. We will continue to move southward scouring the mountains & meeting the Ga. Regiment at a given point. We may continue at this work for a long time & travel far southward. The mountains are covered with these rascals & they should be sent to the proper authorities for summary punishment. The work of climbing the mountains is pretty hard but the men seem to like it—as the country is full of various eatables & all are living in clover. I like the detached position from the main army very much & have enjoyed the trip so far.

The country is full of milk, butter, etc, etc.,—as we are only a small party we have no army to compete with us. The inhabitants of the mountain are very clever and hospitable. We have captured several men with horses, the latter of which animals are in great demand and are pressed into service. I have one in use myself and have been to the top of the Blue Ridge with him caught two conscripts on that day (in company with our Commissary who is a Mississippian). . . . I wish we could remain away from the hubbub of the main army all winter. . . .

The Deserters have made no resistance to us yet and we apprehend none altho' it is said that further southward they are organized into a regular band and will dispute our progress over the mountains. But I believe in no such humbug. The tried veterans among the infantry of Lee's army are a terror to all traitors and will meet with little if any trouble from there. Our greatest trouble comes from the feminine gender, several of that sex having pleaded against the arrest of sons, brothers, etc., whom we have taken up as conscripts fit for duty in the army.

The only trouble attending our separation from the army is the lack of mail facilities. We have no mail communications and I will send this letter by some chance or other. . . .

Believe me, your loving Son
Chars. J. C. Hutson

There were several strategies that unwilling Confederate soldiers employed to help them return home; among the most effective was allowing themselves to be captured by the enemy during the course of a battle. Once taken prisoner, they had the option of taking a loyalty oath, signing a parole, and returning to their family, which was especially easy if their loved ones were already within Union lines. In describing his duty as a sharpshooter, Jeremiah Tate explained the steps taken to prevent such intentional capture. His actions were no doubt intended to keep the army strong by making potential deserters think twice before prematurely surrendering.

Camp Co H 5th Ala Regt twelve months volenteers
Near Orange C.H.
January the 1st, 1864

Dear sister Mary,

. . . The sharpshooters are exempt from all details except Pickett and Drill. we have a hard time of it through the <u>sumer</u> season and in time of Battle as we all ways have to stay in front of the army day and night, and in time of battle the sharpshooters have to bring on the attact, but so soon as the attact becums general they are formed in the rear as gard to keep the men from running out of the fight—sum times we are on poste twenty four to forty eight hours with out being releaved tho it is not so hard now we have two regular organized corps and we take day about and when one corps is on duty the other is restin. . . .

Yours Truly,
J. M. Tate

Lethal force kept the Confederate army intact in the early fall of 1863, just as conscription had done a year and a half earlier. And as long as there was a viable military effort under way, the Confederacy drew support from a fairly wide range of staunchly loyal civilians. Union soldiers appreciated this wellspring of Confederate support when they were detailed to secure the peace. These policing missions opened them to a variety of hostile actions by Southern whites. Women in cities like Fredericksburg could make life difficult for troops patrolling the street, as the private from the Forty-fourth Massachusetts humorously sketched in his rendering of missilelike "Bum-Shells" thrown from the windows of Fredericksburg.

There was nothing funny about the resistance that Dolphus Damuth faced in frontier Louisiana during the Red River campaign. The following letter made clear that service in enemy territory was a dangerous business, even when there was no opposing army to contend with.

Nachitoches
April 3rd, 1864

. . . Yesterday 3 men from the 4 Division went out to a house about a mile from camp and a little beyond the picket line. the owner of the plantation mad his negroes tie them. He marched them out in the woods to Shoot them. He shot one of them (from the 24th Iowa) and the others made good thear escape but one of them was knocked down with the but of a gun before he got away. Cavalry was sent out, but the murderer had left on one of his best horses. I saw the man that was killed after he was brought into camp. It was a horrible looking sight, and his being murdered by a man that pretended to be a Union man made it more agrevating. Gen. Franklin had placed a guard over his premises the night before and given him protection papers. It

Figure 47. "George" lampoons the occupation of Fredericksburg.

> will be a good lesson for the boys that are always Straggling from camp. I hope they will be more carefull in future. . . .
>
> I must close for this time.
>
> Yours &c, Dolph

Confederate loyalists enjoyed two more surges in their collective confidence after the dispiriting Union victories at Gettysburg and Vicksburg. During these periods true believers revisited earlier hopes in their ability to secure Southern independence by holding out against superior force. The first glimmer of optimism came at the Battle of Chickamauga in September 1863, when a concentration of troops helped the Confederates achieve one of their western army's very few victories. Federal troops in this theater were forced to retreat to Chattanooga, where they seemed vulnerable to an extended siege. Yet under the command of U. S. Grant, Northern soldiers avenged their earlier loss by storming a foggy Lookout Mountain in what was dubbed the Battle Above the Clouds. They then staged a successful assault upon Missionary Ridge, a fortified position that had similarly hemmed them in. Union victory came despite the tactical superiority of the Confederates' entrenched defenses.

Several days after this dispiriting battle at Missionary Ridge, Edward Ward of Memphis described how he and other Confederates had undertaken a retreat. The letter opened by noting the slowed communications between civilians and the army and then addressed Ward's despair at missing his parents' visit. The remainder of his note detailed the military setback that dampened troop morale. One result of the failed siege was the resignation of commanding General Braxton Bragg, who had become a symbol of Confederate failure in the western theater.

Camp near Dalton Ga
Dec 8th / 63

Dear Sister,

I received a long letter from you of date Oct 25, which is the last I have received from home. I wrote you a few lines immediately after the fight at Missionary Ridge but as I am not certain you will receive it I suppose I had better give you some of the particulars of our reverse. I gave Miss Tillie a long account of it, which I am in hopes she will receive, as I do not like to waste my sweetness on the desert air. Well, Sis, when you last wrote I think you must have had the blues pretty badly. Now you must be of good spirit, for we have in all our troubles still much to be thankful for. I fear however you can aptly apply to me the old adage of "Physician Heal thyself" for I will confess, that I feel pretty blue myself this morning and by no means in a proper frame of mind to write to my gay—Mischief and fun loving Sister. This is a cold rainy day and having no shelter of my own yet I have gone down to Capt. Campbell's tent intending to devote the day in writing. It has been a long time since I have seen either you or Rose. . . .

The hardest trial I have had to endure was not being able to see P & M when they were out. I really cried when I heard they had gone back—You may think it funny that I should cry, but my spirits from being so high were suddenly lowered so much that tears would come in spite of me. I am now so much in hopes that you or Rose or both will come out and stay a while in Marietta. I think I can get off four or five days to see you. . . .

I promised to say something of the battle. It was a sad reverse, but the actual loss is small and our greatest loss in artillery

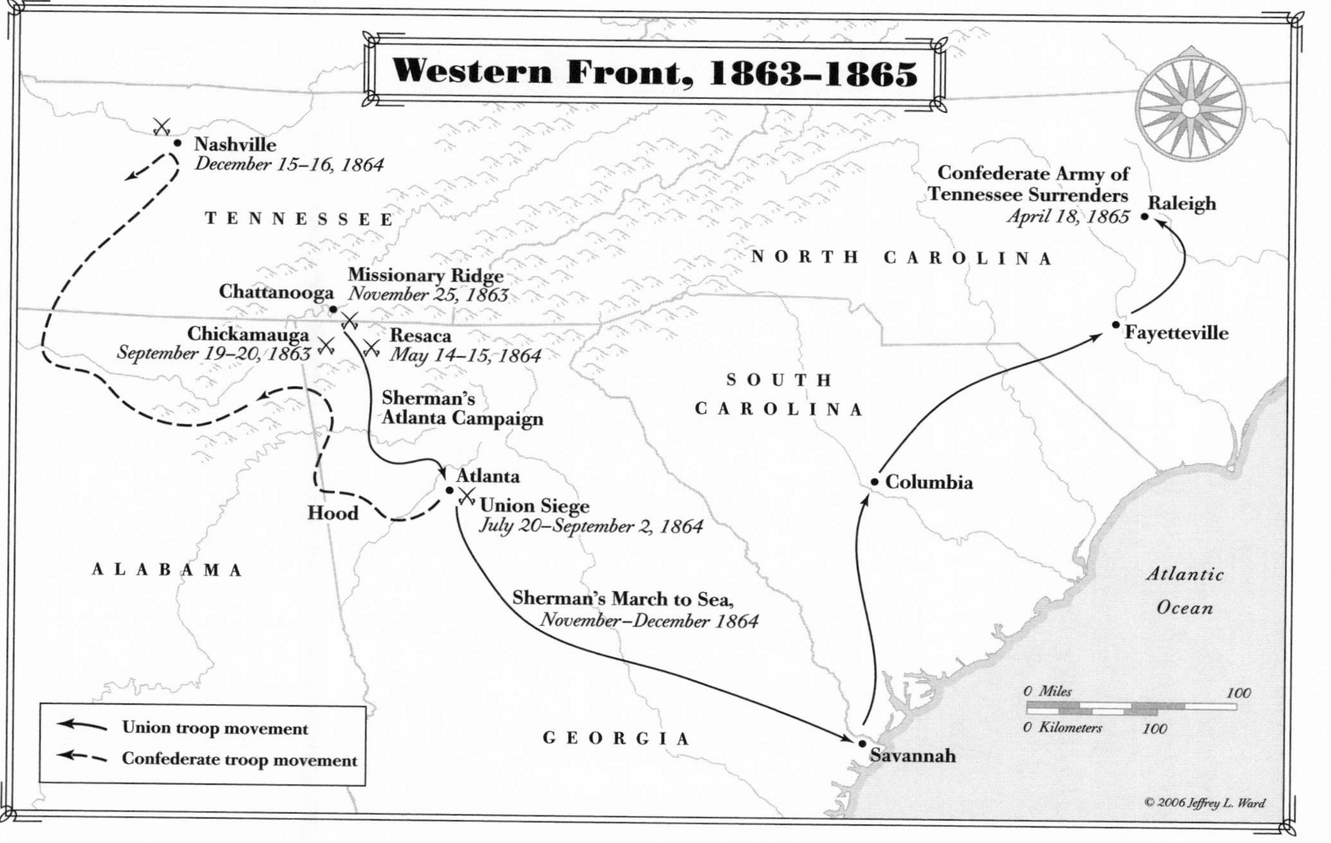

Western Front, 1863–1865
Nashville
December 15–16, 1864
TENNESSEE
Missionary Ridge
November 25, 1863
Chattanooga
Chickamauga
September 19–20, 1863
Resaca
May 14–15, 1864
Sherman's
Atlanta Campaign
Atlanta
Union Siege
July 20–September 2, 1864
Hood
ALABAMA
Sherman's March to Sea,
November–December 1864
GEORGIA
Savannah
SOUTH
CAROLINA
Columbia
NORTH CAROLINA
Fayetteville
Confederate Army of
Tennessee Surrenders
April 18, 1865
Raleigh
Atlantic
Ocean
0 Miles 100
0 Kilometers 100
Union troop movement
Confederate troop movement
© 2006 Jeffrey L. Ward

and prisoners. Missionary Ridge is about a half mile from base to summit. The main force were in a line of rifle pits near the top, but our regiment was made the reserve for a line of skirmishers and were in the Rifle pits at the foot of the Ridge. We could see every movement of the enemy who were in the level plain below. We could see them advancing on us in five lines. Could hear the commands, and saw them with a yell begin the charge. We remained perfectly quiet in the trenches came to a ready and waited untill they were in 500 yards of us when the command fire was given and we opened on them fairly mowing them down. We continued the firing about ten minutes with no loss to ourselves when the enemy flanked us both on the Right and Left and were cross firing at us when the command retreat was given. We soon cleared the trenches and began the ascent up a steep hill side a half mile in length. This was a scene that beggars description. I had not got but a little way up when I got out of breath, and so completely exhausted that I could not step over a log a foot high, but had to roll over it, rest awhile, and then go on. The minnie balls were flying thick around me all the time and in one of these rollovers a ball passed through my new overcoat and my uniform, which would have killed me had I been standing up. Three times I laid down expecting to have either to be killed or taken prisoner. I was so completely exhausted but each time after resting awhile I would go on untill senseless from fatigue and out of breath. I was pulled in at the trenches near the top I had gone somewhat rested here when the order again was given to retreat and we were again flanked. We now found that the whole army was in retreat, and we were to bring up the rear. On the retreat our lot was a hard one. We were continually skirmishing with the enemy and had to wade the Chickamauga River (which was waist deep) three times. You can form an idea how cold it was when the ground was frozen hard. . . .

I feel truly thankful that God in his mercy has again spared me where so many are falling in every fight. I cannot hope to come out safe if we fight again but we will pray to meet again. . . .

How I would like to peep in just to see what you are doing. You must not fall in love with any body untill after the war. It is true I see no end to it, but we may have a good time in the future. Such at least is the prayer of your affectionate Brother,

Ed

Confederates experienced their last sustained upsurge in the spring and early summer of 1864, when an ongoing stalemate produced a correspondingly powerful dose of Northern despair. During this season of fighting, Confederate armies had a greater percentage of veterans since they, unlike Union forces, required soldiers to reenlist when their terms of service expired. The routine of soldiering bred confidence among Southern fighters, but it also led to boredom. Hutson evoked the monotony of yet another year of service in this letter to his brother, who was also a Confederate soldier.

Camp near Orange C.H.
February 19th, 1864

Dear Marion,

I have been here now nineteen days since my return without hearing a word from any of you at Pocotaligo. I have not heard from Barnwell since the 9th. Do you intend to make me a real exile, cut off from every communication?

I have been here so long that I know not what to write to you about. We are comfortable, we have had snow of late, we have been reenlisting, we have been almost freezing & almost melting, we have been drilled from campfires to meet Yankees, we returned, we have been doing nothing, we have been abusing Congress & then praising them for passing such good military, tax, & currency bills, we have had an addition to our strength of 133 Conscripts & recruits, we have had Coffee & sugar issued to us again, we have had scant rations of meat, we have become tired of corn meal . . . we have moved to a new camp when water & wood are plentiful, we have blessed dear old Gen. Lee for giving furloughs extensively, we have had little sickness, we have lost Dr. Fort, who was ordered to Hills' HdQrs, we have got in his place General Robeson, we have the Major sick, the Lt. Col absent trying for the Colncy, but not in a fair way to receive it, we have the O. M. Hewelson away on sick furlough & the

Figure 48. Oil portrait of Edward Ward.

O. M. Leigh, leaving me supreme in these premises but very lonesome, we have myself eating by myself every day & waiting for that box, which was to be sent by you & Mae

. . . we have no more news to tell, we have a desire to be remembered affectionately to all relatives & friends, we have a desire greatly to be with you, we have a desire that you would write to us, we have cause to stop for we have no more to say. We wish you well. we do stop—

Do write soon. . . .

Love to all,
Your loving brother,
C. J. C. Hutson

The war weariness that struck both soldiers and civilians figured in Confederate correspondence even when Southern morale was comparatively strong. The letters that Edward Ward sent home from northern Georgia during the spring of 1864 were a case in point. The dark mood experienced by Ward after Missionary Ridge temporarily brightened with the new year. The appointment of General Joseph Johnston to re-

Figure 49. Daguerreotype of Elmira Ward.

place Braxton Bragg seemed to signal a new sense of opportunity. Many believed that the army would finally have what it took to halt the Union army, which was to be commanded by William T. Sherman during the upcoming year.

But at the moment that his military fortunes seemed to improve, the interactions between Ward and his sister became unusually tense. Neither she nor Ward's friend Rose had been able to visit him despite his earlier requests. The lapse in regular communications meanwhile grew only worse. What most upset Ward, however, were rumors of his sister's activities in occupied Memphis, where the courtship of Federal officers provided Southern women a much-valued opportunity for socializing with the opposite sex.

Camp near Dalton
April 2 / 64

Dear Sister,

As I have an opportunity of sending you a letter I take pleasure in writing although I have not received a line from home since about the first of Dec. . . .

Under such circumstances it is indeed rather discouraging to write at all much less a lengthy or interesting letter. I would have been greatly pleased with one-fifth of the favour of Feb. 6 that George received from you though I can not say the same thing in regard to its contents. From the tenor of your letter I should judge that our city was fast becoming abolitionized and that the ladies could all now associate and be on terms of peace and even intimacy with the Despoilers of their home I can even excuse you from not writing to your brothers in the cause as you do not have time left from your dancing parties and merry making with whomever. Who is there but Yankees, Deserters and worse than these for you to dance with. But I forbear to speak further on this subject only let me urge you if you are guilty of associating with bluecoated fiends for your own and your brother's sake publish not your shame, nor speak exultingly of a deed to those who will hate you for it. We here can readily conceive what a dance in Memphis must be—I never felt prouder in my life than when a gentleman told me that I had two sisters who would never receive any attentions or even Countenance our detested foe. But it may be "times have changed." . . .

Perhaps you are a reconstructionist. I would rather see you fight open and above board against our cause than cloak your enmity under the treacherous disguise of reconstructionist. Excuse my earnestness but this is a subject that more nearly touches my heart—than any other. I have given you my idea of what others think but my dear sister if you have been associating with those fiends in human shape I am certain it was only from thoughtlessness and you will take my advice. . . .

Your affectionate brother,
Ed

This letter was one of the last Ward wrote, since he was killed in the fighting around Atlanta in late July 1864; he was twenty-seven at the time of his death.

Union military leaders realized that defeating Confederate armies mattered for little unless they secured the loyalty of Southern civilians.

This could be accomplished by friendly gestures, such as the courting that went on between Federal officers and Memphis belles, and by the policy of extending provisions to needy Southern whites. There were more forcible means of securing Southern loyalties, of course, and these increasingly came to focus on assuring the complete destruction of slavery. In the following letter, William Brunt explained how he put the vise on the rebellion by frustrating Kentucky masters, who were exempt from the provisions of the earlier Emancipation Proclamation. Slaveholders in this crucial border state continued to claim their rights to human property until late in 1865, when the Thirteenth Amendment to the Constitution banned slavery throughout the entire United States.

Head Qurs Contrb Camp Clarksville Tenn
July 3 / 64

. . . Well Martha Ky feels the smart a little, I think, for two thirds of those Contrabands in my charge are from Ky—I had a ritch joke on a Loyal son of Ky a week before last. Peter Threet of Todd Co Ky came here to get a family of his mothers slaves to return home with him—he plead in vain—they would not go. He then offered me 250 Dollars in Green Backs & said he would give me more if I would persuade them to go home & pledged himself to keep it a profound secret. I let him plead, not taking any offence at the proposition so that I could draw him out fully. I then flattly refused to accept the bribe—telling him it was principle—not money that I came into the service for. He hoped he had not hurt my feelings I told him no he had not—for I expected all Ky loyalists to violate all Federal Orders that did not suit their interest. I judge other mens loyalties by their own hearts. He then begged me not to report him—I told him I came to do my duty—& so far I have done it regardless of friend or foe. & that I should do it in that case. . . . I reported it to the Commander of the Post, he had him arrested & Threet says he did not offer me the money as a bribe. . . .

Our camp is a thorn in the side of Ky for their slaves come here by the score and the able bodied men go into the army. . . . I send the children to school . . . using the fine College building for the Contraband school—that galls the secesh here, they think it an outrage, to take the building erected to educate their children in & use it to educate their slaves in. But I tell them it is just—for many of the scholars are their illegitimate children & have as good a right morally as the legitimate ones. . . .

I am in my glory now, I used to be called an abolitionist. I am one now practically. Please send me your Photograph Martha. Give my love to Each & all your folks. Write soon & Direct to Capt. William Brunt Box 442 Clarkesville Tenn.

Yours Truly in Universal Freedom,
William

Sherman's raid across Georgia in the closing weeks of 1864 was the most dramatic way of breaking the will of Southern civilians. Among the sixty thousand veteran soldiers who marched with the general to the Atlantic coast was Lysander Wheeler of Illinois, who was elevated to the rank of sergeant in the midst of this campaign. Wheeler arrived on the outskirts of Savannah in December and took advantage of resumed mail service to let his family know he was still "right side up." He continued his army travels through the plantation districts of South Carolina in the weeks that followed, and near the end of this five-month tour, he reflected on how the Southern white populace had experienced this famously destructive march.

March 29th [1865]
Goldsboro, North Carolina

Dear Parents, Bro. and Sister

I have been reading over again all the letters 6 in number of Jan 27, Feb 3rd, Feb 12th, Feb 17th, Feb 24th, and March the 2nd received by me Sunday and Monday and I find them so interesting and full of interest for my safety from harm and danger that I am satisfied the care and interest for me at home is ever the same and is always unceasing because you are always in the dark the news you get from me is generally of a month previous and therefore the present is always clouded. . . .

It will certainly be joyful time When war is ended and Peace is once more reigning in triumph, the North is ignorant of the effects of war in Comparison with the South, here it is dead earnest, the women and children feel it as well as the men. Our men cleared the country most effectually through where we passed many miles in width of everything in the eating line and many things besides that were valuable for in so large an army there are many thieves who go in for Plunder and destruction where they could not carry they very often destroyed many a thousand Dollar Piano in Carolina the boys danced a gig among the keys and then broke them to pieces. The inhabitants generally hid things in their Feather beads and Elsewhere in such a style that before the last foraging party had left a house everything was strewed to destruction and it was a common affair to see molasses and all the feathers in the house on the floor. Women and children crying and nearly scared to death. Expecting the next thing to be killed or something worse. Our men must have something to eat, and if one foraging party left Part, the next along would take the remainder. the whole thing beggars description, perhaps these same women and children would come to the Column and the boys would give them enough to eat at least to last while we were passing. What became of them after the Army goes along is more than I can tell, it is a tough matter but if the rebels would rather fight and leave there families to starve it is a matter of their own choosing certainly not ours. I think these moves of Sherman with the Army is doing more to close out the Rebellion than all the fighting that has been done on the Potomac since the War commenced. . . .

Sherman's march through the Deep South served to warn the Confederate citizenry about the consequences of their continued resistance. The resulting collapse of home front support for the war disappointed Southern soldiers who still had confidence in ultimate military victory. Jeremiah Tate still breathed defiance in February 1865, when he wrote the following letter to his sister in Alabama. Accompanying Tate's lingering hopes were his anger at civilian longings for peace and his disappointments with the western army that had been placed under the command of John Bell Hood. Since there was no

Confederate mail service between Petersburg and Alabama, Tate asked a friend named Captain Belcher to carry his note to his family.

On Pickett four miles North of Petersburg
February 1st, 1865:

Dear Sister Mary,

. . . I have no important nuse to communicate as evry thing appears to be quiett hear with the exception of the grate peace rumors, which I fear will turn out as heretofore more fuss than feathers. Vice President Stepens and Mr Hunter of Virginia and Campbell of Alabama left Petersburg day before yesterday bound for Washington on a peace mission.* I hope they may make a compromise and stop the war tho I am not willing to compromise on any terms I want them to contend for our independence to the last. I am truly sorry to hear that the Alabamians and Georgians have becum so dispondent as to want to go back in to the Union again they should indure the pain like the solgers in the field when the danger is nearest and the hour the darkest. That is the time they should brave the storm like a lion and never be discouraged. Mary it is not worthwhile to discus this question further. for if we are whipt it will not be the fault of the solgers especially in this army, it will be the People at Home and Hoods army . . . if they are willing to sacrafise all that is dear to them and submit to Yankee tirants I do not wish to be with them so we will fight on a while longer. . . .

Yours truly,
Jer. M. Tate

The alienation of soldiers from their loved ones was rarely complete. After all, most veterans continued to justify their military service primarily as a defense of home and family. For Charles Hutson, worries about his family became a primary theme of his correspondence late in the war, as Federal troops under Sherman turned north from Savannah to bring

*As Tate predicted, the meeting held on the steamer *River Queen* involving Abraham Lincoln, William Seward, and Confederates Alexander Stephens, Senator Robert Hunter, and Assistant Secretary of State John A. Campbell showed the futility of a negotiated settlement.

the war directly to South Carolina. Hutson's letters during this period show the frustrations that he experienced, in being held in the defense of Petersburg, while his family was forced to flee armies moving through Barnwell Courthouse, a refuge where they had spent much of the war. In the following letter (one of the last of a series of worried notes), Hutson expressed his sense that Confederate fortunes would ultimately be decided by God. He held out hope that even with Federal interlopers drawing near, the family's slaves would remain true to their masters.

Hd. Qr 1st SC Regt, Trenches near Petersburg
March 20, '65

My dear father,

. . . I hope My dear father that you are all well provided with the things of this life and have not suffered at the hands of our enemy—I have been very much troubled about you all but have had to be very patient and quietly await the progress of events. We have heard so much, however, of the barbarism of the enemy's soldiery that we have feared you have had a great deal of trouble and regretted that you ever moved from Barnwell. But surely all things are in God's hand and under his guidance & who can question his wisdom? Our land is sorely pressed but we cannot but believe that God is overruling all. The enemy is determined to subjugate us & refuses to treat with us through any medium of official intercourse. We have only to buckle on the armor of war & to bring this struggle to a final issue.—to determine to live free or die. If God in His wisdom has decreed our subjugation our duty is a sad one but I believe it is our duty to fight to the end. I have a faint hope that we will yet be a free people with our own laws and institutions.

. . . I suppose the Yankees have robbed you of horses and mules etc., Wd. it not be well for you to return to Barnwell CH if it is practicable? You would be near Augusta & we can send letters by express to that City—I hope the negroes have proved true & faithful & may supply all your wants—They can show their loyalty now. . . .

Your ever loving son, Chas. J. C. Hutson—

Tell servants howdie

As Hutson, Tate, and the rest of the Army of Northern Virginia remained in a standoff in the trenches of Petersburg, western troops marched over hundreds of miles of territory, though accomplishing little with such efforts. As a member of this dwindling force, Marion Epperly believed he had a more accurate sense of the army's desperation than was being reported in the few Confederate newspapers still in circulation. His description of the army's loss outside Nashville was fairly accurate in conveying the extent of this crushing Confederate defeat.

Camp near Tupulow, Miss
Jan the 16th 1865

My most Dear Companion,

. . . After three month hard marching and fighting in Ala and Tenn wee cam to this plase which is about 60 milds south of the Tenn River on the Mobeel and Ohio Railrod among the Mississippi swamps which is one of the mudeis part of the counter I have ever been in during the war. Dear Mary I supose you have heard of the Battles was fought while wee was in Ten and no dout have heard Good noos of our Army. I will tell you as near as I can what wee gand and what we lost while wee was round and about Nashville. . . .

I can tell you it was the worst defeat ever befallen our army during the war. This army is in a very bad condition al the men is nearly naked and barfootted our Briggade was on detached survis while we was in Tenn. Wee was at Murphresborrow at the time of the fight at Nasvill we got in one fight while we was thair but did not loos many men we had on kild out of our company and one captuard. . . . I want to get away from I am in hopes wee will get to com back to Va yet this winter Hood is disbanning a Good many Brigades I am in hopes they will disband our Regt. and let us com home a while. I still feel in hopes wee will get to com hom this winter. . . .

So I Bid you farwell for awhile trusting in God to see you soon. I remain your tru Husband as ever.

Til Death,
C. M. Epperly
To my Absent Mary

The Confederate administration of Jefferson Davis remained defiant in the face of such losses. The reelection of Abraham Lincoln in November, the failure of peace talks, and the passage of the Thirteenth Amendment each in its own way stiffened Confederate resolve to fight on if at all possible. From such staunch determination came the Confederates' boldest initiative, a plan to enlist Southern slaves on the promise of providing them freedom at war's end. Such a notion had been aired early in 1864 by General Patrick Cleburne of the Army of Tennessee, though Jefferson Davis quickly helped suppress it. By November of the same year Davis publicly endorsed a similar plan, evoking widespread criticism. The endorsement of General Robert E. Lee gradually changed public sentiment over the coming winter, assuring that the first steps toward enacting the plan would be taken, though not in time to forestall the Confederacy's final collapse.

Marion Epperly was still unimpressed in March 1865, when he took up the topic of black troops in the following letter. While Epperly's primary concern was with the depletion of the western armies, he indicated that the arming of slaves was an act of hypocrisy. From his perspective, the measure represented the Confederacy's last gasp rather than a viable program for winning the war. His letter, like earlier ones, insisted that he provided far more accurate information about military affairs than the overly optimistic Southern press.

Salisbury NC
March the 11th 1865

Dear Companion

. . . wee will leave here today and go to Raleigh the capital of the State. Dear Mary I can't tell whair wee will go from thair. I think wee have marched more and as much as wee can. I doo not no what will Becom of us hair. . . . I don't think that ther is mor than 12 or 14 thousand men in the hole Tenn Armey. in last spring wee had about 44 Thousand. I think wee had just as well give it up. one thing surtain wee ar whipt and badly whipped. the armey is in a heap wors condition than you hear thair it is. They ar putting the Negros in survis but that will not help the Armey a grate many say they don't inten to fight any mor. I don't think our leading men can say aney thing upon the North having thar Negroes in the armey. . . .

Your tru Husband til death,
C. M. Epperly

As Epperly predicted, the spring of 1865 was a season of Confederate surrenders. The most consequential came in April, when Tate, Hutson, Clegg, and the rest of Lee's army ended their part in the fight at Appomattox Courthouse. Over the weeks and months to come, the skeletal remains of the western armies each disbanded after similarly climactic surrenders. Epperly no doubt welcomed the dissolution of the Army of Tennessee, though there was surely a cost for defeat, no matter how disaffected a soldier had become. All Confederate enlisted men struggled to return home, survey the damage, and resume their civilian existences the best they could. Extensive written reflections about the meaning of this difficult process were the exception rather than the rule. Defeat was typically mourned face-to-face with loved ones rather than at long distance through correspondence.

William Clegg, who had always been introspective, was among the few who wrote at some length about the final collapse of the Confederacy. Clegg's comments came in a journal that had tracked with a matter-of-fact precision the business of the Confederate subsistence bureau during the last two years of war. His sense that a story had come to a final end caused Clegg to recover that philosophical streak that was evident in the diary that he had kept through the first year of the war. The last page of this later journal included two final inscriptions. The first seemed disillusioned, the second merely resigned.

> Hope calculates its schemes for a long and durable life, presses forward to imaginary points of bliss and grasps at impossibilities; & consequently very often ensnares men into beggary, ruin & dishonor.
>
> "Let us argue not against Heaven's hand or will, nor bate a jot of heart or hope; but still bear up & steer right onward."

It would be hard to exaggerate the sense of disappointment that such lines recorded, especially when placed beside Clegg's earlier expressions of hopefulness. Countless other Confederates experienced their collective defeat with the same sense of bittersweet resignation, even if Southern white recalcitrance would soon reassert itself during Reconstruction. At the moment that the armies surrendered, there was an overpowering sense of submission to the higher powers of fate. Such a stance helped the war's losers to reckon with how their entire society had been uprooted, how an economy built on slavery was destroyed, and how the deaths of soldiers like the young Edward Ward might have been for naught.

For Clegg, Epperly, Tate, Hutson, and the others who outlived the Confederacy, there would be time to reflect on the cycle of victories and defeats and the endless scenarios that might have led to a different result. Dejection was tempered by a sense of having been a part of history. In years to come, firsthand experiences within the Confederate armies were taken up, debated, and placed in the context of deeply personal losses and gains. Veterans were able to savor even the worst of war, if only to recall the intensity of a period each man carried for the rest of his life.

SIX

Bonds Broken, Bonds Restored

In the year that it took William Woodlin to fill his diary, the war for the Union became a crusade for black freedom, in large part because African-American soldiers like him had swollen the ranks of the U.S. Army. Yet when the twenty-three-year-old private made the last entry in his journal, he all but ignored this stunning development. He turned his thoughts instead to how a written record had become a veteran in its own right.

> [October 31, 1864] I draw my passing notes to a close after a years pleasant companionship in jotting down these passing thoughts hoping that this veteran of 5 battles may have an honored place among the scarred relicts of this present war. I will consigne it to Northern hands; from whom I shall expect that it will be kept for a memorial for coming years; of him who has carried it on the tented field and along 2/3 of the Atlantic Coast 100 miles up the St. John's River & 90 up the James, one more journey and they travels will be ore.
>
> Adieu
>
> Wm. P. Woodlin
>
> Musician of the 8th Regt U.S.C.T. 2nd Brigade, 3rd Divis, 10th A.C. Army of the James. Chapin's farm Virg.: Gen. Birney Divis Comdg.

Woodlin clearly cherished his diary, which traveled with him from Pennsylvania to Florida and then to Virginia. Its importance lay in the solace it provided and the record it compiled. Today's Civil War scholars value his "scarred relict" mostly for its extreme rarity. Handwritten journals kept by black soldiers are among the most unusual of all wartime artifacts, though manuscript letters from black troops are also quite scarce, especially when compared with the surviving correspondence of white soldiers. The most plentiful source of black testimony about Civil War soldiering comes from dispatches that members of the United States Colored Troops (USCT) sent to Northern newspapers. These reports provide a window on the most public aspects of the black soldiers' war. They follow the extensive debate about the struggles of the USCT for equal pay and its heroism in battle. They document black Americans' efforts to set their country's race relations on a new course.

Woodlin himself sought to publicize black achievement through the wartime press. While serving in the ranks, he sent letters to the New York *Anglo-African*, a weekly newspaper, and to the Philadelphia *Christian Recorder*, which published a short note from him during the war's final weeks. In the handwritten journal that Woodlin kept and saved can be found a more personal account of what his experiences represented. Its entries attend to wartime events with no concerted effort to shape popular perception or to comment on the stubbornness of white supremacy among the bulk of the Northern populace. Over some 130 pages, it portrays episodes of enlisted life in the USCT that are difficult to recover by any other means. Its topics suggest that there was no sharp color line when it came to such typical soldiering experiences as receiving mail, complaining about poor food and bad weather, marching ceaselessly, and facing the trauma of combat. Woodlin's commentary on such matters provides a valuable sense of what black and white troops shared in their wartime experiences as common infantrymen.

Yet at the same time, Woodlin's diary establishes what made his experience, and that of other black troops, more than a variation of a common pattern. In a series of passing references, his journal made clear his participation in a world historical struggle to dismantle those inherited systems of slavery and racial caste that had affected practically every aspect of African-American life within the United States. The following excerpts show how Woodlin incorporated these themes on a regular basis, beginning with his contribution to the black press and his interest in the famous abolitionist martyr Owen Lovejoy. Across a range of entries, his diary pursued a running commentary on the differential in pay between white troops (who earned thirteen dollars per month) and enlisted men of the USCT (who at first received a mere seven dollars per month), and he also greeted news of the equalization. In a similarly episodic manner, he noted those slave contrabands who sought freedom from the Florida Confederates who had recently embarrassed Woodlin's unit at the Battle of Olustee.

> [March] 30th [1864] I sent off four letters today one home one to Syracuse one to the Ed. of the Anglo Affrican and one to my brother. . . .
>
> [April] 12th . . . The marsh was sett on fire today. The Doc gave us a very interesting lecture on the death and services of the Late Owen Lovejoy, and ended with good advice to the men in the ranks. A very good speech. . . .
>
> 26th The mail came today with some papers for me and a letter with cheering news from the north. there is some movement in refference to the colored Soldiers. . . .
>
> [May] 6th The Mary Benton came up this morning with the Paymaster on board, who stopped and left his papers and went on: excitement was quite high all the remainder of the day in refference to the smallness of the pay $7 per month.
>
> 7th The pay M. came down this morning and most of the men having backed out of their good desires took the paltry sum of $7 per mo. the larger portion of which will soon be spent in gambling. . . .
>
> 16th The news by the papers is that we are to get 13 per month as white soldiers. rained at night.
>
> 17th We learned to play our two new pieces very nearly. Nothing unusual happened during the day. Wrote the list of all the colored troops raised in the United S. . . .
>
> 21st The Dr. Came back this morning from Fernandina bringing the report that our forces had got in the rear of the

Rebs & drove them from their position at Olustee. I read the law today giving the colored men their pay as white men. . . .

[June] 7th An expedition left camp for a three days tramp. 30 men fell out the first day. the Reg brought in quite a large quantity of cattle & two prisoners who were taken to Jacksonville on the whole it was quite a successful foraging expedition. two adult Contrabands with their children were brought in, as well as a goodly No. of white trash whom we did not keep long. . . .

[July] 26th Got my horn fixed today. Some Contrabands came in from the expedition. a Scout of 160 men went out this morning as far as the Trussel Bridge this side of Finnegan.

27th The Gen* was in here last night but returned before day to Baldwin, as well as some cavalry this morning. 15 Reb prisoners were brought in from Baldwin while 15 contrabands came down on the Hattie Brock. Last evening our Qur' Master came down and took up 7 days rations. first says that we are to leave in three days for some place I know not where the report is that 75 prisoners are on the road here from the front.

28th Rec'd a little mail today. . . . some more contrabands came in this morning and at night the Major came in with the Reg and we played at the Gen's.

The diary's most sustained attention to black troops came in its concluding section, which Woodlin used to tuck away random notes on a variety of topics. On May 17, 1864, he devoted seven full pages to a list of the 157 regiments that composed the USCT at that time. Detailing this new army of black men came a day after he had learned that pay had been equalized between white and black troops. Included in his catalog was a set of basic facts about where each regiment had been raised and whether it was part of the infantry, artillery, or cavalry. Woodlin's primary objective with this list was not so much to describe as to record, however. By the end of the war more than 170,000 African-Americans had served in the USCT.

*The Eighth USCT had by this time come under the command of General William Birney, the son of a leading abolitionist who had been Liberty Party candidate for president in 1840.

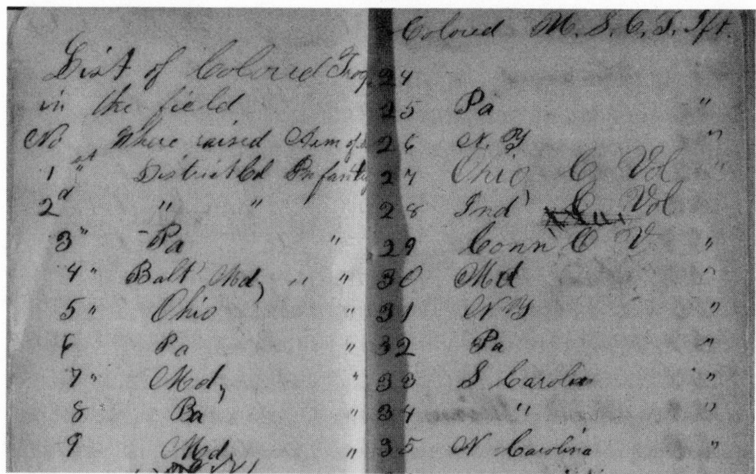
List of Colored Troops in the field
No. Where raised Arm of Service
1st District Col Infantry
2d " "
3" Pa "
4" Balt Md " "
5" Ohio "
6 Pa "
7" Md "
8 Pa "
9 Md "

Colored U.S.C.T. Inf.
24
25 Pa "
26 N.Y. "
27 Ohio C Vol "
28 Ind C Vol
29 Conn C V "
30 Md "
31 NY "
32 Pa "
33 S Carolina "
34 " "
35 N Carolina "

Figure 50. Concluding section of William Woodlin's 1864 diary, composed May 17, 1864.

The story of this mass black mobilization began in the spring of 1861, when General Benjamin Butler of Massachusetts initiated what came to be known as the contraband policy. Butler's order to treat the slaves of disloyal masters as surrendered property revealed the mutual interest that existed between whites, whose primary interest was in saving the Union, and African-Americans, whose main objective was to secure their own freedom. When other Federal commanders copied Butler's policy, a new zone of safety for black slaves was established behind Union lines. As those lines shifted with war's fortunes, a great many blacks attached themselves as servants to Federal soldiers, who were quite willing to relinquish routine military tasks, especially the most onerous, to the newcomers.

White Union soldiers responded to the black presence in a variety of ways, as could be seen in their written comments in diaries and letters and in their general willingness to employ former slaves. Some relied on these men and women to build fortifications, haul materials, cook, and launder, the same sort of labor that slaves provided for the Confederate military effort. But the Union army also relied on contrabands to provide valuable information about local conditions. In his first months of service on the coast of North Carolina, as George Tillotson began to interact with the local black population, he pondered how the Union armies might tap this new source of manpower.

Head Quarters 89th Regt. N.Y.V.
Camp Dickinson, Roanoke Island
March 21st 1862

Dear Lib,

. . . As to the looks of this country I cant see enough of it to call it a country. all I have seen is a little of this island from Ft. Boston to Ft. Huger besides what I can see of the main land across the Croton sound. The inhabitants are a hard miserable looking set what I have seen of them and the contrabands say that most of them are rebels at heart for all they have taken the oath of allegiance.

George

Roanoke Island, N.C.
May 30th, 1862

My Dear Wife,

. . . The question of time that it will take to quash this rebellion appears to be an unsettled one here in camp at least. Some persist in saying that we shall be discharged at no very distant day, while others aver that they don't expect to see home under a year from the time they enlisted and shouldn't be at all disappointed if they served out their whole term of enlistment. I think that the best way to end the concern would be to enlist and arm the contrabands for all the darkeys I have talked with about it say that they would like to fight for the north. . . .

Immagine lots of kisses enclosed. Distribute several apiece to the children and accept a few yourself from your ever loveing,

George

A year later Tillotson reached quite different conclusions about the prospect of arming Southern slaves. His negative view of Lincoln's Emancipation Proclamation was the main factor in his newfound skepticism about the loyalty of black Southerners. Like most other white Americans at the time, he tended to consider African-

Americans in collective terms. As such, he sought to probe their essence as a people rather than consider how the particular circumstances and life experiences of distinct individuals might be compelled by a range of motives.

Suffolk, Va.
Apr 17th 1863

Dear Wife,

. . . We have taken some negro rebel prisoners. One was caught in a tree fireing at our scurmishers, there was a white reb also with him but they killed the white one and captured the black and he declared if he was back there he would fight us just as hard again and also that there was fifteen thousand more like him, who was just as stout as he, and they would fight just as well so you can see how much the niggers want to fight for their own freedom. . . .

Your devoted Husband,
Geo. W. Tillotson

Most whites objected to black troops not because of their loyalties but because of their supposed racial inferiority. The anonymous sketcher of the Forty-fourth Massachusetts conveyed prevailing white sentiments about African-Americans and, by extension, the absurdity of putting them in the Federal army. His sketch was made in the same North Carolina locale where Tillotson had served the previous year.

Figure 51. "George"'s image of "First Colored North Carolina."

The unit he satirized was organized between April and June 1863 and was eventually mustered into Federal service as the Thirty-third USCT. It played a central role at the Battle of Olustee, where its men fought alongside William Woodlin's Eighth USCT and the Fifty-fourth Massachusetts.

The great majority of white Union soldiers took black inferiority for granted, even as they welcomed an assault on the institution of slavery, which they often blamed as the ultimate cause of secession. Antislavery Republicans like James K. Magie regularly operated with a sense of racial superiority, as is evident in the following letters to his wife. The first of these described his interaction with a slave who had sought freedom within Union lines. In the second, Magie mixed antislavery sentiments with pride at being taken as a "massa" himself. This letter shows the recurring conflicts over the rendition of fugitives that erupted between the Unionist slaveholders of Kentucky (and their agents from Louisville and elsewhere) and men like Magie and the colonel of his regiment.

Headquarters 78th Regt. Ill Vol.
Camp at New haven, KY
Jan 21, 1863

Dear Mary,

. . . We have a contraband in camp who makes us a great deal of fun. He is the greatest dancer I ever saw. He joins in our debates and makes a right down good speech. He is employed by the Colonel and cooks, makes fires, washes, etc. He means to stay with us until the war is over and then go to Illinois with us. He is a slave and ran away from Spencer County about 50 miles distant. . . .

James

On board steamer John Groesbeck,
Ohio River
Feb. 2, 1863

Dearest Mary,

. . . Let me whisper you something. Our Colonel is under arrest for refusing to search to the boat for runaway niggers.

The contraband was put in my charge and I have got him yet. The niggers thinks there is nobody like Massa Magie. The Colonel says he means to take him home with him after the war is over, but the nigger says he will go with me. The Louisville nigger catchers would have got him if I hadn't secreted him. . . .

Your own dear husband,
James

As the enlistment of black troops accelerated early in 1863, a major Federal initiative recruited white commanders for each of these newly formed regiments. Some abolitionists demanded that black officers be commissioned and put into positions of command responsibility. Such a step toward racial equality was anathema to the majority of the white North and was thus rejected by the president and his secretary of war. Thousands of enlisted white Union troops were willing to consider becoming USCT officers, and they were driven by a wide variety of motives. For many, gaining a commission would be a way to leave behind the drudgery they experienced as common soldiers. In correspondence with his sister, the Wisconsin soldier Dolphus Damuth explained how personal advancement rather than idealism sparked his interest in joining the USCT. His family's doubts, which he acknowledged in the second excerpted note, may have resulted from their own lingering hostility toward African-Americans, who had been the topic of ridicule in earlier letters. The Damuth family was likely just as concerned with the dangers of the position Dolphus considered for a time but never attained. Confederates warned of reprisals against white men leading black troops, threatening them with prosecution for the capital offense of inciting slave insurrection.

On Board Steamer Charlie Bowen
St Helena, Ark
April 11th / 63

Dear Sister,

I have a few Spare moments I will try and write you a few lines. . . .

I Sepose we will get our pay to day if we do I shall send

some home it is safe thear and you can send some to me any time. Agt. Gen. Thomas* was hear last monday we all went down to the Ft. to hear him he came to see about organizing negro Regts and would give commissions to good men he wanted hard men and must be recommended by the Col. & Cap. of their Regt & Co. Dick Butler thought we would go into it but we was to late for the first regt. The Offices wer all given before the next noon we have been recommended by our Cap. Col & Gen McGinnis our Brigadeere and have sent it to Gen. Prentiss. Charlie is on Prentiss staff and he says he will do all he can for us. I dont want you Should say any thing about to anyone. I dont expect we will get it but there is no hurt in trying. . . .

Yours truly,
Dolph Damuth

May 9th 1863
In camp on the road to the Jackson & New Orleans Railroad
20 miles South of Vixburgh

Dear Sister,

. . . You dont seem to like to have me go into a negro Regt. I will till you how I came to think of it. Dick Butler wanted to go and did not want to go alone. So I told him I would go with him if we both could get commands and even if we did not it would do no hurt to try. I don't think thear is any chance for eather of us thear is over 500 applications now on file and we are away down here. I think it would be quite an object for the reasons that I would get better pay & if I was sick I would be more likely to get home. I don't sepose they up north would think much of any one that would go into one. but it is very different down here. Offercers are going out of white regs into them. I hope you wont worry about it for thear is no dainger of any Such good luck we have got some thing els to do

*Lorenzo Thomas, who was responsible for organizing black regiments throughout occupied areas of the Mississippi River valley.

just now after we get this job done then we will think of some thing els. . . .

I will write again when I have a chance.

Yours Truly,
Dolph

This Sprig was picked by Dave on the Isl. At Grand Gulph

Late in 1863 the Kentucky Unionist William Brunt was among the thousands to receive a new commission within a black regiment, becoming a captain in the Sixteenth USCT. His application for a commission was helped by his impeccable Unionist credentials, which may have won him special consideration from Andrew Johnson, in charge of organizing black regiments in Tennessee, where he served as military governor. It could not have hurt that Brunt also had a deep-seated commitment to remedying the plight of slaves and that he had embraced this mission while working with the freed men and women at Fort Donelson. When Brunt insisted to a friend that "I see an opening in this Negro matter to do a great deal of good," he meant it in the broadest terms possible. His letters conveyed views closer to radical abolitionists than to the bulk of the army rank and file. His correspondence repeatedly expressed enthusiasm for freeing, uplifting, and educating African-Americans as part of a broad national mission. There was a thrill in overturning slavery, which he considered the country's greatest flaw.

While Brunt was full of good intentions, not all his plans were likely to have been appreciated by his fresh recruits. In the following letter, written shortly after he had begun enlisting former slaves at Fort Donelson, Brunt offered an unusual method of proving the valor of his men. While his superiors seemed to have quickly overruled his scheme, the proposal revealed a deeper impulse that was likely to surface in other contexts. Idealistic whites like Brunt may not have realized the burdens that black recruits faced when placed on trial as representatives of their entire race.

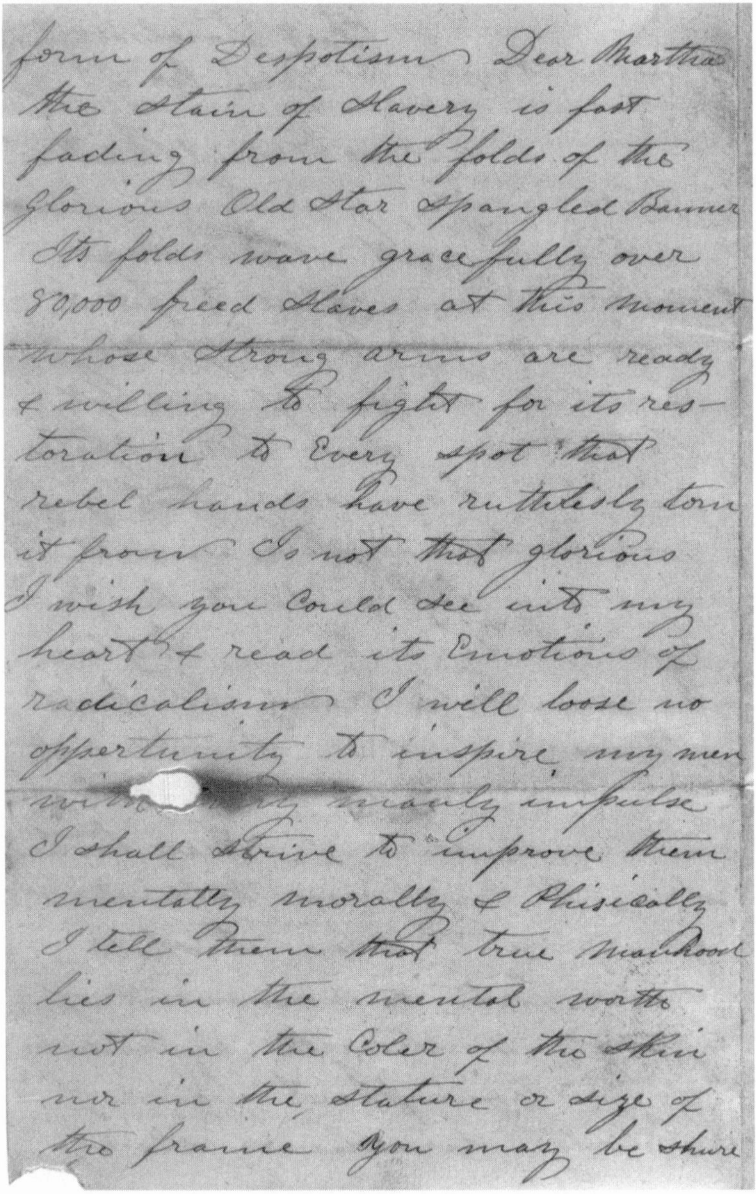

form of Despotism Dear Martha
the Stain of Slavery is fast
fading from the folds of the
Glorious Old Star Spangled Banner
Its folds wave gracefully over
80,000 freed Slaves at this moment
whose Strong arms are ready
& willing to fight for its restoration to Every spot that
rebel hands have ruthlessly torn
it from Is not that glorious
I wish you Could see into my
heart & read its Emotions of
radicalism I will loose no
oppertunity to inspire my men
with [illegible] manly impulse
I shall strive to improve them
mentally morally & Phisically
I tell them that true manhood
lies in the mental worth
not in the Color of the skin
nor in the stature or size of
the frame You may be shure

Figure 52. William Brunt to Martha Winn Cook, December 23, 1863.

[September 13, 1863]

Dear Friend Robert,

. . . Still things look rather gloomy for us at present but clouds and sunshine must alternately follow each other. I think the Federals can stand it as long as the Confederates can. I don't get time to read the news now. You probably know what it is to do what I am now doing. You know how I love to accomplish what I undertake and I have undertaken [to] prove that Negroes can be rendered useful as soldiers. Some think that they wont stand fire. I am going to test them soon by a sham attack taking care to load the Negroes guns with blank Cartridge my self. Iff I can get Col. Hardings consent and some of our soldiers to dress in citizens Clothes I can soon sett that matter at rest. . . .

Yours truly,
William Brunt

Brunt had broad responsibility for those freed men and women who came to Fort Donelson. He later attended to the same challenges by serving as the ranking officer at one of the largest contraband camps in the upper South, just outside Clarksville, Tennessee. Besides providing food and shelter, Brunt established educational and religious opportunities to those black refugees under his supervision. His greatest satisfaction, however, came in enlisting a select group of adult men and preparing them to join an armed struggle against Southern treason. By signing their names (or writing their marks) as volunteers, these men passed to freedom from slavery with the stroke of their own pens. Federal regulations assured emancipation to all soldiers, even if they were left in slavery (as was the case of black Kentuckians) by Lincoln's Emancipation Proclamation of January 1, 1863.

Clarkesville, Tenn
Nov 2, 1863

Dear Friend Robert,

. . . Now for the Glory part. I am enlisting all able boddied ones that wish to enlist. I have sent 154 fine looking soldiers since last Friday week to Major Stearns Head Qts at Nashville. I have enlisted 20 to day and they still come. Oh how theire eyes brighten when they make theire mark to their signature when I tell them that act makes them free as I am. No Masters whip will ever legally gash theire backs again. Their masters henceforth have no more control over them than they have over me. The proportion since I commenced Enlisting has been 64 Rail Road men to 178 soldiers and fully 1/4 of the R road men want to Enlist but are to young to Old or unsound. . . .

From this you can judge of the force that can be raised provided we can get at them. How my heart leaps for joy at this privelige of taking one part of the south to whip the rest with yes to take the cause of the Rebellion to crush it with. . . .

Well my sheet is full. Good night write soon. My love to you & all the boys yours truly,

William Brunt

Brunt followed white conventions by speaking of the "progress of the black race" in unitary terms. But his work in the contraband camp introduced him to black men and women as individuals, and his reports about particular refugees conveyed glimpses of real people like the teenager he described in the following undated letter. The unnamed former slave that Brunt encountered was unlikely to have written his own firsthand impressions of the war. Even if he had learned to read and write as a slave, he would have had few opportunities to preserve any written notes he might have made. For this reason, there would be even less Civil War testimony from slaves than from free African-Americans. Writing produced by men like Brunt furnished an indirect means for later generations to glimpse slaves' immediate responses to wartime revolution.

Dear friend Martha,

. . . A little boy 16 years Old came to camp to see me this morning, that left home last October a year ago, he begged so hard then that I sent him to Nashville to work on the N. Western R Road although my judgement at that time was that it was like sending him to his grave. The lion hearted little fellow went & has returned with 100 Dollars to make his old mother little sister & Brother comfortable—he found his mother & brother at camp unexpectedly—I gave him a pass to go to the country to get his sister & will send him with them to Springfield Tenn. where he has a place prepared for them. He is a Fifer in the 15th U.S.C.T. & has nearly 6 months pay due—in addition to his 100 D. on hand. He has done well.

Farewell for the present.
My love to all,
Truly Your Friend,
William Brunt, Capt. 16th U.S.C.T.

Recruiting among free Northern African-Americans also intensified in 1863. While slaves in the South were drawn to the Union ranks by the presence of Federal troops in their midst, the mobilization of free black communities in the North depended on patriotic appeals and careful organization. The white abolitionist George L. Stearns became a central figure in this process; after filling the ranks of the celebrated Fifty-fourth and Fifty-fifth Massachusetts regiments early in 1863, Stearns worked with a new federal Bureau of Colored Troops to travel across the North in search of more black volunteers. His effort was aided by governors and committees, which mixed pleas to join a crusade for all African-Americans with the lure of sizable bounties. The diarist William Woodlin was among the thousands who responded, and on August 20, 1863, the young musician from Syracuse drew a hundred-dollar bounty that the Pennsylvania government paid for his three-year commitment. Woodlin's decision to enlist in a Pennsylvania regiment was not necessarily a sign of personal ties to that state (though the large black community of Philadelphia did number several individuals with the surname of Woodlin). It was more simply an acknowledgment that the Democratic governor of his own state had yet to authorize such a unit.

Some African-Americans assumed that filling the ranks would prove their patriotism. In numerical terms, the recruiting was a fantastic success, with fully three-quarters of the North's military-age black men enrolling in the fight. Yet the larger white public remained skeptical, withholding judgment until members of the USCT demonstrated their ability to withstand combat with seasoned Confederate fighters.

The Northern press focused its attention on a series of conflicts that tested the mettle of black troops. By the middle of 1863, reports from Milliken's Bend, Port Hudson, and Battery Wagner had vindicated the USCT and fueled black soldiers' claims for equal pay.

Despite their growing combat record, the military competence of black troops continued to be questioned through the summer of 1864. In June of that year USCT units were for the first time moved to the war's most visible theater, where they joined the Union's three-year-old effort to capture the Confederate capital of Richmond and to defeat Lee's Army of Northern Virginia, by then ensconced in the trenches of Petersburg. Charles C. Morey of Vermont knew how elusive a decisive victory in this locale had been since he had witnessed Union failures in Virginia since 1861. He seemed open to the idea that new recruits, whatever their background or skin color, might help complete the job and end the war. The following letter conveyed to his parents a favorable impression of the black soldiers who had arrived a short time before he wrote.

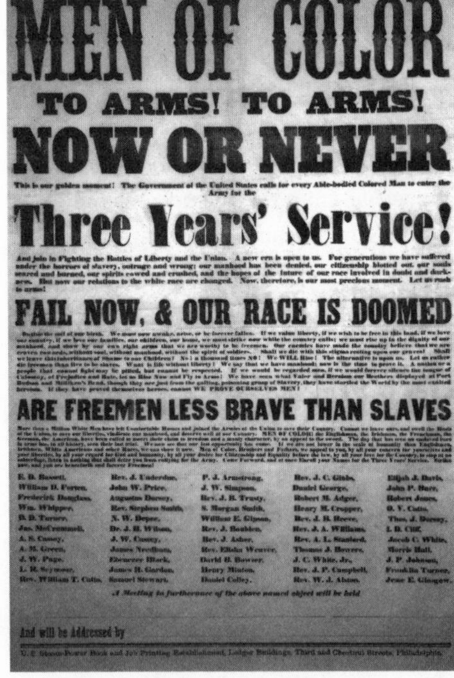

Figure 53. Recruiting broadside for USCT, 1863.

Camp of the 2nd Vt. Vols
June 19th / 64

Dear Parents,

. . . Petersburg is not taken yet and I think we have got hard fighting to do before we get it. we have the three first lines of thier works but they hold us at bay as yet. The negro troops were engaged yesterday and did splendid service. They are just as good soldiers as we have in the field they are well disciplined and make a good appearance and command the respect of the white soldiers. . . . .

Please remember me to all the family and friends and write soon and remember your son in the army of the Potomac,

C. C. Morey

Continuing controversy over black troops played a role in the mid-summer Battle of the Crater, one of the Civil War's most sensational episodes. Union forces had spent several weeks of 1864 tunneling beneath Confederate fortifications. By the end of July officials had decided to ignite an explosion, but not before training regiments of the USCT to charge through the resulting breakthrough. A last-minute decision to advance with uninstructed white troops produced chaos; these white Union soldiers filed into the cavernous "crater" created by the explosion only to be slaughtered by Confederate fire from above. Instead of achieving the decisive assault they expected, Union troops were forced to engage in a costly retreat. This fiasco gave George Tillotson an opportunity to cast doubt on black capabilities as fighters in a letter written the day after the dramatic events he described.

In first line Rifle pits, front of Petersburg
Sunday July 31st, 1864

My Dear Wife,

. . . From common report we knew well enough what was up, though, which was that some forts up in front of the ninth corps was to be blown up, and we were to go and support the 9th corps in the charge on the rebel works. . . . I was woke up just after daylight by the explosion as the rebel fort was blown up and the opening of all the artillery along the lines together with the rattle of musketry which was however a good deal of the time completely drowned by the roar of the artilery. . . .

the report [came] that the blowing up was successful and two or three hundred rebs were thereby killed or buryed alive, and that our men held the first line of rebel works. After some little maneuvering we finally advanced to between the first and second lines of our works from the rear, which was as far as we advanced. . . .

A regt. of negroes came to the top of the hill on the scadda-dle, but an Officer met them there and succeeded in partially stopping them but he had to cut to the right and the left "right smart." To the "brave smart bully petted darkies" I ascribe the disaster of yesterday. A brigade of negro and a brigade of white troops were put both together into captured second line. They say the negroes when charged on scadaddled without fireing a volly. We stayed thar til about noon when the rebs haveing taken back all their lost ground and the 9th Corps having recovered their old lines we marched back but went off some ways farther to the left and lay til near night. . . .

Accept lots of Love from Your True Husband,
George W. Tillotson

A few days after the Crater disaster William Woodlin and the rest of the Eighth USCT were ordered from Florida to Virginia, where they joined Benjamin Butler's Army of the James, then stationed between Petersburg and Richmond. After a memorable trip Woodlin reported his unit's initiation into the constant hostile fire that marked the re-maining months of war.

[Aug] 5th [1864] We got ready by 4 A.M. & moved down to the wharf with the Regt. and got aboard of the Screw Steamer Beaufort. left Jacksonville about 8 A.M. . . .

6th . . . saw a great No. of Pelicans and cranes before we left the mouth of the river. . . .

11th Wind fair all day. We made Cape Henry last evening and

ran into port about 3 P.M. took water aboard left the Ladies & one Officer there and passed on up the James River leaving Newport News to the right. . . .

12th We got Steam up about day light and got under weigh before sunrise. . . . The scenery is very good but the gen' character is Southern quite so. . . . took up the line of march for Gen. Butler's Hd Qur's about 7 miles distant through Virginia dust, which is terrible indeed. Water was very scarce and the evening was enlivened by the Bombardment of Petersburg.

13th The morning was ushered in by the Monitors shelling the woods. things very uncertain about our future destiny. the Guns soon opened on us and some 8 or 9 shells were thrown in on our camp before we could get out of the way. . . . We fell back about half a mile and left our dress clothes and knapsacks and moved in. . . . we started about 11 p.m. and moved across the river on a pontoon bridge and bivouack for the night. Sunrise was ushered in by sharp skirmishing.

The constant harassment from sharpshooters took a toll on the Petersburg front. Yet while Woodlin noted the stress upon troops, he also recorded cherished opportunities to look past the combat, to appreciate the beauty of a vista, and to relish the pomp of a particularly moving dress parade.

[August] 28th [1864] Sharp firing this morning but no regular attack. Washed etc. today our Regt was ordered out on picket. we moved about 9 P.M. the minnie balls flew sharp I can say for they flew very near me before I could cover.

29th A little mail came this morning a letter & paper. nothing unusual happened till night when Our Batteries commenced shelling. so the Rebs answered one of their messengers coming right in to the entrenchments but buried itself so deep that it did not hurt any body; a plenty went over. There were 7 shells concentrated on the Reb Battery at once after which she held up; one gun was dismounted on a Reb work in the afternoon, which they attempted to remount but could not; the firing on the picket posts which is behind breastworks. the Sharp Shooters are very bad here throwing a saucy good ball & at long range to.

30th At night the Band was called up and sent to the rear with the understanding that they were to go on picket no more. there was one man shot through the head during the day by exposing himself. . . .

[September] 13th Things very quiet till near night when there was a fierce fire of pickets and an occasional shell. I went up onto the heights in rear of our Camp & had a splendid view of Petersburg's environs and surrounding country, which included a large portion of the Appomattox River—valley. the real town itself I could not see much of though I saw 5 steeples of churches or some other Public buildings & a lookout. Our lines are very closely pushed up to the confines of P. there appear to be some very fine buildings there of brick. the Heights make it look very picturesque worthy of a painter's pencil. . . .

14th A fierce fire of musketry was kept up all night and about 10 a.m. this morning a fierce cannonading was commenced and kept up for about 2 hours; a No. of men being wounded from our Brigade one shell rooted into our trenches being spent . . . and one struck 2 rods to the right of us against a tree. about as brisk a fire as we have had since we have been here. . . .

16th We practiced this morning. I got a letter from home last night. There was a little firing at noon and a little more in the afternoon. 3 of our men were wounded in the trenches by pieces of shell. One went over our camp [Band] howling. . . .

25th . . . The whole six Regts were ordered out on a Dress Parade in the evening. The Band Played down the entire line & played the Brigade off the field. it was a fine night, there was but one white Regt. present. . . .

26th We were ordered out to Brigade guard Mount this morning, the whole Brigade was inspect by Cos, three at a time. Everything is reduced to order now. . . .

27th Everything is fine today. Duty as usual. Guard mount, etc. We lay in the trenches 3 days doing Picket duty and fatigue & only lost two men killed & they by sharp-shooters & some 6 wounded none dangerously. a very good record. better than the rest of the Brigade.

Woodlin captured the sense of satisfaction that nearly all veterans experienced in successfully facing enemy fire. Even the proudest fighter usually looked forward to the moment when his exposure to danger would end, however. The longing for peace became especially pronounced for those preparing late in 1864 to endure yet another winter of soldiering. This war-weariness caused soldiers on both sides to regard black troops in a more positive light than ever before and to calculate how these new forces might provide a decisive edge in bringing about a final victory.

Dolphus Damuth, in writing home to Wisconsin in the following letters, conveyed how important this issue had become to some Union soldiers. Damuth was at the time stationed as part of the garrison force in Memphis, and in this assignment he might have come into contact with Edward Ward's grieving family. Dolphus addressed the multiple forms of white hypocrisy. After scoffing at Democratic acceptance of black replacements and Southern attacks on Northern "race-mixing," he alluded, in the second letter, to the Confederate proposal to place their slaves in the Rebel armies.

Memphis Tenn.
Dec. 3, 1864

Dear Sister,

. . . The negro troops do all the picket duty and I don't see but what the pro-slavery Dem. like it as well as any one. They are no better to fight than we are. They seem willing to do all they can to help us along in the great work. It is true the war has been a benefit to them. So has it to the white race. It has set as many poor degraded whites free as it has negroes. And the class we call slaves have more or less white blood in the veins. And still the Southern people call us abolitionists and amalgamationists. This war has been a horrible thing and the end has not yet come, but who ever lives to see will say that the blood that has been sacrificed is not in vain. . . .

I cant think of any more to write this time. Good night

From your affectionate
Brother Dolph

Send me a Photograph when you get some taken. Write soon and often.

Memphis Tenn
December 13, 1864

Dear Sister,

. . . You wanted to know how I enjoyed Thanksgiving. Not very well it was on that day that we left Turtle Rock and we lost thought that it was thanksgiving day until nearly night. Next year if I live I shall be at home on that day and then we will all be very thankful and have a good time.

I have reason to be thankful this year. Things look now very favorable for a Speedy peace. I see the South are quarreling among themselvs about state rights and other things. It is hard for them to free and arm their slaves, when slavery was declared to be the chief cornerstone of the Confederacy. Do the Northern Democrats think it right for them to arm the nigers. I notice that the little Mackerals* in this Regt. rais no objections to the nigro troops doing the picket duty around this city but think it a mighty nice thing.

There is a great deal of Changing going on in this place lately. . . .

I wish you could see the pen that I write this with. Tom Speed sent it to me. No more at the present.

Yours &c. Dolph

Union soldiers endorsed black troops for the same reason they voted for Abraham Lincoln: to push the war forward toward a victorious

*This was the belittling term Damuth and others used when referring to the Democratic political supporters of General George McClellan.

Figure 54. Detail of Henry Berckhoff, "Homeward Bound Hop's Landing on the Aquia Creek May 3, 1863."

conclusion and to restore peace across the country. During the final year of the war a good many white Union solders allowed their three-year enlistments to expire, leaving the glory of finishing the job to fresh replacements then streaming in. Few Confederates were allowed to end their service before their armies were beaten and forced to disband. The situation was very different for Union troops, whose homecomings matched the schedule of their enlistment rather than the war's more general progress. It was the spring of 1863, with the war barely halfway over, when Henry Berckhoff's Eighth New York ended their role in the conflict. Berckhoff's last watercolor marked the occasion of their trip home and conveyed how many Northern troops experienced the end of their soldiering careers well before the Union had been assured.

Union soldiers were encouraged to become "Veteran Volunteers" rather than return to civilian life, and the offer came with a sizable financial incentive. For many, the idea of keeping their regiment together was an added inducement, and this motivation was especially strong where unit pride had been sustained by shared triumphs and

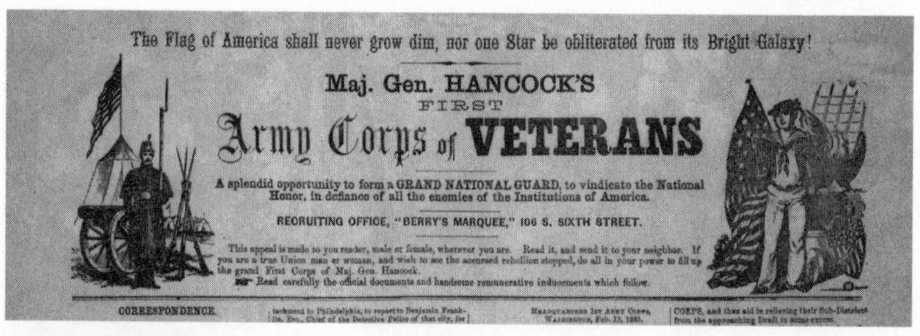
The Flag of America shall never grow dim, nor one Star be obliterated from its Bright Galaxy!

Maj. Gen. HANCOCK'S
FIRST
Army Corps of VETERANS

A splendid opportunity to form a GRAND NATIONAL GUARD, to vindicate the National Honor, in defiance of all the enemies of the Institutions of America.

RECRUITING OFFICE, "BERRY'S MARQUEE," 106 S. SIXTH STREET.

This appeal is made to you reader, male or female, whatever you are. Read it, and send it to your neighbor. If you are a true Union man or woman, and wish to see the accursed rebellion stopped, do all in your power to fill up the grand First Corps of Maj. Gen. Hancock.

Read carefully the official documents and handsome remunerative inducements which follow.

CORRESPONDENCE.

BOUNTIES AND PAY.

THE NET PAY OF A VETERAN VOLUNTEER IN HANCOCK'S CORPS:

For one year, Government Bounty	$400
City of Philadelphia Bounty	400
Monthly Pay from U. S. Government, $16 per month	192
Clothing account yearly	42
Ward Bounty (average)	25
City relief, for families of Volunteers, $6 per month	72
Total	$1121

THE NET PAY OF A VETERAN VOLUNTEER FOR TWO YEARS IN HANCOCK'S CORPS:

Government Bounty	$300
City of Philadelphia Bounty	450
Monthly Pay from United States Government, $16 per month	384
Ward Bounty (average)	25
City relief for family, $6 per month	144
Total	$1303

THE NET PAY OF A VETERAN VOLUNTEER FOR THREE YEARS IN HANCOCK'S CORPS

Government Bounty	$600
City of Philadelphia	500
Monthly pay from U. S. Government, $16 per month	576
Clothing account, $42 per year	126
Ward Bounty (average)	25
City relief for families, $6 per month	216
Total	$2043

Organization to Raise the Brigade.

The Committee who have charge of the organization of the Brigade are:

O. W. DAVIS.
HENRY C. HOWELL.
GEORGE BULLOCK.
DAVID FAUST.
JOHN W. EVERMAN.

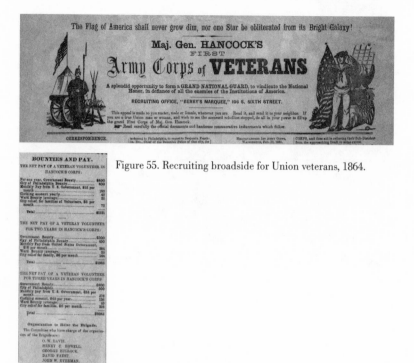

Figure 55. Recruiting broadside for Union veterans, 1864.

sacrifices. Such was the case with Charles Morey's Second Vermont Infantry. When Morey's term expired in the spring of 1864, he committed himself to further service and received a furlough and higher pay. He made the decision when it seemed there might not be much more fighting to do. After he had returned from his leave to the front, his letters began to discuss plans for his own future and for a memorial that might honor the Vermont brigade's commanders. Memories of valor coexisted with a longing for peace, as in this letter conveyed to his family from the outskirts of Petersburg.

March 3rd, 1865
Patricks Station, Va.

My dear Mother

. . . Oh if this war was ended how gladly I would come home to cheer the downward pathway of life, but as I am here can do nothing but sympathize with you and endeavor by letter writing to comfort you all in my power. . . . We have no news in camp of interest but are watching the enemy as a cat watches a mouse and are all ready to spring upon our enemy the moment he tries to escape or lengthen or shorten his lines.

C. Carroll Morey

Morey's string of luck ran out on April 2, 1865, when a canister of grapeshot killed him on his regiment's final day of combat. The fatal wound came on the assault that forced Confederates to give up their entrenched positions and to begin a retreat westward along the Appomattox River. The day after this withdrawal the Confederate government evacuated Richmond, realizing that this city was no longer defensible.

Those who marked Morey's death, at the age of twenty-four, noted the timing of this late sacrifice and drew attention to the fact that he had been among the first seventy-five thousand men to respond to Lincoln's call for troops in 1861. His service was among the longest of any Northern soldier. It had also been among the most eventful, having taken him to nearly all the major battles in the eastern theater. His parents left no record of how they learned of his death, though they may have already known his fate when they received what was the last of dozens of letters that Morey had sent to them from within the lines.

Patricks Station Va.
March 31, 1865

Dear Mother,

Once more I am permitted to sit down and pen a few words. Your last kind letter was duly received. . . .

I think I would enjoy being home very much if the war was ended and an honorable peace once more established but this little job must be accomplished first and we may look soon for important results for Sheridan and all the cavalry the 5th and 2nd corps have gone away around the right flank of the enemy and we occasionally hear their guns booming in the distance—we are under marching orders and expect to move in some direction soon. Last night this corps was ordered to assault the enemy's works in our front this morning at half past four but for some unknown reason to me the order was countermanded and we are still in our old camp but all packed ready to start. We hope and pray that we may be able to strike the death blow to rebellion before many days but perhaps we may fail yet we hope for the best and will work hard for it and trust in God for the accomplishment of the remainder, now is the time that we need divine assistance pray for us that we may accomplish all. . . .

Have not time to write more now. Please give my love to each member of the family and all our friends and All of you write often and accept a great deal of love from your son,

Chas. C. Morey

Lysander Wheeler, the Illinois soldier marching with Sherman, also resolved to stay until the end of the war, but his service ended far more happily than did Morey's. While earlier letters had given details about weakening Southern resistance, those of 1865 indicated the satisfaction that Wheeler and his fellow soldiers experienced as they turned their thoughts toward home. Unlike earlier homesickness, the longings experienced by Northern troops in 1865 were accompanied by a fierce sense of pride, mingled with a continuing acknowledgment of the massive bloodletting of the past four years. There were a series of symbolic moments he took the time to address, noting the fall of the Confederate capital on April 2, Lee's surrender on April 9, and the capture of the fleeing Jefferson Davis on May 10 in southern Georgia. His correspondence brought life and death into dialogue by welcoming the coming harvest, hoping for the execution of Davis, and drawing attention to soldiers' skeletal remains at Spotsylvania.

Sunday Afternoon
May 21st / 65

Camp of the 105th Clouds Mills Near Alexandria Virginia

Dear Parents, Bro, & Sister

. . . it has been one continual string of marching since we left the Chattahoochie River. I never see the men all look so poor as at present. Thank God We had not the prospects before us that we had a year ago. The work accomplished during that

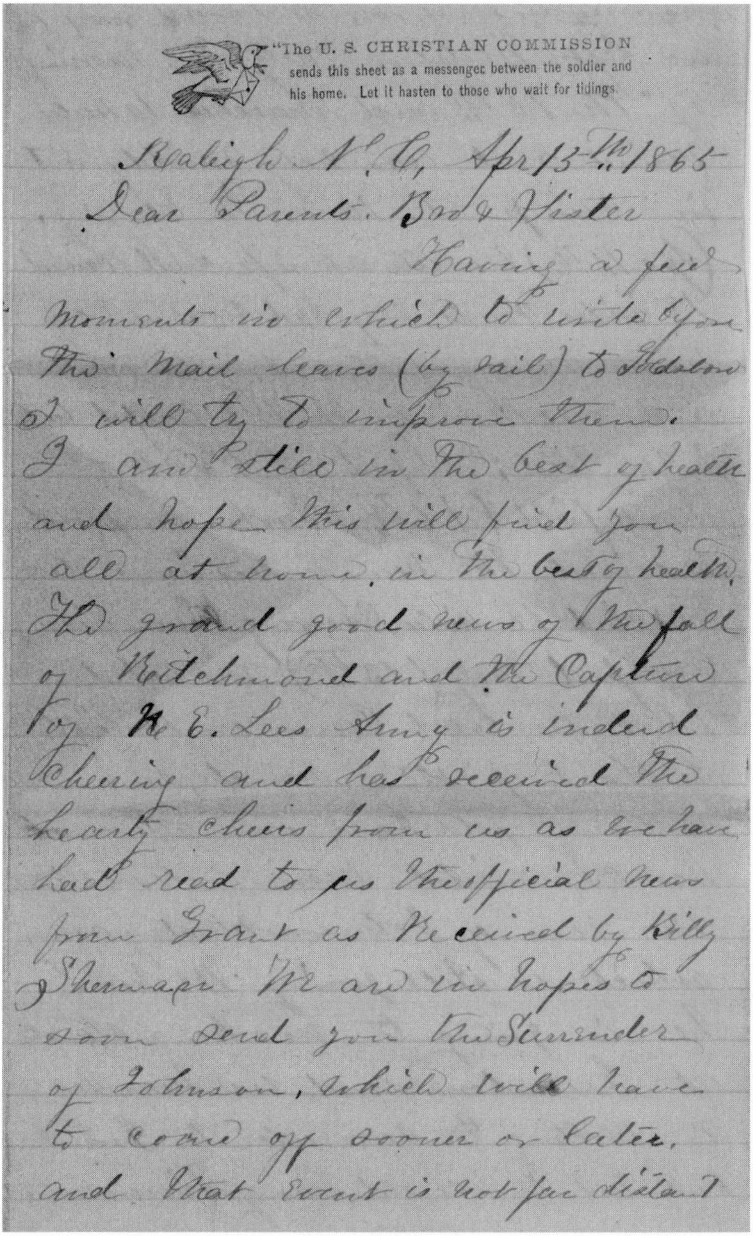

"The U. S. CHRISTIAN COMMISSION
sends this sheet as a messenger between the soldier and
his home. Let it hasten to those who wait for tidings."

Raleigh N. C, Apr 15th 1865
Dear Parents, Bro & Sister
Having a few moments in which to write you the mail leaves (by rail) to Goldsboro I will try to improve them. I am still in the best of health and hope this will find you all at home in the best of health. The grand good news of the fall of Richmond and the Capture of R. E. Lees Army is indeed cheering and has received the hearty cheers from us as we have had read to us the official news from Grant as received by Billy Sherman. We are in hopes to soon send you the Surrender of Johnson, which will have to come off sooner or later. and that event is not far distant

Figure 56. Lysander Wheeler to his family, April 15, 1865.

time has been immense no one better understands it than Shermans boys and therefore no one better appreciates the Word Homeward Bound than these self-same Boys. . . .

Your son and brother, Lysander Wheeler

May 22nd, 1865

Again I write you a few lines this Morning to inform you that I am the recipient of two more letters from home. . . .

We want to get home in time for strawberries and the 4th of July and I am glad you have been so mindful to remember me when you planted the Garden. It wont come amiss. I shall be as hungry as a Dog. You say the Black Currants are doing well Darius you must not eat them all up. You like them so well I expect Mother will have a big loaf of Bread Baked all ready. I hope that she will sit down and eat more hearty than she did at our last meal. How much has occurred since then.

Old Jeff's capture is truly refreshing. We want to see him hung. . . . then We are ready to return to Illinois in triumph how much better we feel to come with our work finished and well done. Truly God has controlled all to his honor and glory how decisive, proud Day for America let her henceforth be jealous of her honor and be careful for the future. I would not have missed contributing my mite in helping to put down this rebellion for a great deal nothing otherwise would ever have satisfied me. I envy not the comforts of those who chose luxury at home in preference of the soldiers Bed & Board including the Dangers of Warfare the risks of war are too many to be enumerated. Many of our Brave boys are sleeping in Death along our winding pathway among the Woods and Swamps of the South. too much cannot be said to their Memory. The Price of Liberty who knows. On the battle field of Spottsylvania (which we passed) the skulls were lying in the road and lay unburried. but I must change the subject. . . .

It is raining here most everyday and is very muddy. I must close with my Love to you each at home.

Your son & brother, Lysander Wheeler

Of all the hundreds of miles Wheeler had marched in the six months of war, the ten or so he took through the nation's capital in late May were perhaps the most dramatic. The Grand Review he described in the following letter was a two-day affair involving some two hundred thousand veterans' troops. Grant's eastern armies went first, followed the next day by Wheeler, Dolphus Damuth, and the rest of Sherman's army.

Washington D.C.
Camp of the 105th
May 26th, '65

Dear Parents Bro, and Sister,

. . . I must tell you a little about our grand review the 24th. We broke Camp near Alexandria at 5 in the morning and started en Route for the Capitol reaching there about 10 oclock, crossing the long bridge which spans the Potomac River (1 ¼ miles). We left the sacred soil of old Virginia and soon came near the Capitol building after halting a little while we commenced the reviewing march down Pennsylvania Avenue to the front of the President's Mansion where the receiving stand was, thence around on another street where we proceed to camp 4 ½ miles from Washington on the Baltimore Pike where we now are and will probably stop until we leave (as the boys say)

To undertake to describe the enthusiasm of the immense gathering to witness a sight (it is probable they will never see the like again) would be impossible for any one in a few words. They were perfectly astonished at the good appearance of Sherman's army supposing we were nothing more than a set of freebooters and marauders who knew how to fight but had lost all good discipline instead thereof (though not as gaudily attired as the Army of the Potomac) we laid them entirely in the shade which is conceded by the Washington Papers and its gay inhabitants. The streets were literally festooned with wreaths of flowers every state of the North had her delegates with huge mottoes of Welcome to the Western heroes of Gen. Sherman's Army. there seemed to be no end to the gratefulness they Displayed towards us. Cheer upon cheer went up as we passed. . . .

My love to each,
Your Son & Brother, Lysander

No such celebrations met the return of Confederate soldiers, of course. Those like Charles Hutson and William Clegg who had been promoted to the rank of officer were taken from official surrender ceremonies to prisons, where they were confined until pardoned for their part in the rebellion. Enlisted men who had not already melted away from the army were formally paroled and allowed to make their way home the best they could. Marion Epperly may have been among the countless men who left the Army of Tennessee before its official surrender. Back in March 1865 he had begun to discuss the opportunities provided by his army's proximity to his home in southwestern Virginia. This letter to his wife indicated that Epperly was determined to quit the life of a soldier as soon as possible, even if it meant risking greater danger than he would face by staying in the army and facing hostile fire.

Chesterville SC
March 8, 1865

My Most Dear Companion,

. . . I haven't written you any letter sins wee left Miss which has been 2 month ago wee have been sent off from home till now. wee have got to whair wee can send letters again. wee are now in about one hundred milds of Va: wee ar now waiting for transportation wee ar going near Danville Va and North Caroliner which will be in a hundred and 20 milds of home. the hole Tenn army is going thair. Sherman is advansing in that direction. wee haven't been in one fight sins wee left Tenn. wee have been faring tolerable well this winter Thou wee have been marching and traveling ever sins last fall. Though I am Very Glad I am Getin as near home as I am I hope there will be som way Provided for me to Get home yet this Spring. I must tell you a little something about Shermans Advans in the State. he has destroid all the Railrode between here and Augusta I can tell you he has plade destruction in this state whair he has went.

I think the people is beginning to feel the effects of this war here in S.C. as well as in Va and other states. Dear Mary, my heart is fild with Uneasiness it has been so long sins I have heard from you an the Children Though I hope when I get a letter I will hear Good noos from you. . . .

Dear Mary if they don't furlow us hom when wee get to Va as they have all the rest of the Soldiers thru here I intend to com any how. if my life is spared to doo soo I had just as soon be kild trying to Get hom to see you and our dear little children as to die in the Confederate army. . . .

Ma God Bless you an ever be with you is my prairs. . . .

C. M. Epperly

Black recruits often had the longest wait for postwar homecomings, since they were generally held more strictly to the terms of their three-year military commitment than white troops were. Even as the Confederate armies disbanded, the need for Union military power remained. The work of occupation and of restoring order in the South became the most pressing military responsibilities. There were also foreign threats to confront, such as that posed by the French emperor Napoleon III in Mexico, where he was working to prop up a New World monarchy by supporting the archduke Ferdinand Maximilian's claim to power. William Woodlin's Eighth USCT was directed to Texas in late May 1865 in order to show American strength on this troublesome southwestern border. These men shipped out a day before the Grand Review in Washington. During this trip, Woodlin suffered from a serious case of sunstroke that left him partly disabled for the rest of his life.

Woodlin's surviving journal indicates he bought a second diary late in 1864, though if he kept a full record of his second year's service, he apparently was unable to preserve it. Evidence of his state of mind does exist, however, in a letter he sent to the *Christian Recorder* of Philadelphia before leaving Virginia. Unlike the more personal writings of his journal, this printed testimonial made an explicit link between Woodlin's wartime efforts in suppressing the rebellion and African-Americans' future within the United States. The contribution he gathered was for the financially struggling Wilberforce University, which been founded as the first college for African-Americans in 1856.

Near Petersburg, Va.
April 28, 1865.

Dear Sir:

The appeal of the Trustees of the Wilberforce University for aid, in the columns of the Recorder, suggested the idea to a friend of our race, of the following collection; and I, as the agent, am happy to state, that the men of the regiment, representing at lest ten different States, have responded to my solicitations with alacrity, and I am enabled to present you, as the result of my labors, the sum of $241, which, if too late for a redemption fund, we desire it to be placed in the endowment. The great changes which are now so rapidly moulding the public mind, have brought us to realize the necessity of intellectual improvement to a much greater degree than ever before. We wish, therefore, to show our interest practically now, so that in days to come posterity may enjoy it. It may be of some interest to you to know that this money was collected on the march after General Lee, from Petersburg to Appomattox Court-house, and some of it the day after his surrender. With this explanation I will close, and subscribe myself respectfully yours,

WM. P. WOODLIN,
Musician 8th U.S.C.T., 2d brig., 2d div.,
25th Army Corps, Washington, D.C.

William Brunt experienced the coming of peace with a mixture of sadness and enthusiasm. The following letter explained how his family had splintered as a result of his officer's commission. This higher rank had allowed his wife to live in the contraband camp, where she became romantically involved with another man during Brunt's absences. This personal disappointment seemed to have been quite difficult for Brunt. Yet he took solace in knowing that personal sacrifices were necessary for the great public changes his service had helped to accomplish.

August 15 1865

Dear Martha,

While I was gone to Iowa, Olive let passion instead of virtue rule her & became inconstant to me—this was indeed painful to hear of & I obtained a Divorce on the 23rd of April last. I treated her kindly—but could not live with her longer nor let her have the children to keep—the court gave me jurisdiction over them & all my property. I kept Olive here until the trial was over & then gave her 100 dollars & sent her home & henceforth we shall be two persons. . . .

All goes well here as could be expected with the Freedmen. I still have charge of their interest at this post and expect to remain as long as I wish to and there is need of me. I like my labor here and will try to do my whole duty faithfully and fearlessly. The noble Chivalry of the South have had to yield. I have very interesting things to write but must defer until my next letter.

Yours truly,
William Brunt

Brunt closed this somber note with a promise of continued correspondence with his friend Martha. There is a possibility that he never kept this pledge however, since this was the last note that Cook tucked away, marking the end of this collection in the late summer of 1865. Whether such letters continued to be sent through the mail or his writing abruptly ended will likely remain a mystery.

For the penmen as a group, there is a similar pattern, since hardly any of these soldiers' collections contain papers written after the early days of peace. The end of their written record was partly a result of these soldiers' return home, where they no longer depended on remote communication to stay in touch with loved ones. Even so, it would be hard to believe that their pens stopped altogether. The main difference of peacetime writing was not its frequency but its worth. As part of the normal order of things, most documents created by civilians would have seemed expendable when compared with Civil War treasures. That they were not preserved for posterity said less about their value than about that of firsthand impressions created amid the whirl of war.

SEVEN

Relics of War

On a fairly regular basis, the mail exchanged between Hillory Shifflet and his wife, Jemima, bulged with contents thicker than the usual ink-lined paper. In addition to her packages of home-cooked food, Jemima sent jewelry, gloves, boots, and a needle and thread that her husband needed to mend his uniform. Her most precious gifts were photographs of herself and their children she sent as a surprise; these moved Shifflet to tears when they were delivered to him after a day of picket duty. His return correspondence also included valued items, especially a regular stream of money. On at least two occasions he also included photographic images of himself, which froze in time his appearance as a proud, albeit deeply disgruntled, Ohio private. None of these personal relics still seem to exist, and if they do, they have been separated from the written artifacts that Shifflet awkwardly produced over the two and a half years of his service. His halting letters now stand alone in conveying his wartime experiences to later generations.

In the early summer of 1863 Shifflet had become a regular enough correspondent to internalize some of the conventions of letter writing and to convey a sense that his written words were as precious as any memento his family could own. He ended one of his most embittered attacks on the Republican Party with explicit instructions to his wife to save all his writing for his later enjoyment. Another note concluded with a rhymed warning against the destruction of his writing:

Remember me when this you see, tho many mils and distans be.
Remember me when far away and dont forget me when you pray
My pen is poor my ink is frail my love to you will never fail,
if you take this in good part, lay it up in your hart
but if you take it in disdain, send it home to me again.

Shifflet's wife did manage to save a dozen or so of his letters, and this testimony allows us to appreciate the challenges faced by an anti–Republican Party army private from the rural Midwest. Jemima had her own reasons for keeping her husband's notes, of course, and these had little to do with their usefulness to later scholars or their in-

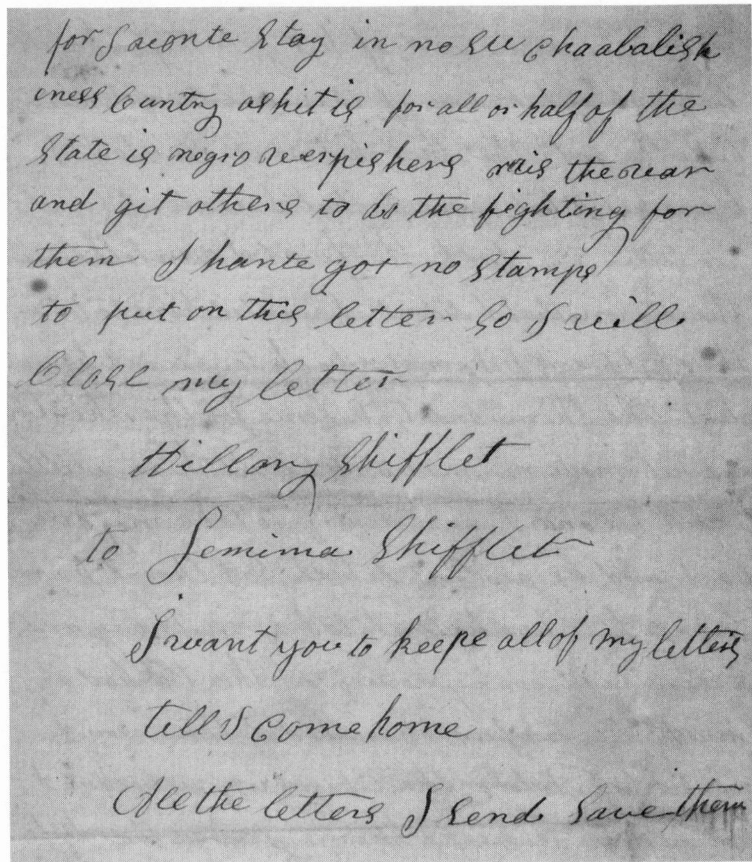

for I aconte stay in no su[c]h abalish
ness Cuntry as hit is for all or half of the
State is negro werpishers rais the war
and git others to do the fighting for
them I hante got no Stamps
to put on this letter so I will
Close my letter
Hillory Shifflet
to Jemima Shifflet
I want you to keepe all of my letters
till I Come home
All the letters I send save them

Figure 57. Hillory Shifflet, to his wife, Jemina, May 3, 1863.

terest to general readers. She likely regretted not saving even more of his weekly reports, since after he was fatally wounded at Missionary Ridge, his body was buried in a military cemetery in Chattanooga, Tennessee. Though it was a comfort that he had a gravesite, it was a burden for a family in Ohio that this stone marker was not closer at hand. Far from the tombstone reared in his memory, Jemima could seek solace in letters that her husband had prepared with his own hand and had intended for her own eyes. For the last decade and a half of her life, whenever Jemima Shifflet took out these wartime messages, she could reckon with her loss and could cling to her husband's scribbled handwriting, even as the tenor of his voice faded from memory.

As Shifflet's example suggests, the lines that connected families during wartime would be a uniquely powerful means of connecting the past and the present once the fighting ended. When armies were in the field, the Civil War turned ordinary Americans into a nation of correspondents, diarists, and sketchers. After 1865 soldiers' families became unofficial archivists who were committed to preserving written relics of war and transmitting them to posterity. We know less about how soldiers' letters, diaries, and sketches were saved than about how and why these items were created. Even so, there are tantalizing hints about how soldier writing figured into a postbellum culture of remembering the American Civil War.

Countless soldiers sent and received mementos, though it is striking how few of these items were saved, especially when compared with the volume of written artifacts that were handed down. There were several reasons that writing was more likely to be preserved than other keepsakes. References to war's gruesome carnage once committed to paper were easier to save than a physical token or trophy. The bone jewelry that Jeremiah Tate sent to his family or the lock of Confederate hair that James Magie mailed after a bloody skirmish in Tennessee lost meaning with the passage of time. In 1864 Charles Morey bragged to his parents about new family heirlooms such as a battle-scarred sword and a hat recently pierced by a bullet. Yet even these items were lost to posterity.

In some cases the historical record accounts for the loss of objects that their owners had invested with special meaning. A series of letters between Morey's father in Vermont and the army bureaucracy indicated that his sword and hat were misplaced or stolen along with the rest of Morey's personal effects, which had gone astray after he was fatally wounded in the Union's final assault upon Petersburg. His parents and siblings could take solace in the return of Morey's corpse to the Connecticut River valley; many survivors of dead soldiers never knew the exact whereabouts of a loved one's body. Edward Ward of Memphis was among the countless buried on the battlefield where he had been killed. Whether or not his corpse was ever recovered and returned to Memphis is unclear. If the body did go missing, this might explain why the Wards commissioned an oil painting of a loved one who had risen through the ranks to become a lieutenant. The portrait of the young Tennesseean was almost certainly based on one of the several wartime photographs Ward mentioned prior to his death outside Atlanta during the summer of 1864.

Each of these wartime fatalities left their most enduring legacy not in their possessions, their gravesites, or even in their images, but in their writing. In Morey's case, the loss of personal belongings was offset by a string of letters and five separate diaries. Lines that Ward, Shifflet, and Smith shared with home were even more potent than their photographs since these could explain themselves and tell their own stories. Words describing particular experiences or expectations conveyed the author's undeniable voice and distinct personality. It should be obvious why families saved these treasures as a way of remembering and of paying tribute to sons, husbands, and fathers. It should be equally obvious why later readers would regard such poignant artifacts with particular reverence and approach them with a sense of awe.

A decade after his visits with soldiers in Washington, Walt Whitman described how writing recalled sacrifice more powerfully than any other relics of war. Documents created in the midst of the fighting, he explained, allowed dead voices to speak with an uncommonly simple sense of tragedy. In one of his most famous prose passages, Whitman reflected on his own notes taken during the war years, when he served soldiers rather than joined them in the ranks. These jotted impressions furnished "a few stray glimpses into that life, and into those lurid interiors of the period, never to be fully convey'd to the future." This comment, along with the rest of his 1875 introduction to *Memoranda During the War*, explained what others may have sensed but were unable to articulate with his blend of concision and feeling. The passing of ten years since the conflict allowed Whitman to gain perspective, which he used to explain how assorted scraps from the past represented a sort of immortality.

> I leave [my notebooks], just as I threw them by during the War, blotch'd here and there with more than one blood-stain, hurriedly written, sometimes at the clinique, not seldom amid the excitement of uncertainty, or defeat, or of action, or getting ready for it, or a march. Even these days, at the lapse of many years, I can never turn their tiny leaves, or even take one in my hand, without the actual army sights and hot emotions of the time rushing like a river in full tide through me. Each line, each scrawl, each memorandum, has its history. Some pang of anguish—some tragedy, profounder than ever poet wrote. Out of them arise active and breathing forms. They summon up, even in this silent and vacant room as I write, not only the sinewy regiments and brigades, marching or in camp, but the countless phantoms of those who fell and were hastily buried by wholesale in the battle-pits, or whose dust and bones have been since removed to the National Cemeteries of the land, especially through Virginia and Tennessee.

Whitman's reflections upon notes recorded in the midst of war led him to explain how these offered a communion that could be found nowhere else.

> Vivid as life, [the notebooks] recall and identify the long Hospital Wards, with their myriad-varied scenes of day or night—the graphic incidents of field or camp—the night before the battle, with many solemn yet cool preparations—the changeful exaltations and depressions of those four years, North and South—the convulsive memories, (let but a word, a broken sentence, serve to recall them)—the clues already quite vanish'd, like some old dream, and yet the list significant enough to soldiers—the scrawl'd, worn slips of paper that came up by bushels from the Southern prisons, Salisbury or Andersonville, by the hands

> of exchanged prisoners—the clank of crutches on the pavements or floors of Washington, or up and down the stairs of the Paymasters' offices—the Grand Review of homebound veterans at the close of the War, cheerily marching day after day by the President's house, one brigade succeeding another until it seem'd as if they would never end.

In short, the stray fragments of scrawled lines were not simply the lifeless remnants of times past. They had a way of assembling themselves in such a way that allowed one to feel deeply nearly the entire history of the Civil War.

Well over a hundred years later Americans collectively experienced the same sort of emotion that Whitman recorded in the 1870s as they listened to the words of what became the most celebrated single soldier letter in American history. In the very first episode of his widely aired PBS series on the Civil War, Ken Burns reached an emotional high point with a slow, somber reading of a letter written by the Rhode Island volunteer Sullivan Ballou to his wife, Mary, in July 1861. In unusually lyrical prose, the note explained Ballou's readiness to die in the service of his country. As the letter ended with Sullivan's affectionate farewell, a television audience numbering in the tens of millions learned that Ballou had paid the ultimate price by being killed the very next day, during the First Battle of Bull Run. PBS offices were in the following days flooded with requests for more information about this strangely unknown poetic document and the fate of its previously obscure author. Over the next decade and a half, Ballou's words and the story associated with them took on their own life. In many classrooms the "Dear Mary" composition has come to rival Lincoln's Gettysburg Address as a potent reminder of what wartime sacrifice meant. This note now provides a vital clue to why so many lives were given in the defense of the Union.

The Ballou letter is only one example of the value that Americans have placed on letters from wartime martyrs. This interest in the most dramatic of all writings has not diminished the appreciation for letters and diaries composed by those who survived their military service and returned home to their families. These veterans shared their exploits with proud and grateful families in person, but they also kept hold of a written record that captured all the glory, hardship, uncertainties, boredom, and losses of army life. As it became ever clearer that these years changed much of the basics of American life, the worth of firsthand written testimony only increased. Documents that had been initially secured in drawers or in trunks were treated with greater and greater care as the events they described receded into the dimming past. Countless soldiers returned to their own wartime writing for inspiration and to relish a retrospective satisfaction. A sizable number resolved to make their impressions available in more permanent form by arranging for their publication.

Memories and relics could comfort, entertain, and remind veterans of the times they had helped make history. In a less exalted sense, recalling Civil War service could provide some with a powerful means of personal advancement. Charles Hutson's minor political career in South Carolina was built on the evident fact of his steady progress up the ranks of one of his state's premier regiments. To have enlisted in the Confederate army became a valued asset for those aspiring to leadership in late-nineteenth-century South Carolina, where efforts to glorify the Confederate war coincided with a fierce effort to restore and institutionalize white supremacy under "home rule." Union service was usually not a prerequisite for leadership in the postwar North, but in a number of cases it could help. James Magie's service assured his continuing involvement with the Illinois Republican Party, which he supported in a series of postbellum editorial positions. Politics apparently was far less consequential for George Tillotson, who became involved with an upstate New York post of the Grand Army of the Republic. This veterans' organization allowed Tillotson to maintain ties with his former military associates rather than to launch or sustain a career. Recollections were their own reward, and these might have been enough to alleviate any lingering bitterness Tillotson had about the wartime typhoid fever from which he never fully recovered.

In most cases, there is a yawning gap between the vivid wartime experiences of surviving soldiers and the haze of their comparatively mundane postwar lives. In several cases, little more is known than the date of a veteran's return and the bare facts of his marriage and death. Not even that much information is available in other instances. Such lack of detail makes it more appropriate to ask questions than to venture conclusions about how wartime experiences affected veterans once they returned to civilian life. Some readers may wonder whether Marion Epperly's view of his service changed and whether he became less embittered about the Confederacy with the passage of time. Others might be intrigued about how recollections of a victorious cause might have helped Damuth, Tillotson, and Magie cope with the disabilities they sustained during war or whether Clegg and Tate ever experienced similar infirmities and regretted not having access to the same disability benefits as Union soldiers. The distinct personalities that these men displayed in their wartime writings make it tempting to imagine what each made of his subsequent life. What truly mattered to them after 1865 must remain an exercise in speculation.

The more one considers such passages from war to peace, the more questions arise. Did William Woodlin and William Brunt become disillusioned over the postwar resurgence of white racism? Did the pride of either of these men suffer from personal setbacks, whether that experienced by Brunt in his divorce or Woodlin in the sunstroke that nearly crippled him? How was it that Berckhoff decided to devote much of his adult life to army service, and why is it that no watercolors after 1863 now exist? Did the sketchbook from the Forty-fourth Massachusetts private still draw laughter after the war had ended? If it did, who was there to share in the jokes and to offer their own?

As time passed and these surviving veterans died in turn, they would be known more for what they managed to record than for any other aspect of what were often long lives. While some veterans took the initiative in preserving their own written records, close family members also played a role in securing their keepsakes. Eventually lines from the war had to be entrusted to those with no personal memory of the 1860s. They then passed to men and women who had neither known Civil War veterans nor heard their stories in direct conversation.

The fate of Jeremiah Tate's letters helps dramatize a familiar pattern. Before Tate died in 1877, he operated a rural Alabama mill and raised a large family of daughters. Efforts to save his letters fell to his sister Mary, who probably felt a sense of ownership in having received them in the first place. She safeguarded these folded notes and their variously improvised envelopes in a trunk that she passed to a daughter, who in turn passed them to her own daughter. By the late twentieth century the dozens of letters describing life in the Army of Northern Virginia were left to the care of Mary's great-grandson, who arranged for them to be opened to historians and to a wider public. This new audience may not have had a direct family connection with the young Alabama private, but they could still appreciate Tate's ability to shed light on the Confederate experience.

By hoarding, safeguarding, and transferring through generations and into the public realm, countless families assured that the writings of ordinary soldiers would constitute a record of past experience that was at once intimate and remarkably thorough. This process did not operate in a vacuum. From the time of the war, the wider public sought out firsthand accounts from ordinary people, finding in the voices of the uncelebrated the best evidence of patriotic service. Beginning in 1861, newspaper editors solicited correspondence from army privates, whose letters featured many of the same observations that they had included in notes to immediate family members. Several revealing military diaries were also published during the war, allowing the general reading public to experience the immediacy that came with regular entries and observations. Among the most successful of these published diaries was James K. Hosmer's *The Color-Guard*, whose author insisted in 1864 that he had initially intended that only his family would read the journal. Only upon their prodding did he agree to share the account of his fighting in Louisiana the previous year with a wider readership. Fewer drawings and sketches by infantrymen were published during the war. When visual testimony based on soldiers' perspectives did appear, as in the case of James Magie's picture of hanged spies, magazine editors emphasized a connection between its authenticity and its origins within the armies.

Collections of transcribed letters mailed home from the front appeared at the war's conclusion, and when they did, they showed that ordinary prose could convey patriotic sentiment even more effectively than verse. What appears to have been the very first anthology of soldier correspondence in American publishing history resulted from the work that Lydia Minturn Post began in 1864 with the cooperation of the United States Sanitary Commission, a volunteer organization that raised money for the benefit of soldiers. Post, who had already been involved with printing civilian recollections of the American Revolution, worked along with the Sanitary Commission to solicit extracts of writing from the soldiers who had made up the Union armies. "It is believed," Post's widely circulated appeal explained, "that much material of interest may thus be brought to light; viz: Thrilling incidents of heroic conduct and self-sacrificing patriotism, and noble sentiments, expressed to mothers, sisters, wives, friends—from camp and field, fort and outpost, ship and gunboat. Persons possessing such records are earnestly invited to respond to this appeal." Post drew heavily on extracts that hailed the Union cause, suggesting that she and her audience were more interested in propagating the war's idealism than in recording the challenges faced by ordinary men in the armies.

War-related publishing tapered off between the war's immediate aftermath and the mid-1880s. During this interval wartime remembrances experienced what the historian David Blight has called a period of incubation, when themes coalesced and recollections hardened into durable forms and conventions. A variety of factors accounted for the stream of war-related writings that found their way into print during the last quarter of the nineteenth century, the single largest being the renewed interest in the Civil War occasioned by a series of accounts published by the popular *Century* magazine of New York. This journal was among the first to publish recollections and retrospective accounts from both Union and Confederate soldiers. Among the sprinkling of actual wartime documents in *The Century* were a handful of letters Walt Whitman had sent to his mother in 1864. Veterans' magazines, regimental histories, and a flood of individual books from the 1880s through the 1910s featured even more letters, diaries, and sketches. The proliferation of such accounts coincided with the raising of the Civil War soldier monuments in countless communities of both North and South.

As the corpus of soldier literature grew, much of it focused on what the Confederate veteran Carlton McCarthy called the detailed minutiae of camp life. The precise details of flags, firearms, uniforms, punishments, and rations entranced military aficionados who both set the agenda for soldier reunions in the late nineteenth century and anticipated the mass phenomenon of soldier reenactments of the late twentieth century. Emphasis on the quotidian details of service marginalized larger issues of motivation and political engagement. Matters

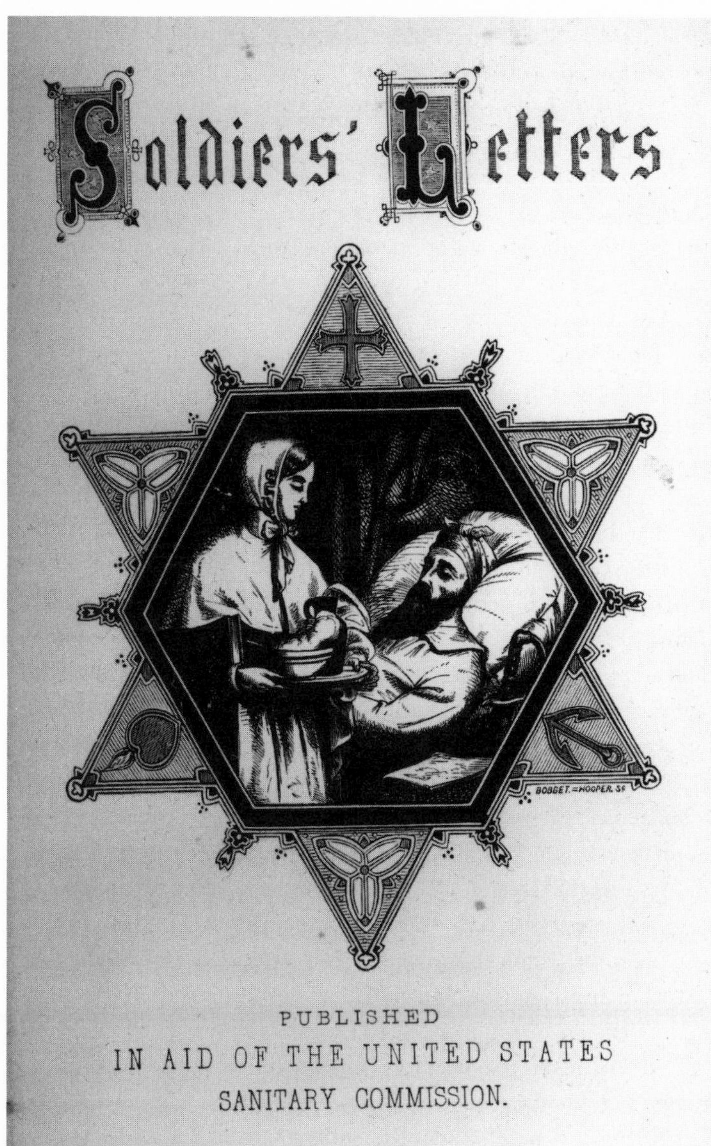

Figure 58. Lydia Post, *Soldiers' Letters*.

of slavery and of partisanship grew less important in the soldiers' remembered war, even while the surviving record indicated how important such matters had been at the time. As popular understanding of the 1860s came to focus on conditions shared by Confederates and white Union troops, it became harder to recognize the factors that had driven these armies to become enemies in the first place.

Once begun, the stream of material devoted to Civil War soldiers never slowed, though its course modified as each new generation worked out its own relationship with this crucial period of American history. The transit of privately held documents into the archives coincided with a growing appreciation taken by professional historians in the army rank and file. The pioneering work done by Bell Wiley in the 1940s encouraged later historians to recognize the worth of soldier testimony and place a premium on those records created at the time (rather than in the retrospective glow of surviving veterans' memoirs). An impressive body of work helped present the Civil War from the perspective of privates. Recently, black troops have inspired a distinct body of historical writing.

The emphasis on common soldiers has assured that Civil War literature draws from a constantly evolving set of key texts. As the body of soldier writing expands through the continuing discovery of privately held sources, new classics of this genre make their way into popular consciousness. The Sullivan Ballou letter itself is a relatively recent phenomenon, having become a popular touchstone only after the Ken Burns production aired in 1991. It seems likely that other treasures await something of the same reception, especially as interest in soldier writing continues to be stimulated by efforts such as the Legacy Project, which actively solicits personal testimony from all of America's wars. Happenstance and good luck can play a role in these new finds, as they did with the reappearance of wartime watercolors produced by Henry Berckhoff, whose work appears in this book, and those of Robert K. Sneden, an even more relentless sketcher, whose papers are now at the Virginia Historical Society. The works of these two quite different New York privates have altered not just how we understand the Civil War but how we see it in the most basic sense.

The written testimony of soldiers, whether conveyed in drawings, letters, or diaries, can appear remarkably fresh despite being nearly a century and a half old. This would not have surprised Walt Whitman, from whom we can borrow one final set of insights. Looking back from the distance of a decade, Whitman characterized the Civil War as a "many-threaded drama" that was simply too intricate and interwoven to be summed up by a single set of stories. When Whitman famously warned that the "real War" would "never get in the books," he seemed to have had in mind the retrospective, overly sentimental accounts then being published, which he associated with the "mushy influences of current times." He was unimpressed by efforts to improve on what already existed and made his convictions clear in his uncompromising statement that the war's "interior history will not only never be written, its practicality, minutiae of deeds and passions, will never be even suggested."

These oft-quoted passages are frequently misconstrued and made to convey more than Whitman himself actually set forth. His summation never concluded that language itself was incapable of describing this most American of all wars. Instead he implied that nothing new would be composed as powerful as what had been recorded at the time. Those who had known war from the inside had already provided the glimpses that mattered, even if their words ultimately never completely recaptured army service itself. Soldiers' contribution to later generations rested in their having lived with the war more completely than they or anyone else could ever fully explain after peace had returned to their common country.

Index of Source Material from the Gilder Lehrman Collection

All the sources featured in *The Soldier's Pen* appear in the following index, followed in each case by the appropriate call number from the Gilder Lehrman Collection. They are ordered chronologically under the name of the soldier who created them. Those marked with an asterisk appear as illustrations; transcriptions of letters are included where appropriate.

TRANSCRIPTION: . . . form of Despotism. Dear Martha the stain of slavery is fast fading from the folds of the glorious Old Star Spangled Banner. Its folds wave gracefully over 80,000 freed slaves at this moment whose strong arms are ready & willing to fight for its restoration to every spot that rebel hands have ruthlessly torn it from. Is not that glorious. I wish you could see into my heart & read its emotions of radicalism. I will loose no oppertunity to inspire my men with every manly impulse. I shall strive to improve them mentally morally and Phisically. I tell them that true manhood lies in the mental worth not in the color of the skin nor in the stature or size of the frame. You may be shure . . .

Letter to Martha Winn Cook, July 3, 1864 (GLC 7006.07), 179–80
Letter to Martha Winn Cook, August 15, 1865 (GLC 7006.11), 220–21
Letter to Martha Winn Cook, undated (GLC 7006.13), 202–203

WILLIAM CLEGG

Selected diary entries for May 24 through October 13, 1861 (GLC 3133), 46–47
Diary entry for June 10, 1861 (GLC 3133), 83–85
* "Rough Sketch of the Battle Field—Bethel Church," June 10, 1861 (GLC 3133), 84
Selected diary entries for October 11 through December 25, 1861 (GLC 3133), 65–66
Diary entry for January 1, 1862 (GLC 3133), 149–151
Diary entry for February 18, 1862 (GLC 3133), 151–152
* Sketch of flower, March 21, 1865 (GLC 3133), 39
Undated diary entry, from spring 1865 (GLC 3133), 186
* Photograph of William Clegg (GLC 3133 collateral file), 150

DOLPHUS DAMUTH

Letter to friends, November 7, 1862 (GLC 3523.14 (2)), 37–38
Letter to sister, March 3, 1863 (GLC 3523.14 (14)), 29–30
Letter to brother, March 17, 1863 (GLC 3523.14 (16)), 127
Letter to sister, April 11, 1863 (GLC 3523.14 (21)), 197–98
Letter to friends, April 15, 1863 (GLC 3523.14 (22)), 38–39
Letter to sister, May 9, 1863 (GLC 3523.14 (24)), 62, 198–99
Letter to sister, June 9, 1863 (GLC 3523.14 (27)), 106
Letter to sister, June 20, 1863 (GLC 3523.14 (28)), 106–107
* Letter to sister, July 5, 1863 (GLC 3523.14 (31)), 130

TRANSCRIPTION:

Rear of Vicksburgh
July 5th 1863

Dear Sister
Yesterday Vicksburgh Surrendered at half past nine you could See white flags on all of thear works it was the happyest 4th of July I ever Saw. We Start this morning for Black River we are going to leave all of our Knapsacks and will take five days rations and will likely be gon that time I dont think you will hear from me till we get back. I feel well and know that the tramp will do us all good

CHARLES J. C. HUTSON

* Letter to Emmeline Colcock, September 1, 1861 (GLC 8165.33), 31

TRANSCRIPTION:

Richmond Va. Sept 1st. 1861
Sunday afternoon

I received your second letter yesterday my dear Emmeline and hope I may have the sweet gratification of answering a third very soon. You may always be assured that it is my supreme pleasure to write often in order that I may express the homage of my heart. Away in this distant land, where I never hear the voice of any gentle lady; amid the stern hardness of men, I find exquisite pleasure in reading the letters of my Em. for they are the reflections of your soul, the pure utterance of a noble heart & they form my best companions. I often think that men left to themselves with no gentle influence to guide and direct their feelings and impulsive natures, with no pure sympathies to soothe a troubled heart, would soon prove victims of selfishness & foreigners to humanity: but I am aware also that the sentiments of their friends, relatives and those most dear to them form a preventive against the influences of a soldier's misfortunes. . . .

I have come over to the city today. . . .

Letter to Emmeline Colcock, September 7, 1861 (GLC 8165.36), 30–32
Letter to sister—Emily McLeod, November 1, 1861 (GLC 8165.43), 56–57
Letter to "Minnie" Colcock, February 6, 1862 (GLC 8165.44), 58
Letter to Richard W. Hutson, July 8, 1862 (GLC 8165.49), 55–56
Letter to his mother, June 28, 1863 (GLC 8165.55), 161–62
Letter to his sister, August 11, 1863 (GLC 8165.57), 163–64
Letter to Richard W. Hutson, November 7, 1863 (GLC 8165.63), 167–69
Letter to Marion Hutson, February 19, 1864 (GLC 8165.65), 175–76
Letter to Richard W. Hutson, March 20, 1865 (GLC 8165.70), 183

JAMES MAGIE

Letter to Mary Magie, January 4, 1863 (GLC 5241.03), 98
Letter to Mary Magie, January 21, 1863 (GLC 5241.06), 196
Letter to Mary Magie, February 2, 1863 (GLC 5241.09), 196–97
Letter to Mary Magie, February 17, 1863 (GLC 5241.12), 15–16, 73
Letter to Mary Magie, March 1, 1863 (GLC 5241.16), 16
Letter to Mary Magie, March 20, 1863 (GLC 5241.22), 126
* View of two spies, *Harper's Weekly*, July 3, 1863, based on Magie sketch (GLC 5241 collateral file), 99

CHARLES MOREY

* Letter to sister, August 2, 1861 (GLC 3523.18 (1)), 21

TRANSCRIPTION:

Bush Hill, Va. August 2, 1861.

Dear Sister Mamie.

Your letter was received last night about 9 o'clk perhaps you can imagine my feelings at hearing from you once more, it is with regret that I hear you do not hear from me oftener for I have written often probably before you get this you have received one written since you wrote yours for I sent one the other day containing the particulars of that awful battle. You earnestly request me to write often and long but we have no conveniences for so doing the only table we have is a barrel since the fight there seems to be considerable discontent but it is all caused I think by the hard march which we have not got over and the poor fare. . . .

* Letter to sister, January 12, 1863 (GLC 3523.14 (3)), 80, 81

TRANSCRIPTION:

The little dots represent the men in the skirmish line and the lines of battle are composed of Infantry, the ground is supposed to be undulating so the skirmishers and all the men in front of the batteries are out of range of our own batteries, the artillery is posted on the highest ground and the Infantry occupying the lowest. Severe fighting does not often last at any one point for a great length of time but is severe for a few minutes then subsides a short time until the forces get a little rested then go at it again. But I guess I have written enough. There is the drum calling the ordiles to the adjutants to receive orders and I have got to furnish 11 men and a sergeant for fatigue and 3 men and a sergeant for guard. So good night for this time. Write soon Charlie

Diary entry for July 8, 1862 (GLC 1921.02), 74

Diary entries for July 1863 (GLC 1921.03), 85–86

* Memoranda written in back of diary shortly after July 1863 (GLC 1921.03), 87

TRANSCRIPTION:

Gettysburg battle was the most severe that I encountered. In July 2nd at dark we took up position on the left flank. At dawn on the 3rd, we looked out from the heights and waited over on the right at Culps Hill there was a cannonade action that began Late in the morning about 10:30 everything was quiet on the battle field. All of a sudden a terrible barrage of cannonfire that seemed to shake the earth right and left of us, caissons exploded scudding fragments of wheels and woodwork shell and shot one hundred feet into the air. For one hour and a half crash after crash holes like graves were gouged in the ground by exploding shells. We were lying in the rear. The heat was terrible. Fifteen thousand enemies stretched a half a mile wide about three ranks deep on the open field. Our artillery opened a tremendous barrage on the rebs, moaning and crying could be heard. Dead bodies straddled all over the field. The biggest victory for the union. Maybe this cruel war will be over soon. Thank God for watching over me.

Diary entries for September 1863 (GLC 1921.03), 133–34

Letter to mother, May 3, 1864 (GLC 3523.18 (8)), 135–36

Letter to parents, May 13, 1864 (GLC 3523.18 (9)), 138–39

Letter to parents, June 19, 1864 (GLC 3523.18 (14)), 205

Letter to mother, September 1, 1864 (GLC 3523.18 (25)), 141

Letter to mother, March 3, 1865 (GLC 3523.18 (51)), 212–13

Letter to mother, March 31, 1865 (GLC 3523.18 (55)), 213–14

* Undated sketch of Morey's tent (GLC 3523.18 (69)), 64

HILLORY SHIFFLET

Letter to Jemima Shifflet, January, 1862 (GLC 2174.02), 17–18

TRANSCRIPTION:

. . . for I wonte Stay in no such abalishiness country as hit is for all or half of the State is negro werpishers. mis the war and git others to do the fighting for them. I hante got no stamps to put on this letter. So I will close my letter.

Hillory Shifflet
to Jemima Shifflet

I want you to keepe all of my letters
till I come home
All the letters I send Save them

DAVID V. M. SMITH

JEREMIAH TATE

TRANSCRIPTION:

Song Ballot The Bonnie Blue Flag
We are a band of brothers and native to the soil
Fiting for the property we gained by honest toil
And when our rights were threatened, the cry rose near and far
Hurrah! Hurrah! for Southern Rights hurrah
Hurrah for the Bonnie Blue Flag that bears a single star

GEORGE TILLOTSON

Letter to Elizabeth Tillotson, January 9, 1862 (GLC 4558.07), 52

Letter to Elizabeth Tillotson, January 22, 1862 (GLC 4558.08), 52–53

* Letter to Georgianna Tillotson, February 16, 1862 (GLC 4558.11), 25

TRANSCRIPTION:

My Dear Daughter Georgianna.

I was glad to here that you took an interest in your papa letters so I thought I would write to you your Ma will read it to you now but you must hurry and learn to read so you can read letters yourself and write them too. You do not know how glad your Pa would be to get a letter from his own dear daughter but I will tel you what you can do you can tell your Ma what to write or what you want to say to me and she will write it for you. You must think of Pa every day, every night when you go to bed, and every time that you wake up in the morning. Be a good girl to babby and Lucy never strike them nor speak cross to them but always be pleasant and kind to them so that they will be kind to you and above all be kind to Ma and mind her for Ma wont tell you to do anything but what you ought to do. and the better children you are the happyer you will be. Kiss Ma, Leon and Lucy for Pa every day and your pa will come back as soon as he can but til then your pa will always remember you.

From your affectionate Father
George W. Tillotson.

Letter to Elizabeth Tillotson, March 21, 1862 (GLC 4558.14), 194

Letter to Elizabeth Tillotson, May 22, 1862 (GLC 4558.15), 91–92

Letter to Elizabeth Tillotson, May 30, 1862 (GLC 4558.25), 194

* Letter to Elizabeth Tillotson, June 14, 1862 (GLC 4558.27), 75

TRANSCRIPTION:

Roaoke Island, June 14th, '62

Dear Wife

I take my pen in hand to endeaver to wright you a few lines. I am stopping now at the Hospitol. I came up here yesterdy The Doctor don't appear to know what what ails me thinks it is only a diseased state of the stumack and bowels but says I am better. I think I shall make a live of it myself. Please excuse poor writing. Write as often as you and I will do the same. This from your most affection husband

George W. Tillotson

Letter to Elizabeth Tillotson, September 24, 1862 (GLC 4558.44), 92–93, 116

Letter to Elizabeth Tillotson, October 14, 1862 (GLC 4558.48), 74

Letter to Elizabeth Tillotson, October 24, 1862 (GLC 4558.50), 116

Letter to Elizabeth Tillotson, January 19, 1863 (GLC 4558.63), 121

Letter to Elizabeth Tillotson, February 5, 1863 (GLC 4558.66), 121

Letter to Elizabeth Tillotson, April 17, 1863 (GLC 4558.83), 195

Letter to Elizabeth Tillotson, October 11, 1863 (GLC 4558.118), 26

Letter to Elizabeth Tillotson, November 21, 1863 (GLC 4558.124), 134–35

Letter to Elizabeth Tillotson, July 31, 1864 (GLC 4558.151), 205–206

Letter to Elizabeth Tillotson, September 21, 1864 (GLC 4558.162), 146

TRANSCRIPTION:

Raleigh N.C. Apr 15th, 1865

Dear Parents, Bro & Sister

Having a few moments in which to write before the mail leaves (by sail) to Goldsboro, I will try to improve them. I am still in the best of health and hope this will find you all at home in the best of health. The grand good news of the fall of Ritchmond and the Capture of R.E. Lees Army is indeed cheering and has received the hearty cheers from us as we have had read to us the official news from Grant as Received by Billy Sherman. We are in hopes to soon send you the Surrender of Johnson, which will have to come off sooner or later and that event is not far distant. . . .

OTHER ILLUSTRATIONS

Acknowledgments

The Soldier's Pen could not have been written without the tremendously supportive staff of the Gilder Lehrman Institute. James Basker, Lesley Herrmann, and Susan Saidenberg proved to be staunch advocates of the project. Sasha Rolon also deserves thanks for administering the institute fellowship that helped to support the early stages of my work. Ana Luhrs and Sandra Trenholm helped me navigate GLC materials housed at the New-York Historical Society and introduced me to a collection marked by continual expansion, in both size and scope. The meticulous research guides that Susan Saidenberg, Sandra Trenholm, and others at the institute have prepared over the years proved invaluable, both as I selected the core group of penmen and then as I worked to assemble these men's stories.

As I began the project and then conducted research in New York City, I benefited from the insight, encouragement, and support of Patricia and Wally Bigbee; David Blight; Kris Collins; Mark Dunkelman; Jack Goodman, Sr.; David Huntington; Robert Knapp; Mark Kornbluh; Steven Mintz; John Stauffer; Harry Stout; and Tom Summerhill. Research funds provided by the Michigan State University History Department and the Office of the Dean of the Faculty at Amherst College helped to defray expenses. Leslie Butler, Peter Carmichael, and Chandra Miller-Manning each read the entire manuscript and provided sage advice. Their contributions went far beyond the specific corrections, additions, and suggestions that sharpened every chapter. Peter and Chandra showed me in their own scholarship how to breathe life into those who fought America's bloodiest and most consequential war. Leslie helped me, as always, to see the bigger picture.

At a late stage of this project, I greatly benefited from leading a research seminar held at the American Antiquarian Society in Worcester, Massachusetts. My thanks go to Joe Cullen, Richard Fox, John Hench, Caroline Sloat, and others who attended that session. Alexandra Lee did superb work as a research assistant funded by the Dartmouth College Presidential Scholars Program.

I did not consult my undergraduate teacher Samuel Hynes while working on this project, but I did keep his books close at hand, and these have been an inspiration. Thomas LeBien was always on the other end of the phone with suggestions and advice. He realized what *The Soldier's Pen* might become well before I did, and I thank him for sharing his superb editorial judgments as the book developed. June Kim helped in countless ways to shepherd my writing toward completion. Everyone else at Hill and Wang worked wonders, not least in understanding and supporting my desire to retain the integrity of these nineteenth-century documents.

The dedication of the book has been the easiest part. Committing the names of Will, Matt, and Cameron to print repays a debt. It marks my appreciation for all the drawing, coloring, and scribbling these three boys have done—and will no doubt continue to do—for parents who are embarrassingly proud of each of them.